GREAT TRAVELLERS AND EXLORERS

PIONEERS

IN

AUSTRALASIA

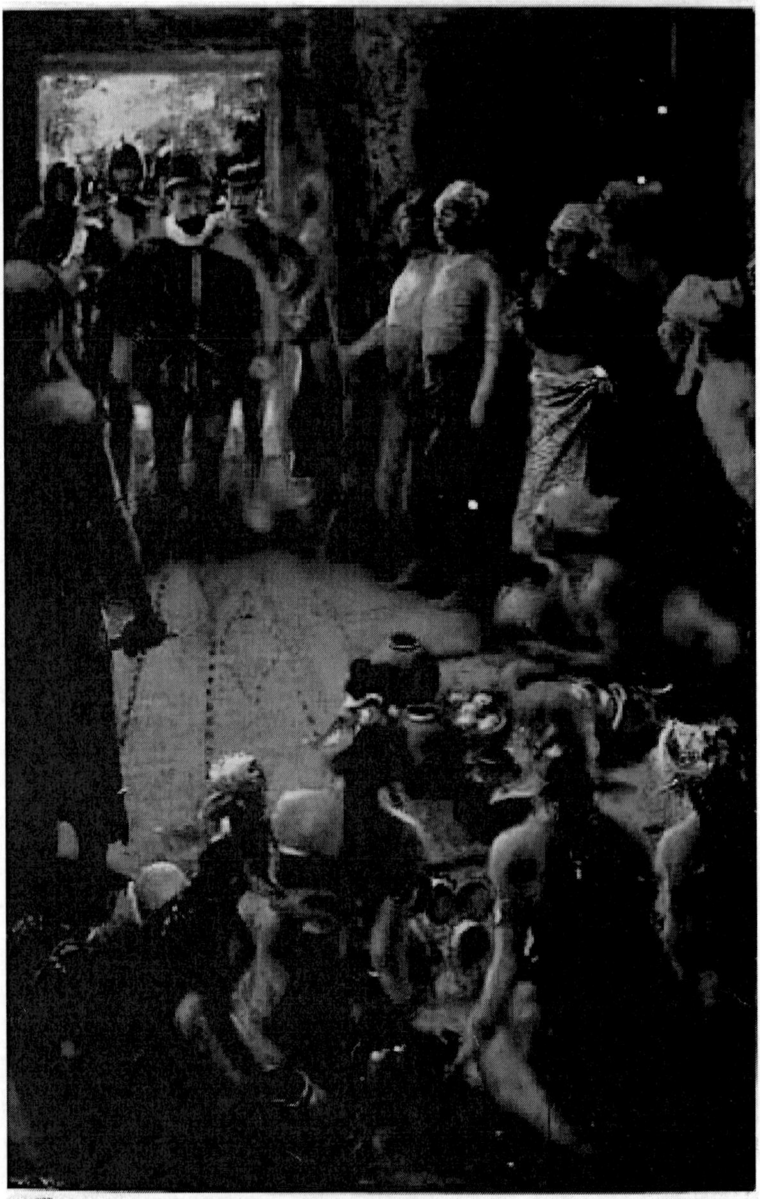

C-457

MAGELLAN VISITING THE KING OF SEBU

GREAT TRAVELLERS AND EXLORERS

PIONEERS
IN
AUSTRALASIA

HARRY JOHNSTON

WITH SIXTEEN PLATES & 3 MAPS

GYAN

Published by

Gyan Publishing House
5, Ansari Road
Daryaganj, New Delhi-110002
Phone: 011-47034999, 9811692060
E-mail: books@gyanbooks.com

Distribution Network
gyanbooks.com
India, USA, Canada, UK, Australia, France

ISBN : 978-81-212-3895-3 (PB)
First Published, London, 1912

2nd Impression 2020

Printed at: Gyan Press, Delhi.

Pioneers in Australasia
Author: Harry Johnston

Great Travellers and Explorers

PIONEERS IN AUSTRALASIA

BY

SIR HARRY JOHNSTON
G.C.M.G., K.C.B.

WITH EIGHT PLATES IN COLOURS
BY ALEC BALL

The Gresham Publishing Company
34 SOUTHAMPTON STREET, STRAND, LONDON

PREFACE

I HAVE been asked to write a series of works which should deal with "real adventures", in parts of the world either wild and uncontrolled by any civilized government, or at any rate regions full of dangers, of wonderful discoveries; in which the daring and heroism of white men (and sometimes of white women) stood out clearly against backgrounds of unfamiliar landscapes, peopled with strange nations, savage tribes, dangerous beasts, or wonderful birds. These books would again and again illustrate the first coming of the white race into regions inhabited by people of a different type, with brown, black, or yellow skins; how the European was received, and how he treated these races of the soil which gradually came under his rule owing to his superior knowledge, weapons, wealth, or powers of persuasion. The books were to tell the plain truth, even if here and there they showed the white man to have behaved badly, or if they revealed the fact that the American Indian, the Negro, the Malay, the black Australian was sometimes cruel and treacherous.

A request thus framed was almost equivalent

to asking me to write stories of those pioneers who founded the British Empire; in any case, the volumes of this series do relate the adventures of those who created the greater part of the British Dominions beyond the Seas, by their perilous explorations of unknown lands and waters. In many instances the travellers were all unconscious of their destinies, of the results which would arise from their actions. In some cases they would have bitterly railed at Fate had they known that the result of their splendid efforts was to be the enlargement of an empire under the British flag. Perhaps if they could know by now that we are striving under that flag to be just and generous to all types of men, and not to use our empire solely for the benefit of English-speaking men and women, the French who founded the Canadian nation, the Germans and Dutch who helped to create British Africa, Malaysia, and Australia, the Spaniards who preceded us in the West Indies and in New Guinea, and the Portuguese in West, Central, and East Africa, in Newfoundland, Ceylon, and Malaysia, might—if they have any consciousness or care for things in this world—be not so sorry after all that we are reaping where they sowed.

It is (as you will see) impossible to tell the tale of these early days in the British Dominions beyond the Seas, without describing here and there the adventures of men of enterprise and daring who were not of our own nationality. The majority, nevertheless, were of British stock; that is to say, they were English, Welsh, Scots, Irish, perhaps here and there a Channel Islander and a Manxman; or Nova Scotians, Canadians, and New Englanders. The bulk of them were good fellows, a few were saints, a few were ruffians with redeeming features. Sometimes they were common men who blundered into great discoveries which will for ever preserve their names from perishing; occasionally they were men of Fate, predestined, one might say, to change the history of the world by their revelations of new peoples, new lands, new rivers, new lakes, snow mountains, and gold mines. Here and there is a martyr like Marquette, or Livingstone, or Gordon, dying for the cause of a race not his own. And others again are mere boys, whose adventures come to them because they are adventurous, and whose feats of arms, escapes, perils, and successes are quite as wonderful as those attributed to the juvenile heroes of Marryat, Stevenson, and the author of *The Swiss Family Robinson*.

I have tried, in describing these adventures, to give my readers some idea of the scenery, animals, and vegetation of the new lands through which these pioneers passed on their great and small purposes; as well as of the people, native to the soil, with whom they came in contact. And in treating of these subjects I have thought it best to give the scientific names of the plant or animal which was of importance in my story, so that any of my readers who were really interested in natural history could at once ascertain for themselves the exact type alluded to, and, if they wished, look it up in a museum, a garden, or a natural history book.

I hope this attempt at scientific accuracy will not frighten away readers young and old; and, if you can have patience with the author, you will, by reading this series of books on the great pioneers of British West Africa, Canada, Malaysia, West Indies, South Africa, and Australasia, get a clear idea of how the British Colonial Empire came to be founded.

You will find that I have often tried to tell the story in the words of the pioneers, but in these quotations I have adopted the modern spelling, not only in my transcript of the English original or translation, but also in the place and tribal names, so as not to puzzle or delay the reader. Otherwise, if you were to look out some of the geographical names of the old writers, you might not be able to recognize them on the modern atlas. The pronunciation of this modern geographical spelling is very simple and clear: the vowels are pronounced *a* = ah, *e* = eh, *i* = ee, *o* = o, *ô* = oh, *ō* = aw, *ö* = u in 'hurt', and *u* = oo, as in German, Italian, or most other European languages; and the consonants as in English.

H. H. JOHNSTON.

CONTENTS

LIST OF ILLUSTRATIONS

COLOURED PLATES

BLACK-AND-WHITE ILLUSTRATIONS

BIBLIOGRAPHY

Magellan's Voyage Around the World. By Antonio Pigafetta. Translated and annotated by James Alexander Robertson. 2 Vols. Cleveland, U.S.A. The Arthur H. Clark Company. 1906. (This is the best work dealing with Magellan's voyage to the Philippines and the after events of his expedition.)

The First Voyage Round the World by Magellan. Translated from the accounts of Pigafetta, &c., by Lord Stanley of Alderley. London. Hakluyt Society. 1874. (This work contains a great deal of supplementary information regarding the doings of the Spaniards and Portuguese in the Pacific and Malaysia.)

Early Voyages to Australia. By R. H. Major. London. Hakluyt Society. 1859.

Tasman's Journal . . . Facsimiles of the Original MS. with Life of Tasman. By J. E. Heeres. Amsterdam. 1898.

Dampier's Voyages. Edited by John Masefield. 2 Vols. London. E. Grant Richards. 1906.

The History of Mankind. By Professor Friedrich Ratzel. Translated from the second German edition by A. J. Butler, M.A. 3 Vols. London. Macmillan & Co. 1896.

The History of the Australian Colonies. By Edward Jenks, M.A. Cambridge University Press. 1896.

Voyage Autour du Monde. By De Bougainville. Paris. 1771.

The Natives of Sarawak and British North Borneo. By H. Ling Roth. London. 1896.

Cook's Voyages. (Original edition in 6 Vols., including plates.) London. 1772, 1777, and 1784.

Captain Cook's Journal during his First Voyage Round the World. Edited by Captain W. J. L. Wharton, R.N., F.R.S. London. Elliot Stock. 1893.

Journal of the Rt. Hon. Sir Joseph Banks. Edited by Sir Joseph D. Hooker. Macmillan & Co. 1896.

Captain James Cook. By Arthur Kitson. London. John Murray. 1907. (This is the best life of Cook.)

The Eventful History of the Mutiny and Piratical Seizure of H.M.S. "Bounty". London. John Murray. 1831.

Gonzalez's Voyage to Easter Island, 1770–1. Translated by Bolton Glanville Corney. Hakluyt Society. 1908.

Terre Napoléon. (The French attempts to explore Australia at the beginning of the 19th Century.) By Ernest Scott. London. Methuen. 1910.

Murihiku. (A study of New Zealand history.) By the Hon. R. M'Nab. New Zealand. 1907. (A most interesting, accurate, and comprehensive work.)

Narrative of a Voyage to New Zealand, &c., in Company with the Rev. Samuel Marsden. By John Liddiard Nicholas. 2 Vols. London. 1817.

New Zealand: being a Narrative of Travels and Adventures, &c. By J. S. Pollack. 2 Vols. London. Richard Bentley. 1838. (Gives interesting information regarding the whale fishery round about New Zealand.)

Narrative of the Surveying Voyage of H.M.S. "Fly". By J. B. Jukes. 2 Vols. London. 1847. (Treats of the exploration of the coasts of Torres Straits, South New Guinea, and Malaysia.)

Narrative of the Voyage of H.M.S. "Rattlesnake". By John Macgillivray. 2 Vols. London. 1852. (This deals with the exploration of South-east New Guinea, &c. Professor Huxley accompanied this expedition as surgeon, and contributed illustrations to the book.)

The Malay Archipelago, &c. By Alfred Russel Wallace. 2 Vols. London. Macmillan. 1869.

A Naturalist's Wanderings in the Eastern Archipelago. By H. O. Forbes. London. 1885.

Life of Sir James Brooke. By Sir Spencer St. John. London. 1879.

PIONEERS IN AUSTRALASIA

CHAPTER I

The General Features of Australasia

In previous books of this series dealing with the achievements and adventures of the pioneers whose journeys led to the foundation of the British Empire beyond the seas, I have described the revelation of West Africa, the exploration of British North America, and the experiences of those who laid the foundations of our knowledge concerning India and Further India. The scope of this last volume brought us to Sumatra, Singapore, and Java: that is to say the western part of Malaysia. I now propose to set before my readers the more remarkable among the voyages and strange happenings which led to the discovery of Australasia, and to the inclusion within the British Empire of northern Borneo, south-eastern New Guinea, the continent of Australia, the large islands of New Zealand, and a good many islands and archipelagoes in the Pacific Ocean. The most convenient general term for this region of innumerable islands, large and small, is "Australasia", since it lies mostly in the southern hemisphere and yet is more nearly connected by affinity or proximity with Asia rather than any other continent.

Yet this title is not strictly correct, for Borneo, like Sumatra and Java, is really part of Asia so far as its geological and human history, animals, and plants are concerned; whereas the Malay islands farthest to the east—such as Timor, the Moluccas, and Jilolo—more correctly belong to a distinct region of the world, of which New Guinea and Australia are the headquarters, and New Zealand, Easter Island, the Marquezas Islands, and Hawaii the farthest outlying portions. But in regard to the landing of Europeans and the order of its exploration, Borneo, like the Philippines, forms part of that "Australasia" which was first reached (1521) from the direction of the Pacific Ocean.

Australasia (it is necessary, if wearisome, to repeat) consists of islands, great, small, and very small; Australia being so large an island that it ranks as the fifth and smallest of the continents. The insular character of Australasia has caused most of the great adventures connected with its discovery and colonization to be extraordinary feats of ocean rather than of land travel. But when we consider the size of the sailing ships, or of the mere junks, boats, or canoes in which some of the journeys were made, and the fact that the home of the explorers was not two, three, or four thousand miles away across the sea (as in the discovery of America and the West African coast), but more than treble that distance; that these hardy adventurers had to reach the unknown islands of the Pacific either round the stormy Cape of Good Hope or the still more stormy Cape Horn in ships on which we might hesitate to embark in order to cross the Bay of Biscay or the Irish Channel: the achievements of the Australasian pioneers in the sixteenth, seventeenth, eighteenth, and early nineteenth centuries become almost unbelievable in their heroism and power of endurance. The *Victoria* of Magellan's fleet which sailed from Spain to the Pacific and back across the Atlantic and Indian oceans was of 85 tons capacity! Matthew Flinders in 1803 crossed the Indian Ocean from North Australia to Mauritius in a schooner of 29 tons! Sir James Brooke sailed in 1883 from the mouth of the Thames to conquer North Borneo from the pirates in a sailing yacht of 148 tons.

Think of the courage that must have been required by a Magellan, a de Quiros, or even a Captain Cook, when they steered into the Unknown from the coast of South America across the broad waters of the Pacific! They had only a limited stock of fresh water: how long would it be before an island or a continent was encountered whereon they could land to replenish their supplies from some spring near the seashore or some stream falling from the hills? They had very little in the way of fresh provisions: when these were exhausted might not their mariners develop that dread disease scurvy,[1] and rot into madness or death? or before arriving at such an extremity mutiny and murder their officers? Food of any kind might become exhausted before fresh supplies could be obtained; and we know from many instances how ready the ship's crew of famished, uneducated sailors was, first to talk of cannibalism, and at last to lay violent hands on an officer or a comrade, kill him, and eat him. Or the undiscovered lands which would be their only resource against a death from starvation, disease, or thirst might

[1] It has been computed that, during the years between 1510 and 1530, the Spanish and Portuguese ships exploring the Atlantic, Pacific, and Indian oceans lost ten thousand seamen from scurvy.

be populated by ferocious man-eating savages (as indeed many of them were) and the landing parties of seamen and officers be promptly massacred. Or it might be a desert island, and the pleasing-looking herbs or fruits be deadly poison, or the strange fish, mussels, oysters, clams, whelks, or turtles prove to be so unwholesome that all who ate of this new fare were prostrated with illness. The gallant little sailing ship—little in our eyes whether its capacity were of 30 or even 400 tons—might be charged by a bull cachalot whale as big as an islet, and then and there spring a leak and founder with all on board. There might well be—and there were—treacherous coral reefs just masked by two or three feet of water on which the vessel would be driven at night-time and break her back. The crew would take to their frail boats and then have a thousand or more sea miles to cross, with oar and ineffective sail, before they could find a landing place and sustenance. Perhaps on the way thither (the giant, greedy sharks following in their wake) they died of sunstroke or thirst, or went mad and jumped into the sea and the shark's maw. Or they did reach some South Sea island—not to be discovered again for a century or two—where they were received as demigods by the astonished savages, but where they had to pass the rest of their lives as savages too; consoling themselves as best they could with a Polynesian wife or husband (for there were women sometimes in these ventures, especially on the Spanish vessels) and the growing up of a half-caste family; but never heard of again in their far-away homes, and ever and anon weeping and crying in vain to Heaven to be restored once more to the fair cities and romantic life of Spain or Portugal, or to the comfort and the orderly beauty of a Norman or an English homestead.

After sailing, sailing, sailing across the equatorial belt of the Pacific Ocean they at length reached—if no disaster arrested their progress—the limits of the known: they came to some part of Malaysia where the natives were no longer naked, black, unreasoning cannibals, or crafty, yellow, naked thieves; some seaport in the Philippines, Celebes, Timor, or Java where they met men of the Muhammadan religion, or even other European Christians who had reached Australasia round the Cape of Good Hope. But the Muhammadans might out of jealousy or of revenge for wrongs they had suffered from other Christians cause them to be imprisoned or murdered, while more often than not the fellow Christians they were greeting after a twelve-thousand miles' voyage half round the world belonged to some nation in rivalry or at war with their own. Then they might be held long years in captivity, or be executed (with or without torture) outright. (Matthew Flinders was imprisoned in Mauritius for six and a half years by the French not much more than a hundred years ago.) At any rate they would probably be refused those sea stores and materials necessary for repairing a crazy ship, and have to face the return voyage across the Indian Ocean, round the stormy extremity of Africa, and through the violent gales of the northern Atlantic with but a slender hope of reaching home, or even of surviving the perils of the sea, in a leaky, worm-eaten ship with splintered masts and rotten sails.

This fifth division of the earth's surface which they had come to explore consisted of an almost uncountable number of islands ranging in size from Australia, with an area of 2,946,691 square miles, New Guinea, which has about 312,330, and Borneo, with another 290,000, to tiny islets like the Fanning atoll, 9 miles by 4, or little Pitcairn, 2 miles square, on which the mutineers of the *Bounty* long hid themselves. The larger islands nearer to Asia were for the most part fragments of a former extension of the Asiatic or Australian continents; even New Zealand (104,000 square miles) must once have formed part of a huge strip of continental land stretching southwards from New Guinea and north-east Australia. But most of the islands of Micronesia and Polynesia (as distinct from Melanesia[1]), though they may have been larger than they are now and have risen out of comparatively shallow seas, were nevertheless always oceanic, that is to say, never connected with any great continent in recent ages.

These small islands are divided into two classes: the

[1] At this stage it may assist the reader if I give in a footnote the principal geographic divisions of Australasia.

Beginning on the west there is *Malaysia*, a term which comprises all the islands of the Malay Archipelago up to the vicinity of New Guinea. New Guinea and the islands and archipelagoes near it constitute the region of *Papuasia*; south of Papuasia is *Australia* (including Tasmania, Lord Howe, and Norfolk Islands, and perhaps New Caledonia); to the south-east of Australia lies *New Zealand*, which dominion comprises naturally and politically the Kermadec islets, the Chatham Islands and Macquarie Island; *Melanesia* is the domain of the dark-skinned people who are half-Papuan and half-Polynesian, and is generally held to include the Solomon Islands, the Santa Cruz, and New Hebrides archipelagoes, and the Fiji group. All the foregoing (together with the Samoa and Tonga Islands) were once connected by land with each other and with the continent of Asia.

North of Papuasia is the division of small islands known as *Micronesia*; it includes the Gilbert, Marshall, Caroline, and Ladrone archipelagoes. Almost in the middle of the northern half of the Pacific is the isolated ridge or shelf from which rises the *Hawaii* or Sandwich Islands, two of which are rather large (for Pacific islands). The Hawaii group is quite distinct from any other, and has never been joined to a continent. Finally, there remains the division of *Polynesia*, which likewise, in all probability, has never been continental, and which includes the separate archipelagoes of Marquezas, Tuamotu, Tubuai, Tahiti (the Society Islands), the Palmyra, Phœnix, and Malden groups, and the remote Easter Island, only 2374 miles from South America. The term "Polynesia" often covers the Samoa and the Tonga Islands, because they are peopled by the Polynesian race; but these groups are in other respects part of Melanesia. Finally, *Oceania* is a convenient term for all the islands, including New Guinea and New Zealand, which lie to the east of Malaysia, to the north and east of Australia.

mountainous or volcanic and the coral or flat islands, also called "atolls", from a word in a South Indian language. Atolls, or coral islands, in the Pacific and Indian Oceans are made by the coral animals (a polyp or minute jelly-fish-like creature living in communities like the cells of a human body), building upwards towards the surface of the sea the lime structures in which they exist. They start, of course, from some reef or submerged volcanic cone which is not far below the surface of the water. The limestone rock which they make out of secretions from the sea water gradually forms an irregular circle of narrow islets, with a lagoon in the centre and one or more deep openings to the sea. Vegetation—always coconuts—slowly covers these coral islands, and at last they become habitable by man. If the land beneath them is rising above the waves, the coral fossilizes into coralline rock and the living coral animals go on building and extending farther out to sea. If the land is sinking faster than the coral animal can build, then by degrees the once pleasant islets become a jumble of barren and crumbling rocks, only haunted by sea birds (but sometimes valuable for their guano), and finally a dangerous reef or shoal.

Of the smaller Pacific islands that are not mere coral reefs and atolls the Hawaii group, the Marquezas, Tahiti, Easter Island, Pitcairn, the Samoa, Tonga, and Fiji groups, the New Hebrides, most of the Ladrones, and one or two of the Caroline Islands are *volcanic*, high, and of recent formation, even though like the New Hebrides and the Marquezas they may rest on submerged extensions of sunken lands. The Solomon Islands are also mainly volcanic, but with the Bismarck archipelago practically form an extension of New Guinea; while New Caledonia is a very old fragment of unsubmerged land, and so is tiny Norfolk Island between New Caledonia and New Zealand. The southern island of New Zealand is, like New Caledonia, a portion of an ancient continent which has never been submerged; and the north island of that dominion is a very volcanic region.

The volcanic islands of the Pacific are always of more importance than the coral, partly because they are larger, but still more on account of their singularly fertile soil, high peaks, good rainfall, and picturesque scenery. They are, in fact, the "summer isles of Eden, set in dark purple spheres of sea", of Tennyson's poem. The climate is almost invariably healthy, the temperature a perpetual summer, with a never-absent invigorating sea breeze. The only grim reminder that there is another side to Nature lies in the occasional hurricane which drives great ships on to the coral or the basalt rocks, which lays low many a dwelling and plantation, or the earthquake followed by the still more alarming tidal wave. In Hawaii there is one of the largest active volcanoes in the world, into the seething crater of which victims used to be thrown as sacrifices to the god of fire. In the New Hebrides and Santa Cruz Islands there are other volcanoes, also active and occasionally emitting great streams of molten lava. This is, or was, also the case in the little islands—mere volcanic peaks rising above the waves—that form a broken chain round the north coast of New Guinea. Here were the "burning islets" so often noted in Tasman's and Dampier's voyages. Weird was the sight of them at night—a great cone standing out of the blue-black darkness, vomiting red fiery gas and red-hot ashes, columns of dense smoke turned gold and orange by the incandescent lava bubbling up and boiling over the crater's lips, and streaming in blazing cascades down the mountain's sides. The thundering discharges of gas, the crackling of electricity, added to the terror of the scene; and yet one can realize that after a time and the passing of many such small active volcanoes the Dutch, Spanish, and English sailors became used to them, and even found the presence of a burning mountain in the dark tropic night a cheering beacon in the pathless seas.

Borneo, Celebes, Buru, Jilolo, and the Spice Islands, Timor, Ceram, the eastern Sunda Islands were, of course, with Java and Sumatra on the west, New Guinea and the Bismarck Archipelago on the east, and the Philippines on the north, *continental* islands; that is to say, fragments of the former prolongation of Asia towards Australia: old lands, large or small portions of which have always risen above the very shallow sea which now separates them from one another. Yet MALAYSIA, like Polynesia, Melanesia, and Micronesia, is very volcanic. Of all its islands Borneo is the least so at the present day, in fact there is no active or recently active volcano in that huge island; whereas the Philippines are occasionally racked with earthquakes and have twelve active volcanoes. Java has a long range of lofty craters—some hundred and twenty-five in all, of which at least thirteen are active. The Lesser Sunda Islands, east of Java, likewise contain many volcanoes: Lombok and Sumbawa are little more than exceedingly large groups of craters, and when the Sumbawa volcano (of which something like 6 cubic miles was blown away) erupted in 1815, its red-hot lava and ashes killed forty thousand of the inhabitants on its slopes. There are volcanoes in Celebes, the Moluccas, Jilolo, and some of the islands off the west end of New Guinea. Timor only shows traces of past volcanic activity. In consequence of its being the most volcanic region in the world, Malaysia is very subject to earthquakes; and these disturbances of the earth's surface not only cause devastating tidal waves on the seacoasts, but in some way affect the atmosphere, provoking fearful cyclones of wind, followed by torrential rain. Similar disturbances of the atmosphere, however, occur frequently before or after the rainy season. Borneo is frightfully hot—perhaps hotter all the year round than any other country—but it is less afflicted with devastating winds. Nearly all Malaysia has a tremendous rainfall, though one or two islands, such as Flores and parts of Timor, have a rather drier climate, more suggestive of northern Australia. As a rule, however, Malaysia, in consequence of its perpetual summer under an equatorial sun, its rich alluvial soil—often of that peculiar richness associated with volcanic materials—and its plentiful rainfall, is clothed with a primeval forest which for luxuriance can scarcely be matched in West Africa or Brazil. These lands have been styled "the gardens of the sun"; "enormous forcing houses crammed with vegetation"; "great zoological gardens, full of rare and curious beasts". Here may be seen many species of palms: the gloriously beautiful Cyrtostachys palm of Java, with vividly red sheaths to the fronds and flower stalks, and bright yellow inflorescence changing to scarlet fruit; the creeping, climbing palms (the "rattan" or *Calamus*); stately Areca palms (which produce the betel nut, and the smaller species the "cabbage", so often described by travellers in Australia and the Pacific islands); useful Sago palms (*Metroxylon*); the sugar-yielding *Arenga*; the toddy or "rum" palm (*Caryota*); the Nipa, used for thatching; and, of course, the Coconut. As one travels eastward into the Pacific, this variety of palms thins out until at last only the Coco nut remains on the coral islands.

Of the other far-famed trees of the Malaysian forest there is the tall Duriān, with its evil-smelling, delicious-tasting fruit; there are stately, evergreen oaks, chestnuts, and mulberries; many kinds of fig trees—some growing like the Indian Banyan, with dependent roots that reach down from the far-spreading branches and form a grove of trees in time; others that live like grey, snaky parasites writhing about the trunks of victim trees, which in time they strangle; there are giant laurels, cinnamon laurels, huge myrtles, clove myrtles with their intensely aromatic flowerbuds, caoutchouc trees producing indiarubber, nutmeg trees, with their fragrant spice which so early drew traders to the most eastern part of the Malay Archipelago; and there are trees of sweet-smelling wood like the sandalwood and the *Aquilaria* or eaglewood, others like the damar-attam (*Hopea*), which produce a valuable glass-like resin; there are two or more kinds of big-leaved Breadfruit trees (*Artocarpus*), yielding their farinaceous, fig-like pods; and Artocarpi of a creeping habit whose branches are covered with small fig-like fruits remarkable for their gorgeous coloration — scarlet spotted with white, scarlet and purple, white and orange. Bamboos, often of huge girth, grow everywhere; orchids of incredible loveliness in colour and strangeness of form fringe the great boughs of the forest trees, which also afford harbourage to parasitic aroids of fantastic appearance; the glades are full of pitcher plants, ground orchids, brilliantly-coloured Cannas, "Grains-of-Paradise", calladiums with painted leaves, and wild bananas, with their beautiful, glossy, emerald-green fronds, or in some species with vividly coloured flower spikes. The marshy places are thickly grown with rushes resembling the papyrus of Africa; the shores of estuaries and low-lying coasts are the domain of tall mangroves and of the pandanus or screw pine—a semi-aquatic tree of the tropical parts of the Old World, which, with many aerial roots, and long, pointed, sword-like leaves, is distantly akin to the palms, and in Australasia produces fruit which is much eaten by the natives, especially in the Pacific Islands. These dense jungles of mangrove, pandanus, and other trees growing in the mud and brackish water —the habitat of mud-hopping fish, and numbers of large, brightly-coloured shore crabs, some so blue and so white and glossy that they are called "porcelain" crabs—were often a great barrier to the early explorers on the coasts of Borneo, Celebes, and Timor, besides being a prime hiding place for the *praus* of the Malay pirates. In the dense forests the lianas and climbing plants are a remarkable feature in the pictures of triumphant vegetation —pictures of which my untravelled readers can gain some faint idea by ascending the winding staircase in the great Palm House at Kew Gardens and looking down on the complex assemblage of tropical trees and plants. In these Malaysian woods there are many species of wild vines, with small brightly-coloured grapes; there are exquisite wreaths of the climbing asparagus—*Smilax*; festoons of climbing ferns, of the various kinds of pepper that hang their clusters of aromatic seeds from tree to tree, of the ipomœas (convolvuluses), passion flowers, bignonias, jasmines, purple and scarlet loranthus (a kind of mistletoe), and many climbing peas and beans, remarkable for their delicate or brightly-coloured flowers, which often exhale a delicious scent. In the higher parts of Java, Borneo, the Philippines, and even of New Guinea there are jungles of rhododendrons with vivid crimson blossoms. It is, however, a common mistake to suppose that the entire surface of the Malay islands is covered with

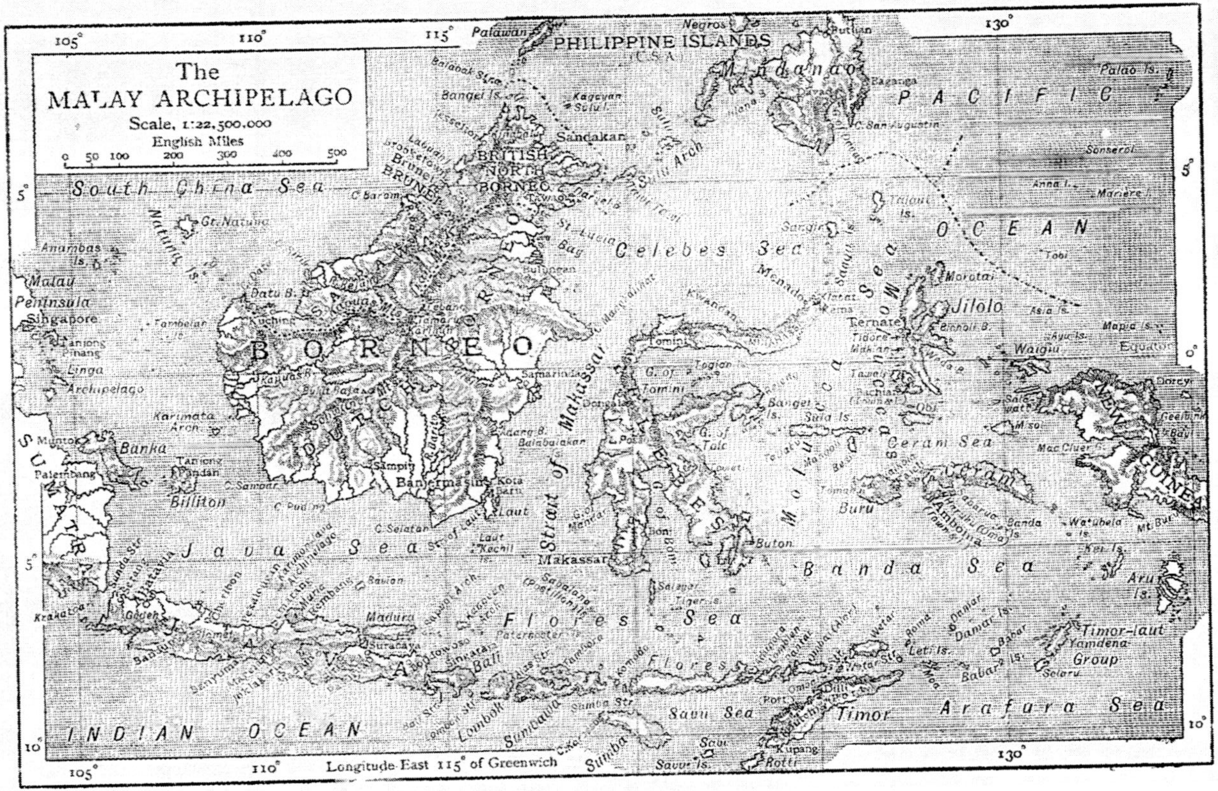
The MALAY ARCHIPELAGO
Scale, 1:22,500,000
English Miles
0 50 100 200 300 400 500
PHILIPPINE ISLANDS
South China Sea
BORNEO
BRITISH NORTH BORNEO
Celebes Sea
PACIFIC OCEAN
Java Sea
Flores Sea
Banda Sea
Strait of Makassar
Ceram Sea
Savu Sea
Arafura Sea
INDIAN OCEAN
SUMATRA
NEW GUINEA
Longitude East 115° of Greenwich

primeval forest. Considerable spaces have been cleared for cultivation, or after such clearing have relapsed into jungle; and this jungle is either a second growth of poor and scattered trees or more often a coarse and luxuriant grass. In the hilly interior of Dutch Borneo there are dry moors, deep in sand and sparsely covered with scrub. On the high plateaus and the mountain ranges of Flores and Timor considerable areas are open, treeless spaces, but covered instead with low-growing herbs, offering to the eye spectacles of brilliant colour when they blossom during the rainy season.

The splendid vegetation of Malaysia extends throughout New Guinea and the adjacent archipelagos, but with a diminution of species eastwards and a gradual infiltration of Australian forms, such as the *Eucalyptus* (a relation of the Myrtle family), the Casuarinas,[1] and the Araucaria conifers. More and more attenuated, the Malaysian flora spreads out over the tropical Pacific islands, wearing itself out finally in Hawaii, to which the sandalwood and a few other Malayan trees extend; and Pitcairn Island, where, however, the few Malayan species may have been anciently introduced by man.

The larger and more western islands of the Malay Archipelago have a fauna of beasts, birds, and reptiles, fish and insects, spiders and land crabs as remarkable as the wealth of their flora, and next to Africa the richest in the world. Here may still be seen—in Borneo—the wild Indian elephant and a two-horned rhinoceros; in Java there is a tiger and a small form of one-horned Indian rhinoceros. In Borneo exists the large red-haired ape

[1] A tree in appearance like a conifer, but in reality belonging to an isolated and very peculiar sub-class of flowering plants, distantly akin to oaks and catkin-bearing trees.

called Orang-utan; in Java there are smaller anthropoid apes known as Gibbons. Java and Borneo both have a handsome wild ox, the Banteng, besides more or less wild long-horned Indian buffaloes. The smallest and most remarkable of all the buffaloes is the Anoa, found only on the island of Celebes, and a larger but similar short-horned buffalo is found in the Philippines. Nearly all the islands have wild swine—generally of a type near to the wild boar, but with a very long head—the parent form of the domestic pig of Polynesia. But the queer island of Celebes, and Buru, which lies to the east, possess the strangest pig in the world: the Babirusa, a type with—for pigs—a small and slender head and (in the male) tusks which grow up and out through the cheeks. In Borneo there is a large monkey with an immense drooping nose; in Celebes a creature called the Black Ape—an intermediate form between baboons, macaques, and the higher apes. The macaque monkeys—creatures with short tails and bare faces, rather like small baboons (the Gibraltar monkey is a macaque)—are very common throughout Malaysia, extending as near to New Guinea and Australia as the islands of Buru and Timor. The other monkeys belong to the *Semnopithecus* genus, the long-tailed sacred monkeys of India. One of these found in Borneo is a combination in colouring of black, white, and chestnut red. The more northern and western of the Malay Islands possess a few strange lemurs, a large flying creature, the colugo, allied to lemurs and bats, and the Tupaias or squirrel-tailed Insectivores. Deer, without any white spots and related to the Sambar type of India, are found in the Philippines, Borneo, Java, the eastern Sunda Islands as far as Timor, Celebes, and the Moluccas; and in the Philippines there are spotted deer like the hog deer of India. Carnivorous mammals are represented more especially by a small tiger and a leopard in Java, the Clouded tiger of Borneo (a kind of leopard), several small cats, numerous civets, a small bear, and wild dogs. Cats and civets extend their range to Timor and the Philippines, and a civet—probably brought by the Malays—is found in Celebes. The fruit-eating bats or flying foxes are very large, often attaining to 5 feet across the wings. Their range extends eastwards beyond the Solomon Islands to north-east Australia and the New Hebrides. Nearly all the Pacific islands, including New Zealand and Hawaii, have bats of their own, but they are insect-eating, and very often day-flying. In the eastern islands of Malaysia begin to appear the marsupials of Australia, but until New Guinea is reached there is only one type to be seen, the Cuscus—a kind of phalanger akin to the "Opossum" of Australia.[1] There are porcupines, squirrels, and many strange rodents of the Rat family in western Malaysia. Peculiar genera and species of rats penetrate not only to New Guinea and the Solomon Islands, but also to Australia. The native rats of New Zealand and the Polynesian islands, however, have been introduced by man, chiefly for food.

The wealth in birds in Malaysia makes the naturalist's and artist's mouth water! There are no vultures, but several types of eagle—amongst them, in the Philippine Islands, a very large monkey-eating eagle with a huge, narrow beak—and some very handsomely coloured kites and hawks. Amongst the parrots are the gorgeous

[1] The real opossums are only found in America. Phalangers are woolly haired lemur-like marsupials, living in trees, which have their thumb and big toe opposite the other digits for grasping, besides a tail with a prehensile tip. In the arrangement of their teeth they are distantly related to kangaroos, which are really only phalangers, whose far-back ancestors have taken to a life on the ground.

crimson Eclectus, the lovely Lories, and those "white parrots"—Cockatoos—which furnished so much amazement and delight to the early Italian voyagers. But the strangest looking of all the parrots are the black cockatoos, peculiar to New Guinea. The peacock reaches to Java but not to Borneo, but in Borneo and Palawan there are superb pheasants and peacock-pheasants, and most of the Malaysian islands possess wild jungle fowl. Peculiar to Malaysia and Australia are the Megapodes, a family of gallinaceous birds allied to the Curassows of America, and which hatch their eggs by depositing them in mounds of decaying vegetation. There are very large cuckoos, the size of big pheasants; but perhaps the most remarkable bird groups in their Malaysian developments are the Hornbills and the Pigeons. The Fruit Pigeons of this region transcend description in their exquisite tints of peach colour, green of several shades, crimson, purple, and maize yellow. One kind is jet-black and pale-cream colour. These fruit-eating pigeons extend their range into New Guinea, Australia, and the Pacific Islands. In New Guinea there is the celebrated Victoria Crowned Pigeon, largest living of all the tribe; and in the Samoa Islands, without any near relation, the *Didunculus*, or Little Dodo —a ground-frequenting bird (which has since taken to the trees) that shows us how the large Dodo of Mauritius developed from the ordinary fruit-pigeon type. The Kingfishers of Malaysia are also very wonderful, and reach their climax of development in the New Guinea region. Some species are remarkable for their long storklike beaks, their long racquet tails, and superb plumage of ultramarine blue, purple, and white.

But the crown of glory which rests on eastern Malaysia and New Guinea in regard to bird life has been bestowed on this region because of the presence here—and here only, together with the north extremity of Australia—of the Paradise Birds. These marvels of creation, which are fast becoming exterminated by the agents of the wicked plumage trade, and without any opposition from the Dutch, German, or British Australian Governments of these countries, first make their appearance to a traveller coming from the west when he reaches the island of Jilolo or the Aru Islands, neither of which groups is very far from New Guinea. The Paradise Birds do not extend their range to the Bismarck Archipelago. East of the Solomon Islands there are fewer and fewer species of birds. Two Lories and three or four Parrakeets are found in Fiji, a beautiful blue and white lory inhabits Tahiti, together with a species of parrakeet. An ultramarine-blue and purple lory is found in the remote Marquezas archipelago, the farthest prolongation eastwards of the Malayan fauna. The other land birds of the Polynesian islands are pigeons, thrushes, flower-peckers, starlings, shrikes, babblers, a screech-owl, one or two plovers and rails, a sea-eagle, and two or three species of ducks. This seems to represent the totality of the resident birds of the Pacific islands east of Fiji and the New Hebrides. The birds of the Hawaii archipelago are very peculiar and have come thither chiefly from America. They include a peculiar family of starling-like birds—the *Drepanidæ*—celebrated for the beauty of their plumage which, in fact, has led to the extinction of several species.

The reptile life of Malaysia comprises many strange and remarkable forms, but, like the beasts, birds, and freshwater fish, it thins out in variety of species as the traveller crosses the boundary line between the Malay islands of Asiatic affinities and those belonging more to the Australian region; while, of course, in Polynesia reptiles are very few, or absent altogether. One or two species of harmless snakes are found as far eastwards as Fiji and Samoa. No land reptile of any kind exists in Tahiti or in Hawaii. Perhaps the biggest Crocodile in the world[1] (*Crocodilus porosus*) is found in all the great Malay Islands, and its range extends through New Guinea to the Solomon archipelago and Fiji, and to the extreme north coast of Australia. A much smaller—barely 7 feet long—crocodile with a long, narrow muzzle is found in northern and north-eastern Australia, and is quite harmless. Borneo has a peculiar gavial (fish-eating crocodile) with a very narrow snout. Large Pythons—perhaps the biggest known to science—extend over the same Austro-Malayan region, but do not reach lands to the east of New Guinea and Australia. Their place in the Melanesian islands of the Pacific is taken by small Boa snakes of a harmless nature. A prominent reptile in the life of the aborigines in Austro-Malaysia is the Monitor lizard, nearly always miscalled by Europeans "Iguana". This Monitor is the largest of the lizards, with a long, flexible tail, and sometimes as much as 8 feet in length in its Melanesian types, and is not infrequently mistaken for a crocodile by Europeans. It has very sharp teeth and can give a severe but not a very dangerous bite, its most powerful weapon being its whip-like tail. It is often eaten by the natives, and in its turn devours their fowls. Curiously enough, there is a *real* iguana in the Fiji Islands—one of the puzzles of animal distribution, for the Iguana family of vegetable-eating lizards is otherwise confined to Tropical America and Madagaskar. The seas of Malaysia

[1] A specimen 33 feet long has been recorded.

and of Polynesia (as far south as the New Zealand coasts) swarm at times with different types of real sea-serpents, that is to say, snakes that live entirely in the water and resort only to the shore to give birth to their young, which are born alive. These sea-snakes are of the Cobra family and are very poisonous. They are sometimes brightly coloured and marked in bold patterns.

Very different in climate, flora, and fauna to Malaysia and Polynesia are the great southern lands of Australia and New Zealand, together with New Caledonia and Norfolk Island. The northern, eastern, and south-western coast regions of Australia have a fairly abundant rainfall —quite as much as that which prevails in the more southerly of the Malay islands. But the centre, south, west, and north-west of Australia is much of it an almost hopeless desert, though not such a complete sandy desert as may be seen in Mongolia and northern Africa. The vegetation of this dry region of Australia consists mainly of a close-growing, spiny-seeded grass — the celebrated *Spinifex*. There are also gouty-looking Baobab trees like those of Tropical Africa. In New Guinea, where the rich flora contains not a few Australian elements, there are mountains rising considerably above the line of perpetual snow[1] both in the south-east and west, and many of the volcanoes, active and extinct, of Malaysia attain altitudes of over ten and eleven thousand feet. There are mountains nearly as lofty in the Solomon Islands, while in New Zealand we have the superb Southern Alps (12,349

[1] The New Guinea mountains are the highest in Australasia, higher than any land between the Himalayas and the Andes. They rise to over 16,000 feet in the west of New Guinea, and nearly 14,000 feet in the east. High mountains are common features on the great Malay islands. They rise to over 10,000 feet in Celebes and the Philippines, to 13,700 feet in North Borneo, and to altitudes of over 11,000 feet in Java, and nearly as high in Timor.

feet at their highest), which give a magnificent display of snow peaks and glaciers. But much of Australia is flat and undulating, and the highest mountain in that continent is only 7328 feet. Another thing which marks off Australia from the rest of Australasia is the complete absence of active volcanoes. But this is only quite a recent fact in its history, for at periods scarcely more distant than fifty thousand or sixty thousand years ago there were still volcanoes in the eastern part of the island continent vomiting out boiling lava and red-hot ashes, even after the land was inhabited by man. Still, as compared with Malaysia, Polynesia, and northern New Zealand, Australia is a very stable region, not persecuted by earthquakes or the present results of volcanic activity.

Its flora, like its fauna, is so peculiar that it constitutes one of the most distinct and separate regions of the world. There are a few patches of forest in the far north-east which are almost Malayan in their richness, and which contain quite a number of Malay types; and in the extreme south-west the Araucaria pine forests attain a certain luxuriance of growth. The predominant tree throughout Australia is the Eucalyptus, a peculiar development of the Myrtle order (anciently inhabiting Europe), which extends into New Guinea but not into New Caledonia or New Zealand. The Eucalyptus genus in Australia develops something like one hundred and fifty species, some of these trees 200 feet high, like the splendid Jarra timber, others—the Mallee scrub—making low thickets of 12 to 14 feet above the ground. The Australian "pines", important in the timber trade, belong to the genus *Frenela*, (which is akin to the African *Callitris*), to the cypresses, the yews, junipers, and to the genus *Araucaria*, the "Monkey Puzzle" type of conifer. These Araucarias are also met with in Norfolk Island, New Caledonia, and on the mountains of New Guinea. They furnish the Norfolk Island pine, 200 feet high and 30 feet in girth; but the equally celebrated Kauri "pine" of New Zealand belongs to the quite different genus *Agathis*. The "She-oaks", "swamp-oaks", "beef-wood", "iron-wood" trees one reads about in the literature of Australia, are all species of Casuarina trees. (The Casuarinas form a separate sub-class of flowering plants. See note on p. 27.) There are no real oaks in Australia, but there is a kind of beech tree in the south. A type of tree most characteristic of Australia is the Acacia in various forms, but not looking at all like the Acacia of Africa and India with its pinnate leaves. The three hundred kinds of Australian acacias mostly develop a foliage which consists of long, undivided leaves. They are famous for the beauty and odour of their yellow blossoms, and under the incorrect name of "Mimosa" are now widely grown all over the world where the climate is sufficiently mild, just as the *Eucalyptus globulus* or Blue Gum tree of Australia has been spread by cultivation far and wide through Europe, Asia, Africa, and America. But Australia has comparatively few palms,[1] and those chiefly in the north-east, and no bread-fruit tree (except where introduced). Conspicuous objects in the landscape are the "Grass trees" (*Xanthorrhœa* and *Kingia*)—plants allied to lilies and rushes. The Grass tree has a great bunch of wiry-looking leaves at its base, out of which rises a straight smooth stem like a long walking-stick. This is surmounted by a spike of white flowers. The *Doryanthis* lily grows to a height of 15 feet from the ground. Another conspicuous object in the "bush" is the splendid Flame

[1] See p 241.

tree, with bunches of crimson flowers (*Brachychiton*, a genus of the *Sterculiaceæ*, distant relations of the Baobab and the Mallows). A common sight in the well-watered regions is the Australian "tulip" (nearly everything in Australia is mis-named)—the great red Waratah flower, really a kind of *Protea*. To this same order (*Proteaceæ*), which is so well represented in Australia and South Africa, belong the beautiful-foliaged *Grevillea* trees and the celebrated *Banksia*, a shrub named after Sir Joseph Banks, and found in Australia and New Guinea. In the marshes and creeks of Queensland there are superb water lilies with leaves 18 inches in diameter. The gouty Baobab trees of the desert have been already mentioned.

Beautiful scenery is only to be met with in Australia in the mountain ranges of Queensland, New South Wales, and Victoria, and in the vicinity of Perth (south-west Australia). Here there are glades with superb tree-ferns, but the mountain peaks above the tree zone are bare and desolate. A large proportion of the interior is a dismal flat of scrub and stones, its monotony only broken by 6- to 20-feet-high mounds of the Termites or white ants. A good deal of the north coast is obstructed by forests of mangroves—a dismal-looking tree with its dull-green, leathery foliage, grey-white stems and pendent air-roots.

An interesting feature, however, in Australian scenery is the Great Barrier Reef. This is the remains of a former north-eastward extension of Australia—an immense coral reef stretching out for several hundred miles from the coast of Queensland in the direction of New Caledonia and the New Hebrides. This reef of visible and sunken rocks acted as a great barrier in the past, and prevented timid navigators from finding the north-east coast of Australia and establishing its separation from New Guinea. But the reef is of importance to commerce, for it maintains enormous quantities of the Trepang or Sea-slug, a creature which makes delicious soup and is passionately liked by the Chinese. [It is not really a slug but a relation of the star-fish, and is called scientifically a Holothurian.] The Great Barrier Reef is famous for the variety and almost incredible beauty of its corals and of the painted and decorated fish, anemones, and crabs of these shallow waters. It is, in fact, a region of such wonderful and strange beauty that one can only hope it will some day be made a kind of national aquarium by the Commonwealth of Australia, and constantly visited by those who like to gaze on the marvellous animals of a tropical coral sea.

The rocky coasts of Australia and Tasmania (besides those of the Philippines and the Pacific Islands) are remarkable for their abundant supplies of oysters, clams, whelks, and other shell-fish, which for ages have been a great food supply to savage man,[1] who had in fact merely to take at low tide what nature offered to him, at very little trouble to himself. Some of the clams (*Tridacna*) are enormous, measuring 3 feet and even 5 feet across the upper shell.

The crocodiles, pythons, and monitor lizards of Australia have been already alluded to in the description of Austro-Malaysia. There should, however, be mentioned in addition the long-necked tortoises of the continent and the turtles of the seacoasts. Australia once produced immense horned and armoured tortoises, but they became

[1] And since the discovery of Australasia began, a sustenance for shipwrecked mariners.

extinct soon after man entered this remote land. There are no vipers or rattlesnakes in Australia; all the poisonous snakes (and there are many) belong to the Cobra family. The most singular in appearance of the living land reptiles is a very large Agama lizard (the *Chlamydosaurus*), which is as much as 3 feet long, runs or hops on its hind limbs, and when angry erects a huge frill of leathery skin round the chest and shoulders. Another equally strange form of the Agama family is the Moloch lizard, about 1 foot long, with a very small mouth, but protected by the covering of its skin—a mass of sharp spines, thorns, and knobs. Its skin is not only very rough, but very absorbent, so that it will suck up water like blotting paper.

The beasts and birds of Australia are, in most cases, peculiar to that continent. The former belong almost entirely to the marsupial sub-class, that is to say, they consist of creatures like the Kangaru, Phalanger, and Thylacine (besides the Opossums of America), which, after the young is born, place it in a pouch on the outside of the mother's stomach, where it is kept until it is able to forage for itself. In many respects these marsupials evince a low organization, and really resemble, in their jaws and teeth, primitive mammals of ancient times discovered in fossil in Great Britain and North America. New Guinea also possesses some of these marsupial types, derived probably from Australia. The most widespread of these is the Spotted Cuscus, a phalanger with a woolly coat, the male of which has large black or brown spots on a cream-coloured ground, while the female is uniform brown. This animal ranges through the easternmost Malay islands from Celebes to New Guinea and north Australia, while another species,

THE BIGGEST OF THE KANGAROOS

(From a specimen sent from Australia to the New York Zoological Park)

the Grey Cuscus, is found as far east as the Bismarck Archipelago and the northern Solomon islands. These outlying groups of islands to the east of New Guinea also possess a flying Phalanger, but otherwise no marsupials penetrate into the Pacific islands beyond New Guinea and Australia. For the rest, New Guinea has Short-legged Kangarus (*Dorcopsis*), Tree Kangaroos (*Dendrolagus*), Striped Phalangers, Dormice Phalangers, Flying Phalangers, Feather-tailed Phalangers, Ring-tailed Phalangers, a species of white-spotted Dasyure ("Marsupial Cat"), and several forms of insectivorous marsupials ("Bandicoots" of the genera *Phascologale* and *Perameles*). But the true Kangarus—especially the big species—the Banded Ant-eater, the Wombats (which look like huge rabbits), the Koala or Tailless Phalanger (the "native bear"), the striped marsupial wolf or Thylacine, the Tasmanian Devil, the Marsupial Mole, most of the Dasyures and Bandicoots, are confined in their distribution to Australia and Tasmania, Tasmania being the richest part of Australia in marsupial types.

But this region, in common with New Guinea, possesses mammals still more primitive and interesting than the marsupials—the egg-laying sub-class, which contains the two existing forms of Echidna (Porcupine Ant-eater) and Duckbill. The Duckbill, a furry creature the size of a large cat, with the jaws converted into a leathery beak, is only found in the south-east of Australia and in Tasmania. The Echidna and Duckbill do not produce their young alive, but lay eggs from which the young are hatched. Apart from these marsupials and egg-laying mammals, Australia possesses only a few species of the higher mammals: a wild dog, a number of rats—aquatic and terrestrial—and bats; besides, of course, seals on the coasts and rivers, and the strange Dugong.[1] The bats are both of the insect-eating and fruit-eating kinds, and have probably flown over in recent times from New Guinea. From the same direction likewise have travelled the Australian rats, some of which have taken to a water life. As to the Dingo or Wild Dog, that may have been introduced by the early human inhabitants who came to Australia from Malaysia, but it has inhabited Australia for a very long period, though it did not reach Tasmania. It is related to a wild dog of Java. There is said to be a wild dingo in New Guinea.

Australian birds are very noteworthy. In the extreme north there is the Cassowary, which elsewhere is only found in New Guinea, the Bismarck Archipelago, and the Island of Ceram. Nearly the whole of Australia, however, was at one time frequented by the Emu, a large, flightless bird only second in size to the Ostrich. The Emu once extended its range to Tasmania as well as to Kangaroo Island, off the south coast of the continent. The Parrot order is more abundantly represented in Australia than anywhere else. In New Zealand and the tiny Norfolk Island there are species of a remarkable type of Parrot —the Nestor—which has a very long beak, not deep, like that of other parrots. The family of brush-tongued Lories is represented in the island continent by many beautiful forms. Here also developed originally the Cockatoos, which have since spread to New Guinea and the eastern Malay islands. The True Parrots and Parrakeets are well represented in New Guinea and Australia, and assume in some cases the most lovely and delicate coloration

[1] The Dugong, very commonly met with in the early stories of Australasian adventure, is an aquatic mammal, the size of a large porpoise, which belongs to the order of the Sirenians. It frequents the shores of estuaries and seacoasts with plenty of seaweed. It is a vegetable feeder only. See p. 165.

Amongst other noteworthy Australian birds is the Lyre Bird, in two or three species. This is a distant connection of thrushes and warblers, the size of a pheasant, and with very pheasantlike habits. Although the colour of its body is simply brown of various tints, the male bird has a most remarkable tail, the larger feathers of which exactly reproduce the form of a lyre. This creature is one of the minor wonders of the world, and it is therefore surprising that the great Commonwealth of Australia should take no measures to prevent its extermination at the hands of thoughtless and ignorant settlers, for, unlike the cockatoos, it does no damage to crops.

Australia also possesses the Black Swan, and it has a strange-looking, long-legged Goose, which has scarcely any web between its toes. There are numerous Eagles and Hawks, but there is no Vulture. There is also no True Crow, but there are Choughs and many crow-like developments of the Shrike, Oriole, and Starling groups, and in the extreme north of Australia, besides one or two Birds of Paradise, there are the singular Bower Birds (really belonging to the same family), who build little palaces and ornamental gardens of sticks, shells, feathers, pebbles, and other bright and attractive objects, as places in which they can go through their courtship ceremonies. The mound-building Megapodes or Brush Turkeys (which do not hatch their eggs by sitting on them, but bury the egg in a mound of decaying vegetation) also inhabit eastern and northern Australia, and are the only representatives there of the gallinaceous order. Amongst Kingfishers is the celebrated Laughing Jackass, which lives not on fish but on insects and carrion. Australia has no Woodpeckers, no Hornbills, no Cuckoos, and no True Pheasants, and a good many other bird families are remarkable for their absence from this region.

The scenery of New Zealand, in contrast to that of Australia, is nearly everywhere beautiful—as nature made it—though the modern settlers have robbed the island of much of its loveliness by cutting down the forests recklessly, destroying the ferns, and shooting the song birds. In the North Island of New Zealand are the most remarkable examples of volcanic activity, and this region has, or had—for they sometimes disappear in earthquake convulsions—beautiful crater lakes of deep blue or emerald green and terraces of congealed lava or pumicestone that assume lovely tints of pink, pale yellow, green or bluish grey.

The trees and plants of New Zealand have a character quite as peculiar and distinct as those of Australia. Amongst them grow beech trees similar to those of South Australia, and allied to the beeches of South America. There are only two species of a single genus of palm (*Rhopalostylis*), but there are many conifers allied to those of New Guinea and South America rather than to the conifers of Australia. The Kauri "pine" (*Agathis*) has been already mentioned. None of the conifers of Australia, New Zealand, New Guinea, and New Caledonia are "pines", "cedars", or "firs". The members of the pine family are entirely restricted to the Northern Hemisphere. The magnificent "pines" of New Caledonia and its adjacent islands are Araucarias ("monkey puzzles"). Besides an abundance of ferns (including the bracken), the undergrowth of New Zealand is chiefly composed of Veronica bushes, of fuchsias, and calceolarias. New Zealand has no deserts, and is blessed with a constant and a fairly abundant rainfall. It is as unlike Australia in appearance as it could well be, and much more resembles in general appearance our own country of England or the southernmost parts of South America.

New Zealand and New Caledonia were evidently cut off from their ancient connection with the New Hebrides and New Guinea before mammals had spread in that direction. New Zealand was entirely without any form of beast, except bats and seals, when first colonized by the Maoris; but this Polynesian people brought with them in their canoes a rat which they bred for eating, and a small, foxy-looking, domestic dog. Of the bats there are two kinds: one a small nocturnal bat, allied to the European Pipistrelle; and the other a very remarkable and isolated form, a "day" bat (*Mystacops*), which climbs about the trees, has very narrow wings, and does not fly much. The seals on the coast, which made New Zealand so attractive to the American and English whaling ships, consisted of a "Sea Bear" (*Otaria*), the Sea Elephant (now extinct), and four other large Antarctic species of true Seal. New Zealand had no great variety in species of birds, which belonged mainly to the Goose, Rail, Eagle, Parrot, Honeyeater, and Corvine groups. Amongst the most noteworthy of modern New Zealand birds are the Kaka Parrot of North Island and the handsome Kea Parrot of the South Island (both of the genus *Nestor*). The last-named has lately taken to attacking sheep. Another very interesting form is the *Stringops* or Tarapo Ground Parrot (sometimes called the Owl Parrot). The Huia is a chough-like bird with orange wattles and a beak which, though straight in the male is sickle-shaped in the female. The Tui Honeyeater or parson bird has two delicate white plumes below each cheek. But it is the extinct birds which will always make New Zealand interesting.

Amongst these was the largest type of bird which has probably ever existed—the Moa. We now know that besides Moas with long necks and small heads, which stood about 12 feet high, and were bigger than ostriches, there were other and much smaller types of the same order. One of these still survives: it is the so-called wingless Apteryx, which comes out at night, and with its long beak searches for worms. These Moas, of many sorts and sizes, probably still lived in the three islands of the New Zealand dominion when they were first discovered by the Polynesians; but being without any adequate means of defence, and quite unable to fly, they were soon exterminated, only the nocturnal Apteryx remaining. It is possible that these great ostrich-like birds reached New Zealand from the direction of Queensland and New Caledonia. [New Caledonia possesses one bird, which is found nowhere else in the world, though it has relations in South America. This is the Kagu, a pretty, grey, heron-like creature, which is really a sort of dwarf crane.] Two other remarkable bird developments once existed in New Zealand: a large, flightless goose (*Cnemiornis*), and a huge, thick-set Harpy Eagle (*Harpagornis*). This last no doubt fed mainly on the Moas, and died out when they became extinct.

New Zealand has only one kind of frog, no snakes, no tortoises, and only one true lizard (a Gecko), but it possesses all to itself an indigenous reptile of the greatest possible interest. This is the Tuatera (or *Sphenodon*), now restricted in its range to three or four islets off the northernmost coasts of New Zealand. Once this creature, which is about 3 to 4 feet long, ranged over the whole of New Zealand. It has been killed out mainly by the white settlers, and unless some effort is made will soon have disappeared altogether. This would be a great pity, for it is one of the most interesting of living things. It is the scarcely changed descendant of a very early order of reptiles which came into being millions of years ago and inhabited Europe and Asia.

CHAPTER II

The First Human Inhabitants of Australasia

At some date of unknown remoteness—it may be a hundred or two hundred thousand years ago—a primitive type of man entered the island continent of Australia, coming from New Guinea and the islands of the Malay Archipelago. The period in human history was perhaps so distant from our days that the geographical conditions of the Malay Archipelago were not precisely what they are at the present day; islands now separated by shallow seas may have been joined one to the other, the southern projections of New Guinea and the northern peninsulas of Australia may have been much closer together, so that men, though living a life of absolute savagery representing the lowest grade of human intelligence, were nevertheless able, by making use of floating logs or roughly fashioned rafts,[1] to enter the Australian continent and to pass from

[1] Dr. W. E. Roth, writing to the Royal Anthropological Institute in 1908, describes the existing canoes on the northern and eastern coasts of Australia as being of two kinds: that which was made from a single sheet of bark, folded in its length and tied at the extremities (the sides being kept apart by primitive stretchers), and that which was hollowed by fire and stone axe from the trunk of a tree. But he implies by his further remarks that these "dug-out" canoes were originally obtained by the black Australians from the Melanesian or Negroid people of Papuasia, who are several degrees higher in mental development than the Australoids. He also alludes to rafts possessed by the northern and eastern Australians (the Tasmanians had somewhat similar ones), made of logs of white mangrove tied together at both ends, but in such a way that the rafts were narrower at one end than at the other. On top was placed some seaweed to form a cushion to sit on. These are propelled either like punts by means of a long pole, or are paddled with flattened stumps of mangrove or similar trees from the water side. In the tropical regions natives will make a rough-and-ready raft out of three trunks of the wild banana tied together with rattans or flexible canes.

New Guinea eastwards and southwards into the nearer archipelagos of the Pacific. Although, doubtless, changes have taken place during the last hundred thousand years in regard to the distribution of land and water between south-eastern Asia and Australia, and even over the surface of the Pacific Ocean; and although islands or islets may have since subsided that once served as stepping-stones for adventurous savages: nevertheless there cannot have been within this period of time—which is scarcely a second in the age of the planet on which we dwell—the rise of any continuous land surface between the continent of Asia and the great Malay islands, on the one hand; and New Guinea, Australia, New Caledonia, the New Hebrides, and Fiji, on the other. Because if there had been any such continuous land connection within the last two hundred thousand years, sufficient to effect the peopling of Australasia by the human species without the need of crossing straits and narrow seas, there would have come into these regions as well as Man many examples of the modern animals of Asia. But, as we know, the south-eastern part of the Malay Archipelago and all Australasia and the Pacific islands are singularly deficient in the types of mammal now existing in Asia. In New Guinea, Australia, and the Malay islands to the east of Celebes and Bali, there are no monkeys, cats, wild oxen, or deer (excepting in the Moluccas and Timor), no apes, bears, insectivores, squirrels, elephants, rhinoceroses, or tapirs. Elephants, tapirs, apes, tigers, and rhinoceroses got as far east as Java (though the two first are now extinct there), and if there had been continuous land connection from that region eastwards to New Guinea and Australia, which made human emigration thither possible without crossing the sea, then these other large mammals would have equally invaded Papuasia and Australia. That they did not penetrate farther east than Java shows that a broad sea strait must have intervened, and the fact that this strait—or rather a succession of straits—did not prevent the Tasmanians, the Negroes of New Guinea and the Bismarck Archipelago, and the aboriginal Australians from reaching the lands in which the Europeans found them living three hundred years ago, shows that when they set out on these migrations from Malaysia eastward they could not have been without some knowledge of human arts and inventions, since they must have been able to fashion and use forms of transport across broad stretches of sea, such as logs or reeds fastened together into rafts, or water-tight vessels made out of the bark casing of fallen tree trunks.

Nevertheless, though of the same human species as ourselves, the Australoids[1] and Tasmanians[2] belonged to the lowliest living types of mankind, both physically and mentally. We know from various researches and evidence of cave deposits, bone and shell heaps, that these races had inhabited Australia and Tasmania for a very long period, that they did not originate in the southern continent, but evidently came from Asia; and that their nearest relations at the present day are the savage forest tribes of India and Ceylon, and in the past — most wonderful to relate—the ancient races of Britain and the continent of Europe. In his skull features and his very simple handicraft the Tasmanian resembled closely the people who lived in Kent and north-eastern France one to two hundred thousand years ago, in the warm inter-

[1] It is more convenient to give this name to the dark-skinned Australian aborigines, inasmuch as the term "Australian" now means a white man of European ancestry.

[2] The Tasmanians have been extinct since 1876 or 1877.

c 487

AN AUSTRALIAN ABORIGINE NAVIGATING A RAFT

vals of the Great Ice Age. When races of superior intellect and bodily strength were developed in Europe and northern Asia, the ancestors of the Tasmanians and the Australoids were driven forth into the forests of Africa and southern Asia. From out of the Tasmanian type was specialized the Negro of Africa and southern Asia. But the unspecialized Tasmanian meantime was either extinguished by stronger races or was pushed on, ever farther and farther eastwards and southwards, until first Australia, and lastly what was once the southernmost peninsula of Australia—Tasmania—was his last refuge. The Australoids followed in the Tasmanian's footsteps, and became the native race of the Australian continent, prevented or discouraged from crossing over into Tasmania by the sea passage—Bass's Straits—which had been formed between Tasmania and the mainland. Other Australoids and Tasmanians no doubt populated New Guinea and the great Melanesian islands (as they had done all Malaysia). Here, however, they were followed up by the Negro, and in course of time Papuasia (as New Guinea and its surrounding islands is called) became almost as much a domain of the Negro as Africa. Primitive Negroes (mixed in blood with Australoids, and forming thus the Melanesian type) travelled as far eastwards and south as Fiji, the New Hebrides, and New Caledonia. They may even have reached New Zealand before the Polynesian Maoris came, and in a half-breed with the Polynesian they extended their ocean range as far as the Hawaii archipelago. They populated the Philippine Islands,[1] and all the other islands of the Malay Archipelago, even as far out at sea as

[1] Here being dwarfish in stature they are styled Negrito, a Spanish diminutive of Negro. The pigmy negro type is not confined to the Philippine archipelago, but reappears in some of the south-eastern Malay islands and in New Guinea.

Micronesia, except—curiously enough—Borneo, and perhaps Java.

The Negroes or Melanesians improved on the rafts and bark canoes of the Tasmanians and Australoids by inventing and perfecting the "dug-out" canoe. This is made of a single tree trunk, hollowed out by the use of fire and the chipping of stone axes.

In Micronesia and Malaysia these Negroids soon became mixed with or exterminated by the early Mongolian type of man which, originating somewhere in High Asia, invaded Europe, America, south-east Asia, and Malaysia, assisting in time to form that race of mysterious origin and affinities, the Indonesian or Polynesian, whose invasion of the Malay Archipelago and Pacific islands occurred long after the coming of Tasmanian, Australoid, Negro, and Mongol, yet may have been as far back as five or six thousand years ago. The Polynesian's ancestors produced very considerable effects on these regions by bringing to them the first fruits of the white man's civilization which we associate in Europe and western Asia with the New Stone Age, or the period beginning perhaps twenty thousand years ago, in which men began to make beautifully finished stone and bone implements and set themselves to domesticate animals and to cultivate plants.

Among the Maoris of New Zealand, the people of Samoa, Tonga, Tahiti, one or two islands off the west and the north-east of New Guinea, and the Sandwich Islands (Hawaii), there are, or rather were, types amongst the Polynesians, strikingly European in form, feature, and mental characteristics. I write "were" with the intention of alluding to the days when there were no European settlers in these regions who could have modified the population by intermarriage. The languages spoken at the present day by all more or less pure-blood Polynesians betray a resemblance and affinity with the Malay dialects and languages of Java, Sumatra, and the Malay Peninsula. It would seem, therefore, as though Malaysia was the original home of development of the Polynesian race, and that this remarkable people, celebrated for their fearless navigation of the ocean in well-constructed canoes, with masts, sails, and outriggers,[1] arose from some southward migration of the White Man (Caucasian) when he was emerging from the condition of the savage into the beginnings of civilization; a stage which is understood by the use of the term Neolithic, or the stage of perfected stone implements. Here in Malaysia the Caucasian type (which in ancient times populated much of northern and eastern Asia) mixed with the Mongol or Yellow Man, with the Negro or Black Man, and perhaps even with what remained of the generalized Australoid stock; and the result was the Polynesian as he is seen to-day: a tall, well-developed specimen of humanity with a reddish or yellow skin, large eyes set horizontally in the head, a well-formed nose and chin, straight hair (finer than that of the Mongol and with some tendency to curl or undulate), slight beards in the men, and a good brain development. In some respects these Polynesians recall in appearance, in mind, and in culture the aboriginal inhabitants of the three Americas, North, Central, and South. Indeed, if natives from the Upper Amazon, Southern Chili, or California were put alongside Polynesians from New Zealand, Tahiti, or

[1] The seafaring vessels of the Polynesians were as much of an advance on the dug-out canoes of the negroid Papuans as these last were superior to the rafts and bark coracles of the Australoids. The chief feature in the Polynesian canoe was the out-rigger, sometimes double. This was a long piece of wood floating on the water parallel to the canoe and fastened to two poles or sticks projecting horizontally from the side of the canoe.

Samoa it would not always be easy to pick them out at a glance. Where the Amerindian differs from the Polynesian is in being absolutely straight-haired and having features slightly more Mongolian, so that there is a still greater resemblance in body and mind between the Amerindian of South America and the Micronesians of the Ladrone Islands, the Dayaks of Borneo, or the Malays of the Malay Peninsula. The indigenes of North America obviously contain a great deal of Caucasian blood, from ancient migrations coming from north-east Asia, and therefore sometimes resemble Polynesians more than they do the Mongols of northern Asia.

Many students of the unwritten history of the human past are now inclined to believe that by the aid of islands since submerged individuals of the Malay and the Polynesian races must have penetrated in ancient times into Central and South America, carrying with them the beginnings of Neolithic culture and many new ideas in religion. Such theories derive some support from a comparison between the arts of Borneo and other islands of the Malay Archipelago, and of the Pacific islands and those of Central and South America.

Amongst the many problems of the past which we are unable at present to solve is why, if the Polynesians could colonize every island or islet in the vast Pacific, including New Zealand and Easter Island, they should have had so little effect on the development of Australia. In travelling east and south from their original homes in Sumatra, Jilolo, and the islands north of New Guinea, the Polynesians might just as easily have landed on the coasts of Australia as on those of New Zealand. But though such landings almost certainly took place, nearly all record of them is lost, and they had very little effect on the physical and mental character of the dark-skinned Australian aborigines. As a matter of fact, for some reasons connected with ocean currents and prevailing winds, the line of Polynesian migration seems to have been from west to east across the more equatorial regions of the Pacific, north of New Guinea, and afterwards from east to west, north-west, south-west, and due north. New Zealand was colonized by the Polynesians, not from the direction of New Caledonia, but from Samoa and Tonga. These Maoris (as they are now called) came at no very ancient date—perhaps not more than six hundred years ago;[1] but there may have been earlier Melanesian invasions from the direction of Fiji.

The aborigines of Australia at the present day are usually divided into two main sections, based on language, affinities, and other evidence. It is thought possible that the southern half of this division is the more primitive, and that the northern half has received here and there some modification by occasional attempts on the part of Hindu adventurers from Java, or Malay, Polynesian or Papuan

[1] There are legends and evidence—such as shell heaps—in New Zealand indicating that the islands were first populated by a Papuan race akin to the peoples of New Caledonia and New Guinea. This is difficult of belief because of the isolated character of New Zealand and the exceedingly stormy seas which cut it off from other lands to the north and west. Yet the existence of a negroid element among the Maoris of New Zealand is undoubted. It may have been due to the earliest Polynesian invaders bringing with them slaves and captives from Fiji. That the Maoris kept slightly in touch with the world of Asia after their colonization of New Zealand is shown by the discovery some years ago in the interior of New Zealand of an Indian bronze bell dating from about the fourteenth century A.C., with an inscription on it in the Tamil language of southern India. It was a ship's bell belonging to a vessel presumably manned by Muhammadans, probably Malays. Either, therefore, a Malay ship or one from the south of India discovered New Zealand some six hundred years ago, or reached the Melanesian or Samoan islands of the western Pacific, and there left its bell to be carried off to New Zealand as a treasure. The Malays certainly traded to the New Hebrides. It should also be noted that in many other outlying Pacific islands besides New Zealand, there are traditions and even the remains of implements to suggest a former wide migration eastward of the Negroid type—even as far as Hawaii.

seafarers, to settle on the inhospitable coasts of north-western, northern, and eastern Australia.

It is in any case practically certain that the Malay people were the first discoverers of Australia from the point of view of civilized man and of definite human history. The Malays are mainly of Mongol affinities. They belong to that great division of humanity which includes the peoples of Indo-China, Tibet, China, Japan, Mongolia, and Arctic Asia and America, and which is characterized by narrow, somewhat slanting eyes; a small, straight, narrow nose; high cheekbones; lank, coarse head hair, and a relative absence or scarcity of hair on the face and body. But the word Malay must be understood in two senses in this and other books treating of Australasia. It means in a general sense the Mongolian race which populates so much of the Malay Peninsula and the Malay Archipelago (extending on the north-east to the Philippines and Formosa); and in a more restricted sense a tribe and language which originated in the Menañkabao district of central Sumatra. The Malay language is a member of the great Malayo-Polynesian group which may have been created by an ancient fusion, many thousand years ago, between the early Caucasian (White men) invaders of Sumatra and the Mongolians who followed them. At the present day the languages of this group range from Madagaskar in the south-west to Hawaii in the north-east, to Formosa in the north, and New Zealand in the south. An early mingling of the Mongolian Malay and the Caucasian or Indonesian[1] inhabitants of the Malay Archipelago produced probably not only this widespread family of languages, but the remarkable Polynesian peoples of the Pacific.

[1] Indonesian is the name applied to the light-skinned people of Caucasian features found in Sumatra and Papuasia.

Yet although the Malays proper spoke this Polynesian type of language (so very different from the Mongolian languages of Indo-China) they remained chiefly Mongol in their physical features. But their close association with the Indonesian or Caucasian type of people in Sumatra seems to have inspired them with some of the energy and culture—especially in the matter of navigation—which was already carrying the hybrid Polynesians far ahead in the colonization of the Pacific islands. At several epochs these Malays left their native Sumatra on oversea adventure. They seem firstly to have visited Ceylon, southern India, and the Maldiv Islands. Then much bolder sea journeys, perhaps in outrigger canoes with mat sails, took them, via the Seychelles, to Madagaskar—it may be more than two thousand years ago. Later migrations eastward brought them to the coasts of the Malay Peninsula and islands, where they became the celebrated "Sea Gipsies" —the *Orang laut*, or Men of the Sea, who lived almost entirely on board their canoes, and only came on shore to trade or to plunder. Finally arose a warlike Malay tribe of eastern Sumatra (Menañkabau), who, becoming converted to the Muhammadan faith about six hundred and fifty years ago, left Sumatra to become a conquering, colonizing, trading people, who in the course of some four hundred years had settled on the coasts of the Malay Peninsula, Borneo, Java, and the other Sunda islands, Celebes, the Moluccas, Philippines, and the north-western parts of Papuasia, and had founded kingdoms, spread everywhere their Muhammadan faith, and everywhere between Sumatra and New Guinea imposed their own Malay dialect as a medium of intercourse and commerce. In these wonderful adventures—which may have carried them and their civilization as far east as the New Hebrides.

besides spreading still farther products of the Indian world, such as the domestic fowl,[1] the orange, lime, and betel pepper-vine—they undoubtedly discovered the north coast of Australia about five hundred years ago, and communicated their discovery to the Chinese, the Arabs, and finally the Portuguese and Dutch.

Assisted by Persians of the Persian Gulf, the Arabs of southern and western Arabia revealed East Africa and Madagaskar about the beginning of the Christian Era, and before this period had found their way to western India, Ceylon, and even the Malay Peninsula. After the convulsion and awakening caused by the promulgation of the Muhammadan religion, Arab voyages to the Far East (largely instigated by the merchants of Persia) increased to a remarkable extent; and wherever the Arabs went they endeavoured to spread the faith of Islam. Thus, as early as the thirteenth century, the Arab religion, dress, and customs had been introduced into the Island of Borneo, into the north of Sumatra, and the south of the Malay Peninsula. By 1470 the whole of Java had been converted to the Muhammadan religion, and the great mass of the Malay people became ardent advocates of that faith.

The Arabs, of course, belong to the Caucasian subspecies: they are emphatically White Men in body and mind, though their skin colour may have been darkened by ages of exposure to a hot sun and by occasional intermixture with the Negro. But they have gradually grown to be distinct in cast of mind and sympathies from the peoples of Europe; and the institution of the Muhammadan religion separated them still more widely from the world of Greece, Rome, Paris, Lisbon, and London. Until the

[1] The domestic fowl had even reached New Caledonia but not any part of Australia or New Zealand.

fourteenth century of the Christian Era they and their Persian allies monopolized the whole of the trade which had grown up between Asia, Malaysia, and Africa on the one hand, and Europe on the other. Then the movements of the Mongols and Tatars in central and western Asia, and their temporary respect for and curiosity concerning Christian Europe, enabled Italian commercial travellers to penetrate to the farthest parts of Asia. Thus there reached Europe not only more or less accurate descriptions of Java and Sumatra, but vague hints as to a "great Java" which lay to the south and was a whole continent in itself. These hints became more precise at the beginning of the sixteenth century, when not only had the Malay Archipelago been traversed almost to the limits of New Guinea by adventurous Italians, but French and Portuguese navigators may even have been driven out of their course by storms, and obtained some glimpse of the Australian coastline.[1]

The definite revelation of Australasia will be dealt with in succeeding chapters. Meantime, before we begin to review the historical discovery of the Australian continent and the islands and islets of Malaysia, Papuasia, and of

[1] In my volume on the Pioneers in India and Southern Asia I have referred to the story told to Ludovico di Varthema by a Malay captain of the vessel in which he travelled, according to which Malays had penetrated southwards into seas where the ice obstructed their passage, and the day in wintertime became shortened to a period of four hours. This would look as though the Malays had anticipated us in Antarctic discovery.

The names of the French voyagers who may have sighted Australia in the first half of the sixteenth century were Binot Paulmier de Gonneville, who, sailing across the Indian Ocean after rounding the Cape of Good Hope, was blown out of his course and landed on the shores of a great island, which he believed to be Terra Australis (perhaps only Madagaskar); and Guillaume le Testu, who, starting apparently from Marseilles in 1530, also rounded the Cape of Good Hope, and in directing his course for the Spice Islands apparently stumbled on the coast of West Australia. The southern continent is certainly indicated on an old French map of 1542, now in the possession of the British Museum. But this discovery of the Provençal sailor is based on slender evidence.

the Pacific, let us first of all realize what were the conditions of life amongst the savage or semi-savage inhabitants of these regions before they came into contact with the men of strong minds and strong bodies who left western Europe from the sixteenth century onwards to found colonies in the new worlds of America and Australasia.

In the sixteenth century the distribution and condition of the native races in Australasia and the Pacific islands stood thus: Java was thickly populated, far more so than any other island in Malaysia. This population consisted almost entirely of a short, yellow-skinned people of MALAY speech and more or less of Mongolian type, but with some ancient Hindu intermixture. In the mountainous regions of the interior was a forest-dwelling race—the Kalangs—(now extinct), a wild people, supposed to be negroid but in reality more like the Australoids. Java, colonized some two to three thousand years ago by the Hindus, and at a later date much visited by Arabs and Chinese, had attained a high degree of civilization (of a very Indian character) when first visited by Europeans in the fifteenth and sixteenth centuries. Under the Dutch from the seventeenth century onwards it became the great centre of Malaysian commerce.

Borneo, on the other hand—a very much larger island—was in a less advanced stage of culture, except on the north coast, along which both Indian and Chinese—and, later, Arab—civilization had come into play. North Borneo was a very old colony of the Chinese, and under Arab influence after the thirteenth century had become a region of considerable wealth and power. The Muhammadan religion had spread over the North Bornean kingdom of Brunei and thence to Palawan and the Sulu archipelago, between Borneo and the Philippines. The Malays from

Celebes wielded a considerable influence over the south coast; but all this Eastern civilization did not penetrate far into the interior, which was inhabited mostly by a Mongolian people (like the Malays and Indo-Chinese in appearance) generally known as Dayaks. Other tribes were distinguished as Dusuns, Muruts, Bukits, Kanowit, Kayan, Sagai, Madangs, Punans, Kennias, &c. All these interior peoples led a life of relative savagery, though they were very artistic, and never allowed complete nudity in either sex. They were not cannibals, but they had a passion for head-hunting and for the collection of skulls, which they preserved and decorated, and to which they attached some religious significance. In their appearance, their weapons (such as the blowpipe), arts, and industries, and this practice of head-hunting they offered most striking resemblance to the Amerindians of equatorial South America. Curiously enough, so far, there has been no trace whatever found of pre-existing Negroids or Negritos in Borneo, though this race once predominated in the neighbouring Philippine Islands, and is found in the Malay Peninsula and even eastern Sumatra. There are slight traces of Negroids in the population of the great island of Celebes, to the east of Borneo, and, with the exception of Java, in all the other parts of Malaysia. The island of Celebes, like Java, was a region of considerable Malay civilization when first reached by Europeans. The people here (except the wild forest tribes) had elaborate dresses, steel weapons and implements, were skilled in weaving, embroidery, gold and silver jewellery work, and shipbuilding. On the whole, Java and Celebes were the two most advanced of the Malay islands in the arts and industries and the amenities of civilized existence when Europeans first sailed amongst these wonderful islands of spices, of Malay pirates, of cockatoos, hornbills, and buffaloes.

In Palawan (in which live the most exquisitely beautiful peacock pheasants), and the Sulu archipelago—between Borneo and the Philippines—the natives were all Muhammadans and much under Arab influence; but in the rest of the Philippine Islands the Malays and the older Mongolian peoples dwelling on the coasts were civilized pagans, a good deal under Chinese and North Borneo influence, while the interior was tenanted mainly by the wildest pigmy Negritos, who were strong enough in numbers to keep the yellow-skinned, straight-haired people from colonizing the forested mountains. After the Spaniards came and put firearms into the hands of the Malays, the Philippine Negritos soon got the worst of it, and at the present day only number about twenty-four thousand in Luzon and Mindanao out of a total population of nearly eight millions. Unfortunately the arms and ammunition thus obtained by the Malays in the Philippines and Borneo turned them into a bold race of pirates, who began after the commencement of the seventeenth century to prey on the commerce of Malaysia and the China Sea.

The eastern islands of the Malay Archipelago—Timor, Flores, Buru, Jilolo, Ceram, and their adjacent groups of islets—were peopled by mixed races, partly of Malay and partly of Negrito or Papuan stock. In the mountainous interior of the larger islands the natives were still wild and naked pagans, but little distinguishable from the Papuans of New Guinea. But the coast population was mostly Muhammadan, or about to become so, and more or less derived from Malay settlers. In some cases, perhaps, they represented a Mongoloid stock older than the Malay and related to the Micronesians farther to the north-east.

PAPUAN OF SOUTH-EAST NEW GUINEA, NEAR PORT MORESBY

(From a drawing by the late Professor T. H. Huxley)

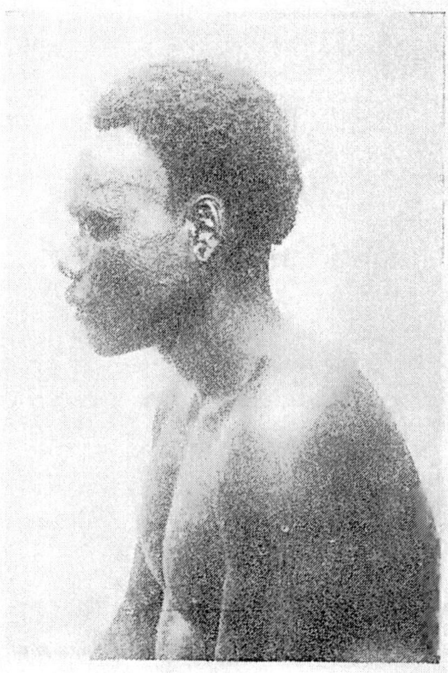

OCEANIC NEGRO TYPE FROM THE NORTHERNMOST SOLOMON ISLANDS

(From a photograph)

These MICRONESIANS were the peoples of the Mariana or Ladrone, Palao (Pelew), Caroline, Marshall, and Gilbert Islands. They were of mixed elements, partly Polynesian (which is to say semi-Caucasian), partly Mongolian, and in some degree Papuan, but many of them bear a remarkable facial resemblance to the Amerindians of North and South America. This may arise partly from the partial colonization of these archipelagoes of small islands in the western Pacific by immigrants from Japan and China, mostly shipwrecked mariners. This intermixture has imparted a "Tatar" look to some of the Micronesians, just as the same facial features in the Amerindian are undoubtedly derived from ancient migrations taking place in prehistoric times from Siberia and Japan into north-west America. On the whole the Micronesians are most nearly allied to the Polynesian group of peoples to the south of them, though their languages form quite a separate group. Before Europeans discovered them they ignored the use of metal; their implements were made of stone, of sharks' and whales' teeth, of sharp-edged bivalve shells, of cane, and wood. They had a great reverence for stones, both as objects of worship and as money. This feeling would almost seem to be due to the remembrance of more remote times, when there dwelt in these and perhaps other Pacific archipelagoes a wonderful race of stonebuilders, who may have been the Caucasian ancestors of the modern Polynesians and akin to that European Neolithic race which ranged across the Old World from Ireland to Korea, and over the Australasian islands from Sumatra to Easter Island.

A section of these Neolithic stonebuilders seems to have sojourned for a time in the Caroline Islands, one of the Micronesian archipelagoes. Here they constructed forts, palaces, quays, out of immense blocks of stone, shaped ready hewn, so to speak, by the hand of Nature: for they were cubes and four-sided prisms of basalt (like the formations at the Giant's Causeway in Ireland), the remains of ancient volcanic eruptions on the larger islands of the Caroline group. Besides the stone buildings (which were erected, like all ancient stonework, by placing block on block, without any binding mortar between) this vanished race constructed artificial canals and harbours. Their prosperity and civilization seem to have come to an end—perhaps they emigrated to America and founded some of the prehistoric civilizations there—through the partial subsidence of the Micronesian islands. Many of these ancient stone buildings are now partly under water, and there is other evidence which shows that these and other Pacific groups of islands were larger in extent several thousand years ago than they are now. The modern Micronesians may be in part descended from the great race of stonebuilders, but they have much degenerated in civilization, as has been the case with the people of Egypt and the Amerindians of Peru and Mexico.

New Guinea, four hundred years ago, and its adjacent islands, large and small, of Waigiu, Aru, Timor-laut, the Admiralty Islands, the Bismarck Archipelago (once known as New Britain and New Ireland), and the Solomon Islands were peopled almost entirely by NEGROIDS, that is to say by Oceanic Negroes, Papuans, and Negritos, similar to the inland populations of the eastern Malay islands. The Papuans were a tall race, with abundant bushy hair of woolly texture and with arched, almost Jewish noses. Their skins were very dark, and their appearance (except for the high nose), their noisy dispositions, love of excitement and laughter, reminded travellers very much of African Negroes. The Oceanic Negroes of the Bismarck Archipelago only differed from the Papuans in being more "negro", with more tightly curled hair and flatter noses. The Negritos were like the pigmy Negroes of Africa. But here and there on the coast of New Guinea, or on the islands off it, were obvious Polynesian settlements of old times, and even on some isolated island a people quite pale skinned and Caucasian in appearance.

The inhabitants of the Solomon Islands, the New Hebrides, of New Caledonia, and the Fiji archipelago are allied to the Papuans more than to any other stock, but are usually known as MELANESIANS.[1] Their characteristics when first discovered by Europeans (which for purposes of accurate description was not much more than one hundred years ago) were not quite so "negro" as those of the Papuans and the Negritos. They had dark, almost black skins and broad noses, but the head-hair was less tightly curled and grew to greater length. They had often the very prominent brow ridges of the Australoid, and some indications also of mixture with a higher race —the semi-Caucasian Polynesian—and were no doubt the result of an early mixture of all these types. The civilization of the Melanesians was somewhat higher than that of the Papuans, but inferior to the arts and industries and social life of the POLYNESIANS. They had developed agriculture to some extent, and amongst cultivated plants had the taro yam (a kind of Arum with tuberous roots), the Sweet potato (a Convolvulus), the sugar cane,

[1] This word is derived from two Greek roots meaning "Black Islanders". There is much difficulty in deciding what is Papuan and what Melanesian when classifying the peoples of the Solomon Islands and Bismarck Archipelago. There is a strong infusion of Melanesian blood in Hawaii.

the Bread-fruit tree,[1] the banana, the coconut palm, the sweet roots of a tree-lily (*Dracæna*), and the fruit of a Pandanus; perhaps also the Kava pepper vine. They possessed as domestic animals a pig of an east Asiatic species and a dog of a type like the pariah dog of India or the Dingo of Australia. They also had fowls of a game bantam type, which no doubt had been brought eastward by Malay traders till they passed from island to island into Melanesia, and even to most of the Polynesian islands *except* New Zealand. In New Caledonia there were fowls of a big breed but there were no pigs or dogs. [The domestic fowl was even found in the remote Easter Island when it was first visited by Europeans, but had not got beyond that to South America; neither had the American maize, tobacco, or other cultivated plants reached the Pacific islands till they were brought there from Asia or Europe in recent times.]

Melanesians, like Polynesians and Papuans, lived much on a fish diet if dwelling anywhere near the sea. The Papuans of New Guinea do not seem to have known the Bread-fruit until modern times, though that tree was the

[1] The Bread-fruit, which will often be referred to in these pages, is a tree of moderate height (*Artocarpus incisa*). With its near relative, the Jack fruit, it is a member of the Mulberry order, and consequently a distant relation of the figs. Dampier gives the following description of the Bread-fruit of the Pacific Islands: "It grows on a large tree as big and as high as our largest apple trees. It has a spreading head full of branches, and dark leaves. The fruit grows on the boughs like apples; it is as big as a penny loaf . . . of a round shape, and has a thick, tough rind. When the fruit is ripe it is yellow and soft, and the taste is sweet and pleasant. The natives of this island (Guam) use it for bread; they gather it when full grown, while it is green and hard; then they bake it in an oven, which scorches the rind and makes it black: they scrape off the outside black crust and there remains a tender thin crust, and the inside is soft, tender, and white, like the crumb of a penny loaf. There is neither seed nor stone in the inside, but it is of a pure white substance like bread. It must be eaten new, for if it is kept above twenty-four hours it becomes dry, harsh, and choky . . . this fruit lasts in season for eight months in the year." Mr. John Masefield, who has edited the best and the most recent edition of Dampier, compares the flavour of Bread-fruit to "apple sauce".

most important staple of life in so many Pacific islands, and under another name appears anciently to have been a favourite article of food in the Malay Archipelago. There was, however, no Bread-fruit among the New Zealanders, though they had sweet potatoes, taro yams, and gourds. Likewise the New Zealanders omitted to take the pig with them from their original home in Samoa: perhaps, however, the pig had not then reached those islands from the west. The New Zealanders ate their dogs, and the domestic dog throughout Oceania was bred for eating, and not merely as a hunting companion. Like the Dingo of Australia, and the domestic dogs of Negro Africa, the breeds of Malaysia and Polynesia could not bark. In Melanesia and most parts of the Pacific, including New Zealand, one or more species of rat were much in request as food, and were introduced by these different races of men into almost all the islands, including New Zealand.

All the Melanesians, like the Papuans of New Guinea, and the Negroes of the Bismarck Archipelago, were thorough-going cannibals, and this vice—the eating of human flesh—infected some of the Polynesian peoples, especially the New Zealanders. Cannibalism probably existed at one time in all the Polynesian islands, but had died out in most by the time they were discovered by Europeans, only remaining as a well-established custom in New Zealand and throughout Melanesia. The New Zealand Maoris used after one of their inter-tribal battles to collect the bodies of their slain enemies, cut off their scalps and right ears, and offer these first as a sacrifice to the gods. Then a row of cooking pits were dug on the right hand "for the gods" and on the left for humans. The eyes and the brain were removed from a dead warrior, and were eaten raw by the chief man of the victorious party. When the cut-up bodies of the vanquished were cooked, the chief's sons and relations first, and the whole of the army afterwards, fell on the meat cooked on the left-hand row of pits and devoured all they could at a sitting. The right-hand section of the feast was presided over by the priests and the contents of the pits partly consumed by them, and partly carried off to be stored against future requirements. What was left over on the left-hand side was packed up in baskets and sent to friendly tribes, who by accepting and eating the remains of these slain men took the side in the quarrel of the victorious force.

In Fiji human flesh was, above all, the food of chiefs, but everyone partook who could. Slaves were captured in war or purchased from other islands and were carefully fattened up for the table.

Cannibalism was partly an act of revenge, a desire more completely to extinguish a fallen enemy, and in part a sacrifice to the gods of the victorious tribe, or it began as an act of atonement or propitiation to win the favour of a deity. In New Caledonia and New Zealand—perhaps also in Fiji—it was often provoked by mere hunger for meat, a hunger less easy to satisfy than in the large islands of the Bismarck Archipelago and the mainland of New Guinea, where there were the great Cassowary birds, large fruit bats, tree kangarus, phalangers, and an immense variety of pigeons.

In religion there was mostly this difference between Melanesians, Micronesians, and Polynesians: the two latter had castes of priests who devoted themselves to the conduct of religious ceremonies, and were often unmarried; whereas amongst the Melanesians and Papuans there were no priests, anyone—usually the chief of the village or tribe

—being competent to sacrifice to the gods, or to conduct the semi-religious ceremonies (so like those of Negro Africa) connected with birth and death: most of all, the solemn rites observed in the initiation of boys and girls into the duties of adult life on their entering manhood or womanhood. The dwarf Negroes or Negritos of New Guinea and the islands to the west had very little religious belief; the Papuans more, but not so much as the Melanesians of the Pacific archipelagoes. These last, no doubt, had been taught and influenced for many hundred years by the Polynesians. All these peoples believed in a variety of gods, devils, spirits, and fairies. (The Fijians even believed in water-babies!) Sometimes the supernatural being was the soul of a deceased hero or chief, canonized after his death, and still working for or against the survivors in the form of a shark, a turtle, a fish, snake, or lizard.

Stones and trees were worshipped as the form or the home of a god; so were lizards, snakes, birds, the sea, a volcano, the sun, the moon, stars, and vault of heaven. Nearly everything of fixed form had a soul, was alive, was connected in some way with the spirit world. A belief among Papuans, Melanesians, Micronesians, and Polynesians in the immortality of human beings was almost universal. Only perhaps among the Negritos was it absent or "not thought about".

As to the arts and industries, all this region lay outside the range of metal-using countries, except where iron had been introduced by the Malays, as on the north-west coasts of New Guinea and the islands of the Malay Archipelago. Otherwise the races of Australasia and the Pacific were still in the Stone Age. The Papuans and Melanesians, however, had a great feeling for art and colour. They carved wood most skilfully with chisels made of bivalve shells, or stone adzes. There was a great tendency, derived from Malaysia, especially in New Guinea and Melanesia, to build houses on piles, with platforms rising high above the ground: a most convenient architecture both for defending the dwelling against attack (by drawing up the ladder of approach) and for raising sleeping places above the range of mosquitoes, centipedes, snakes, and damp. In some parts of New Guinea the people constructed their houses high up in the forks of great trees, and used rope ladders to ascend and descend.

But in Polynesia and those island groups to the east and north-east of New Guinea much influenced by the Polynesians, the houses were mostly built on the ground, sometimes with a stone floor, or were raised on a mound of earth. They were usually oblong in shape, and of considerable length, with a roof of thatch or palm leaves in shape like a long boat turned upside down. In the Solomon Islands the houses (occupied by several families) were occasionally as much as 70 feet long and 40 wide. The thatched roof was in some instances carried right down to the ground, in other cases it formed a veranda supported on posts. But in parts of New Guinea and the islands adjacent to its eastern half, in Fiji and New Caledonia there were round or oval-shaped huts, looking like hayricks. The houses of the New Zealanders had firm walls made of slabs of wood, and one small window facing eastward. There was a porch over the door. In the southern part of the great South Island, near the snowy mountains, there were winter houses made by excavating a square or oblong pit in the ground and roofing this over. In wintertime a fire was lighted inside this underground dwelling, and the temperature under the heavily thatched roof became very high, whilst it was freezing outside; but as the dwelling was unventilated it was often unwholesome for its occupants. Except among the wildest Negritos and Papuans, there were in every village a club house and a guest house, or the two uses combined in one large dwelling. And on this club house the men of the village lavished their best ideas of art and decoration. The beams and posts would be handsomely carved and painted, or even inlaid with beautifully coloured sea shells; mats woven of palm fibre or grass covered the walls, and the timbered floor might be lacquered with some vegetable varnish. Similar decorations were bestowed on their temples and their chiefs' houses.

The furniture consisted of little else than a rude bed made of slabs of wood covered with matting; chairs or stools were carved out of solid blocks of wood, or made from bamboo sections. The fireplace was a thick cane basket covered with clay. Canes or reeds and the invaluable bamboo equally made light but firm frames which did duty as tables in Polynesian households, but the Melanesians were usually content with mats and stools for all furniture. Pottery—baked clay—was made by the Melanesians and by most Papuan (but not Negrito) and Micronesian tribes; it was also known to the Polynesians, but for some reason had in late centuries almost gone out of use, its place being taken by wood vessels, gourds, the halves of coconuts, and the shells of clams. Still, the manufacture and use of clay pots were retained by the Polynesians of Easter Island. Food was cooked by placing it between hot stones, which were then sprinkled with water, and the whole thing covered over till the food was steamed and cooked. Water was boiled in wooden vessels by dropping in red-hot stones.

Sharp knives in New Guinea and Melanesia were made from splinters of bamboo. The ground was tilled and prepared for cultivation all over these Oceanic regions by wooden implements—pointed stakes, forked branches made into hoes, flat slabs rubbed down into smooth spades. Papuans (but not Negritos)—still more Melanesians, Micronesians, and Polynesians—were industrious agriculturists, and besides food plants they cultivated bright-coloured flowers (such as the crimson Hibiscus) and the paper Mulberry tree, from the bast of which they obtained the famous *tapa* "bark cloth", as also from the bast of fig trees and a relation of the Bread-fruit. There was no loom or idea of weaving anywhere, except here and there on the coast of New Guinea and in the Santa Cruz Islands (near the New Hebrides), whither it may have been introduced by Malay seafarers. But the plaiting of leaves, rushes, and fibre was carried to a fine art by all these Oceanic peoples. In New Zealand the Maoris made much use of the now-celebrated New Zealand flax, the fibre of *Phormium tenax*, a liliaceous plant related to aloes.

Not having any metal (as already related), axes were made of chipped flakes of obsidian (a glassy, flint-like volcanic stone) or of other stones ground to a sharp edge, or of hard, sharp-edged bivalve shells, or sharp-edged bones from the flattened spine of the tortoise or turtle. Terrible instruments for slaying and beheading were devised from the lower jawbones of large fishes, with saw-like rows of recurved teeth; or by implanting razor-edged sharks' teeth into the sides of wooden swords. Daggers with saw-like edges were made from the spines of the ray or skate, as well as from very hard wood rubbed down into a sharp cutting edge by sharks' skin. Spears and pikes were also made from hard wood and sharpened by burning the point in the fire. Or the point of the spear was made from the bony spines in the tail of the great Ray fish, or the wooden haft of the spear was fastened to a sharpened stone or obsidian blade by means of resin. Bows and arrows were in use nearly throughout New Guinea and most of the adjacent island groups; also in the New Hebrides. But they had not been introduced into New Zealand, and had fallen into disuse in most parts of Micronesia and Polynesia, though they were originally used by all these Oceanic peoples. In the eastern Melanesian islands slings were employed to hurl stones. Clubs and throwing sticks were common Papuan and Melanesian weapons, some of the former as executioners' weapons being fitted with stone heads. Shields scarcely penetrated to Polynesia, but were much developed and most fantastically carved and painted in New Guinea and some of the western Melanesian islands. In the northern parts of Oceania armour made of fibre, cord, or matting, and helmets of fibre, wood, or basketwork were worn, but more for ornament than to shield the head.

The Negritos, Papuans, and most of the Melanesians went about in complete, or almost complete, nudity before they were influenced by the Malays or by Europeans. On the other hand, the Polynesians were scarcely ever seen without some covering; they had, in fact, a sense of decency which was almost entirely absent from the negroid races of Oceania in their primitive condition. But whether or not clothing was worn for a covering or for propriety, the men, and in a lesser degree the women, of all the Oceanic races were passionately fond of ornaments. The more highly developed Polynesians decorated the face and body of men and also women by tatuing; that is to say, by pricking the skin with a sharp implement and rubbing in some colouring matter. The Melanesians and Papuans, however, were more addicted to what is called "cicatrization", that is to say, slashing the skin and raising permanent blobs or blisters by introducing some irritant. The more or less bushy hair was dressed sometimes with great elaborateness. Necklaces of teeth (human, dogs', pigs', kangarus', phalangers', fishes', and whales'), of seeds, shells, pebbles, bones, and pieces of wood were worn, together with armlets, bracelets, and anklets; so also were girdles of plaited fibre. The brightly coloured feathers of birds entered largely into personal adornments—in breastplates, masks, head-dresses, and robes.

All these Oceanic races possessed musical instruments, chiefly drums, flutes, Pan pipes, and slabs of resonant wood. They loved singing—especially the Melanesians—and dancing.

In both Melanesia and Polynesia—even also in Australia—there were the rudiments of picture writing, which in Easter Island became developed into regular hieroglyphics.

All the Oceanic peoples, except the dwarfish Negritos, were fond of birds, partly owing to their love of colour and partly due to a sense of the poetry of nature which thrilled them all, the handsome Polynesians most of all. In Easter Island the pretty little terns, or "sea-swallows", were tamed and trained to perch on the men's shoulders. Some of the island pigeons were partially domesticated. In New Guinea and the big islands near by a great admiration was felt for the fantastic Hornbills, and to wear a hornbill's head and casque was a privilege of brave men only. The New Zealanders regarded their parrots as semi-sacred. They would seem, however, in the earliest days of their settlements on these two great islands, to have exterminated the gigantic Moas. Perhaps, however, Nature had already begun the killing off of most of these flightless birds before man came on the scene. Certainly some Moas survived to the coming of the Polynesian New Zealanders from Samoa and Tonga; for the legend goes that, when the earliest pioneers of these adventurous people returned to Samoa with proofs of the discovery of a vast New Land in the southern ocean, they brought with them the bones and feathers of a gigantic bird.

Most of these Oceanic peoples had some idea of a currency, except in the savage interior of New Guinea; that is to say, there were objects used in trade which had a more or less fixed value, such as, in some island groups, the red hair-tufts from the necks of fruit bats, parrots' feathers, the feathers of the starling-like *Drepanidæ* (in Hawaii), brightly coloured shells—or, in others, pieces of bark cloth, rolls of matting, beautiful seeds, disks, pieces or points of shells strung on fibre (like the wampum of America), or the teeth of dolphins, whales, dogs, phalangers, and boars; also the vertebræ of the Dugong. (See p. 40.) In Micronesia the currency was more in objects like stones, either large "millstones" made of a yellowish limestone in Palao Island; or small red stones, polished pebbles, enamelled beads of unknown age and origin, prisms of polished, baked, red clay (known as *brak*), bits of glass or porcelain (obviously from China).

How were the Oceanic peoples living, from a social point of view, before the advent of the European? The Negritos of New Guinea and those which lingered in the interior of Malayan islands like Buru led an absolutely savage existence scarcely superior in intellectual level to that of the ape. They were hunters dwelling in the dense forest on grubs, termites, wild fruits, roots, and edible leaves; on the flesh of such birds and beasts or monitor lizards as they could snare or slay. They built rough shelters as temporary dwellings, and wandered from one part of the forest to another in search of food. They were expert at catching fish or climbing trees after birds' nests or honey, but they had no canoes, no implements, no religion (only a vague belief in a life beyond the grave), and no ceremonies connected with birth, puberty (or the "coming of age"), marriage, death, or burial. They belonged to the human species, but were primitive human types who had degenerated rather than advanced, and were almost drifting back into the life of the beast.

Then there were the jolly, ferocious, excitable, laughter-loving vigorous Papuans, with their nearly black skins, their mops of frizzled hair, their big arched noses and tall, well-made bodies. The Papuans lived in small tribes and passed their lives raiding other tribes, eating their captives, hunting ground kangarus, tree kangarus, phalangers, cassowaries, Birds of Paradise, parrots, and Crowned pigeons. They came to trade with the Malays on the coasts, where sometimes they settled down under Malay sultans. As often as not, however, they would turn treacherous, fall on some band of traders (if they could take them at a disadvantage), slay, and eat them.

On parts of the north-west and north-east coasts of New Guinea, as on some of the outlying islands of the Jilolo group and of the Bismarck Archipelago, there were settlements of Caucasian-like people, called by anthropologists INDONESIAN—a term scarcely distinguishable from Polynesian. They were of the same stock as the similar folk (with faces like dark-complexioned Europeans) to be met with on the islands off western Sumatra. These Indonesians had broadened out into Polynesians eastwards of New Guinea. They had mingled in most of the Melanesian islands with the primitive Negroes, and had introduced many new ideas in religion, warfare, and art. They were a little less cruel, perhaps, than the Papuans. In the extreme limits of their range to the north-east—Hawaii archipelago—and to the south-east—Easter Island—they had developed a considerable civilization, though it is by no means certain whether they were the first inhabitants of those islands (the existing Hawaiians, according to their traditions, came from Samoa and had only been in the Hawaiian archipelago for about nine hundred years when they were discovered or re-discovered by Captain Cook). They may have been preceded in both groups by the ancient race that built in huge blocks of stone, but which either passed on to America or died out, leaving, however, its mixed and slightly degenerate descendants in the Polynesians, who from some such centre as the Marquezas Islands and Tahiti spread westwards to Samoa, and thence to nearly all the Pacific islands.

Both in Easter Island and in Hawaii the development of religion was a development of terror. The common people were especially harassed by their belief in evil spirits waiting to torture them cruelly after death (a belief engendered in the Hawaii archipelago by the terrible earthquakes and the active volcanoes with their seething craters). And at any moment they were liable to be seized by the priests, the nobles, or the king to be offered up as human sacrifices to the gods of sky, earth, mountains, and sea. The priests and kings or chiefs (and in some islands a king or chief was not merely a high priest as well, but was often worshipped as a god during his lifetime) had immense power over the community by being able to establish "tabu". To declare a thing or a person "tabu" was equivalent to saying that it was sacred, under the protection of the gods—might not be touched, drunk, eaten, smelt, or even looked at, without risk of death, through the action of some supernatural force or as a punishment administered for impiety by the human authority. This practice penetrated to New Zealand and spread its influence over much of Melanesia. It could be wielded with great benefit in keeping the people in order, but it also checked their enterprise in many directions, and was shockingly misused by both priests and chiefs for their own advantage.

All the Oceanic peoples were immoral, and their numbers were slowly decreasing in the Pacific islands as the result of superstition, vice, and selfishness. In order that there should be no scarcity of food in the smaller islands families were often limited to one or two children, many infants being killed at birth. They were particularly averse from daughters, so that in not a few tribes and communities the women were much fewer than the men, perhaps only one woman to four men; thus not a few of the men (priests, generally) were unmarried. Women were very unfairly treated, as is frequently the case among barbarous peoples. They were often forbidden to eat the more nourishing forms of food, in case there should not be enough for the men. In Hawaii, for example, they were put to death if caught eating bananas, coconuts, or the flesh of pigs or turtles. Their husbands (in Tahiti and Samoa) sometimes made them wean their children and bring up instead young pigs or puppies. (A similar practice is referred to in my book on the Pioneers of Canada in regard to the rearing of young bears by Amerindian women.)

Wars were constantly being waged between island and island, tribe and tribe—especially in the Melanesian division of Oceania. In the western Pacific, indeed, the lives of the natives, before the establishment of the White Man's rule, was one perpetual acquaintance with terror. At any moment in the offing might appear the war canoes of an enemy, and ensue the sudden invasion of a village, the defeat of its fighting men, the cannibal feast on the bodies of the slain, the carrying off of the young women and children into captivity, there perhaps to be fattened up and killed for more cannibal feasts. Or when bathing and swimming (which nearly all these people delighted in) they might be seized and devoured by sharks; or their islet or island coast was suddenly swamped by an enormous tidal wave, or a mighty earthquake swallowed up the village in an earthcrack or landslide; or red-hot ashes and burning lava from a suddenly active volcano destroyed several communities; or hurricanes devastated their settlements and swamped their fleets of canoes. It is true that they never suffered from cold (except in New Zealand), and seldom from famine; for the sea provided bountifully fish and edible seaweed, there were the sea birds' eggs on the rocks, innumerable oysters, clams, sea slugs[1], crabs, langoustes, and prawns; there were pigeons, parrots, rails, plovers, ducks, on most of the smaller islands, and a bewildering abundance of bird life in New Guinea and the big islands. There was the Bread-fruit tree, there were bananas, yams, the invaluable coconut—giving food and a wholesome drink; and in New Zealand, where tropical products were mostly lacking (though the Maoris introduced sweet potatoes and taro yams), there was the bracken fern, which from root stems yielded a palatable

[1] Holothurians, a starfish-like creature, called in commerce *bêche de mer*.

substance like that sago which in west Melanesia and Fiji, as in Malaysia, was an important article of diet.

Yet in spite of an abundant food supply and a genial climate, these Oceanic peoples suffered a good deal from disease before the Europeans came. There was leprosy, which was a terrible plague in some islands; there were various forms of germ fevers introduced into the blood by mosquitoes; smallpox had come from the west, spread by the Malays. Mostly these primitive Oceanians led short lives; and if they were mainly merry and irresponsible, these spells of light-heartedness, of dancing, immoderate feasting and drinking, song-singing, love-making, gambling, and living the life of mermen and mermaids in the foaming breakers of a warm sea, alternated with heart-breaking struggles against the forces of nature, panics in regard to new diseases, terrors of unseen devils, torturing sacrifices to malevolent gods, murders, cannibal feasts, poisonings, and enslavement.

In this description of the condition of man in Oceania I have made no allusion to Australia and Tasmania, for the reason that the natives of the southern continent (of which Tasmania recently formed an outlying peninsula) differed so remarkably from the peoples of the Malay islands, New Guinea, Micronesia, Melanesia and Polynesia (including New Zealand) as to require separate treatment.

The aboriginal Australoids are the most primitive, the least improved of existing human races: although peculiarly developed in some points, they are the lowliest form of real mankind known to us. They were considered at one time to be the descendants of a brutish but big-brained type, a veritable "ogre" which dwelt in Europe some hundred thousand years ago: the Man of Neanderthal. But this impression was wrong; the Australoids more nearly resemble the less specialised, ancestral human race of Europe. Australia was originally peopled by two distinct types of men: the Australoids and the negroid Tasmanians. These last had the curly black hair and depressed noses of Negroes, though they were also akin to the Australoids; which last people, except that they are dark-skinned and brutish-looking, are remarkably like savage white men! They have head-hair which is neither lank like that of the Mongolian nor frizzly or tightly curled like the "wool" of Negroes and Papuans. Unlike the Papuans, moreover, and still more unlike the smooth-skinned Mongolian and Amerindian, the Australoid has much hair growing on the face and body, as is often the case among European and Indian peoples. But they also exhibit a feature present both in primitive man and in the modern European—an exaggerated projection of the brows, of the bones of the forehead which shade the eyes. The stature is not much below the European mean, but the lower limbs are usually short and rather slender. The forehead is retreating, the large jaws prominent, and the teeth bigger in proportion than in other races of modern men.

Considering the great area of the island-continent on which the Australoids must have lived for many thousand years, there is considerable uniformity of physical appearance amongst them, and a general resemblance in the structure and sounds of their languages, though these last are divisible into two main groups: those of the north and north-west, and the speech of the remainder of Australia. In considering their language, to some extent, and still more in examining their rudimentary arts and religious ideas, it is obvious that the people of the north-east of Australia have been visited for centuries by Malays,

Papuans, and even Polynesians, yet that none of these superior races succeeded in getting a permanent foothold.

So far as any sense of shame was concerned, the Australoids of both sexes went quite naked, or merely wore a girdle round the hips, to which strings or strips of fur were attached; but in cold weather or at night they put round their shoulders cloaks made from the skins of marsupials, skins sewn together after being scraped, softened, and dressed. Their own bodies they decorated or mutilated in various ways, such as knocking out two of the upper front teeth, passing a bone nose pin 5 or 6 inches long through the septum of the nose, cutting off the end joints of their fingers, and marking the skin of the upper arm, chest, and belly by terrific scars of raised skin. This was "cicatrization", so often referred to in describing the skin decoration of savages, especially the negroes of the Congo basin. The Australoids did not tatu their bodies (with pin-pricks and paint) like the Polynesians and Malays. They painted their skins for warfare or for ceremonial dances with red and yellow ochre, white and grey clay, and black mineral substances or charcoal. Also the men would gum to their bodies the white down or fluff of certain birds and beasts.

They had no agriculture, and no domestic animals but the Dingo. This dog they kept as much for eating as for hunting. Although each tribe occupied a definite area, they had scarcely any settled homes or permanent villages. They roamed about looking for food, and living for days, weeks, or months alongside their food supply, which consisted of the produce of the chase—kangarus, phalangers, wombats, koalas (tailless phalangers), emus, bustards, swans, parrots, and pigeons; fish, snakes, lizards, turtles (on the coast), and shellfish. They ate a good many

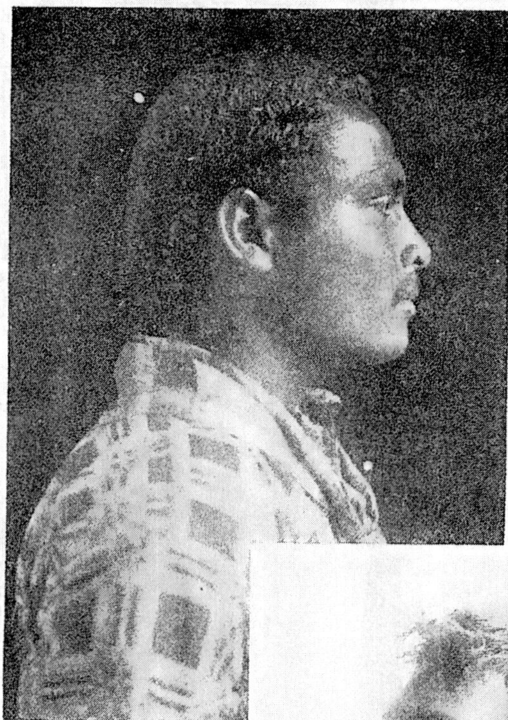

A TYPICAL POLYNESIAN

(A man of Tongatabu, Tonga Archipelago)

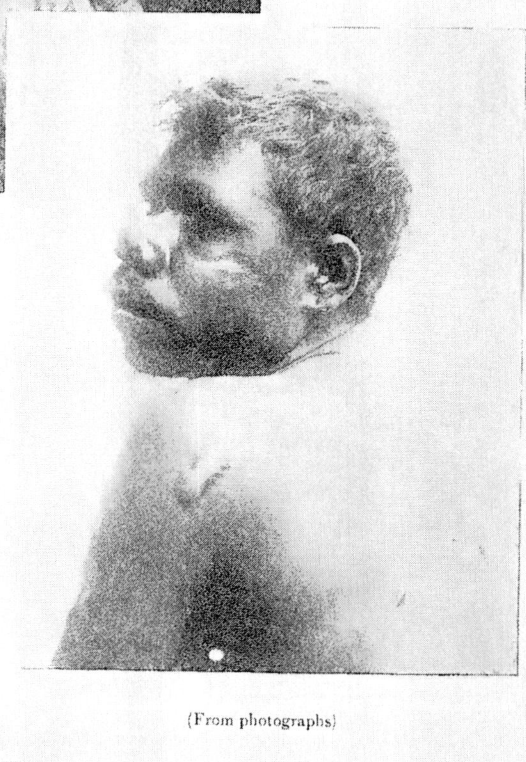

AN AUSTRALOID TYPE FROM NORTHERN QUEENSLAND

(From photographs)

insects—fat-bodied moths, beetle grubs, termites (white ants), the pupæ of real ants, and the larvæ of bees. Honey was, of course, much liked and much sought after, and from it they made with water a sweet drink which sometimes became slightly fermented like mead. Their women obtained from the ground wild yams, truffles, and the roots and tubers of various plants or the seeds of others. They cooked their food by broiling, by baking in the ashes, and by the use of hot stones. Although they did not know tobacco till the Europeans introduced it, they already possessed the idea of inhaling the smoke of other dried leaves through a bamboo pipe, and chewed some leaves for their soothing qualities.

When hard up for food, they occasionally became cannibals, and after an inter-tribal fight the slain were generally eaten. They had a vague sense of religion, believed that there was a life after the grave, that men's spirits mostly went to a land beyond the visible sky, and sometimes returned again in the bodies of newborn children. But some of these men—famous chiefs in their day—stopped in the sky and became gods. There was one principal God, who was sometimes identified with the creator of all things, and who might be seen at night time in the form of a very bright star. Much of their religion was associated with the discipline of the community, and was manifested in elaborate dances. Nearly every clan or tribe had "medicine" men—individuals who were learned in the customs and laws of the tribe, and who had some rough knowledge of medicine and surgery. Their tribal organization was based on the association for common purposes of defence of a number of groups, which last were either united by family ties or formed a brotherhood because they all inherited or adopted the same "totem"[1] or crest. It was usually forbidden for a man to marry a woman who belonged to the same clan or totem group as himself; he must secure a wife from another coterie. Marriage was actually or generally pretended to be an affair of capture, though frequently based on a bargain; and the unwilling young woman was sometimes dragged to her new home by the hair of her head, or knocked senseless by a club and then hoisted on to her husband's shoulders. The women, in fact, were very badly treated, and did all the hard work of the community.

The Australoids when first discovered were a degree or two farther advanced than the "Eolithic"[2] Tasmanians. They were, in effect, in a "Palæolithic" stage of culture, similar to that of Europe some fifty thousand years ago. Their weapons and utensils were made of wood, stone, and bone. They did not know the bow and arrow, but used a rather elaborate wooden rest for throwing their spears with greater force than by the unaided arm. The spearhead was either of finely pointed hard wood, carved with notched barbs, or it was a separate piece from the haft and made of stone, bone, or shell, tied strongly on to the haft, and further fastened by resinous gum. This gum from the Eucalyptus trees was very useful for attaching the blades of stone axes and knives to their handles.

But the Australoids were specially celebrated for two things: their "bull-roarers" and their "boomerangs". The bull-roarer was a carved and flattened piece of wood or stone something in the shape of an axe blade. At the

[1] The "totem" system is explained in my work on the *Pioneers of Canada.* The totem was some animal, plant, or natural object chosen as the imaginary ancestor or symbol of the clan.

[2] "Neolithic" means the age or stage of highly finished stone weapons and implements, "Palæolithic" refers to an earlier period when the stones were very roughly shaped, and "Eolithic" means the very dawn of culture, when the stones were merely broken fragments, not artificially shaped at all.

narrow end of this implement (which had a sacred character, as it was usually inscribed or painted with the "crest" or device of the clan's totem) were indentations, to which a piece of fibre string or strip of hide could be tied. The "churinga" (as it was called in south-east Australia) was then whirled round and round in the air till it made a loud booming noise. This the women were persuaded was the voice of a spirit, and only youths after their initiation, or full-grown men, were in the secret. [All over the world of savagery in ancient times, and in the few places where savages now remain, women have been very easily "gammoned", and have been made to believe much nonsense which the men invented to scare them and keep them in submission.]

The boomerang was a wooden throwing stick, very thin and flat, and curved or crooked in the middle. Although more or less flat in surface, it nevertheless had a slight twist, a little like the plane of a bird's wing. Hurled flatwise through the air it was a very effective weapon; and some kinds, if they did not hit the object aimed at, would return and fall near the place from which they had been thrown. But both boomerang and bull-roarer, though they seemed very novel and unusual to the early pioneers in Australian discovery, were really not peculiar to this savage people. They have existed in many parts of Negro Africa, and even anciently in Europe, India, and in Egypt.

The houses of the Australoids were rough shelters of sticks, fronds, and grass. In warm weather the natives did not bother to put up huts, but slept with their feet towards the fire and their heads against a low wind screen of boughs and grass. The aborigines of Australia had some gift for painting and drawing objects, and had even invented a rough alphabet of symbolic signs or primitive writing, with which they marked their "message sticks" or churingas. These message sticks, in fact, were the germ of letters.

Finally, it might be mentioned that, even when first discovered, Australia—an island continent of 2,946,691 square miles—was very sparsely inhabited, and the bulk of the population was confined to the districts near the seacoast. If there are, as is sometimes computed, one hundred thousand aborigines still living in Australia at the present day, there were probably not more than double that number a hundred years ago. They did much to limit their own increase by killing or abandoning their children; they were often engaged in civil wars; in times of scarcity they turned cannibal. What, however, is so remarkable about this isolated people is their having gone on living with very little change or improvement in the life which was that of our ancestors fifty thousand years ago. While the races of Europe and northern Asia have tried so many experiments, have achieved so many conquests over nature, have had such a marvellous insight into the workings of the universe—have, in fact, for ten thousand years or so, been leading the lives of demigods, the Tasmanians and the Australoids have been content just with the day's provision of food, a fairly dry sleeping place at night, a little fighting and dancing, lovemaking of a more or less brutal kind, and a span of life which, owing to its excessive hardships and the callous if not cruel treatment of the men and women past their prime, was seldom more than fifty years. They have, it is true, seen God in the stars, and they have felt like us the tragedy of death and the hope of a resurrection; but, unlike us (their far-off cousins, whose "Tasmanian" and "Australoid" ancestors stayed in Europe), they achieved no conquest over nature, their lives were scarcely better than the lives of beasts.

The Tasmanians shared some of the physical features of the Australoids. Like them they were dark-skinned—a very dark brown—and of brutish appearance, especially in the women. The men were usually better looking than the females, but both alike represented perhaps the lowest type of humanity which has been known to scientific men in a living state—for they just lived long enough to be photographed. The Tasmanians were distinctly more negroid than the Australoids. They were of medium height. The nose was broader, shorter, and more depressed than that of the Australoid, and the hair inclined to be tightly curled. They looked, in fact, with their long and large upper lips, their receding chins, projecting brows and jaws, big teeth, woolly hair, small, deepset eyes, and hairy faces and bodies (even the women had slight whiskers) like the most primitive form of *Homo sapiens*, and the joint ancestor of the Negro and the European.

Probably they entered north-eastern Australia at a very remote period, and were pushed down by the succeeding Australoids into the south-easternmost extremity of the continent—first the peninsula, then later the island of Tasmania. They were then (and they remained) in the lowest stage of human culture, like the Negritos or pigmy Negroes of Malaysia and Africa. They had no dwelling good enough to be called a hut: merely a circle of sticks stuck in the ground with their points converging. On to the top of these bent wands was thrown a mass of fern or grass, which made a rough thatch. Or the savages contented themselves in fine weather with a mere wind shelter of branches and bark strips. Whenever there was a cave or a cranny in the rocks handy to their hunting ground, they lived in that. They had no agriculture and no domestic animals, not even the Dingo or semi-wild dog of Australia. They lived much on shellfish, on the cray-fish of the streams, and the flesh of kangarus and other marsupial beasts, and such birds as they could bring down with their throwing sticks; though they also ate roots, fungi, fruits, gum, and the sweet sap of certain trees. This even they sometimes allowed to collect in hollows at the base of the trunk till it became slightly fermented. Their method of cooking was by broiling over a fire or placing the dead beast to cook in its skin in the hot ashes. Their only weapons and implements were heavy stones used as hammers; flaked stones—big chunks of sand-stone with sharp edges, held in the hand as scrapers or choppers; long stakes, their points sharpened and hardened by being charred in the fire, and their stems straightened by heat and pressure; stems of small trees fashioned into rough clubs; and short, straight, thin but heavy sticks used as missile weapons for hurling at birds or small mammals.

Their language was never properly written down by the Europeans. It is described as being full of rough sounds and not possessing a great number of words, but we really know very little on the subject. They were without any sense of shame, and if they wore any clothing it was for warmth or ornament. As a matter of fact, it was limited in the men to strips of kangaru hide tied round the neck or ankle, and other pieces of hide which were fastened round the legs like gaiters when travelling through thorny bush country. The women tied an un-dressed kangaru skin round the neck and waist, in which they carried' their babies. Both sexes wore necklaces of shells, flowers, or seeds; and the men decorated their hair with kangaru teeth. The bodies—especially of the men—were anointed with kangaru fat and coloured with red ochre, and this red dust and fat were also rubbed into the hair and beard.

They had no religion, other than a vague belief in a life after the death of the body. Yet they were not cannibals, as was the case with the Australoids and the Oceanians; and they treated their women better than did the brutal Australoids. But their tribes or clans were constantly at war with one another, and this fact rather than any scarcity of food was the cause of their being in small numbers after many thousands of years of settlement in this large and fertile island. At the end of the eighteenth century—when Tasmania was first explored by Europeans—it was estimated that the aborigines numbered a total of between six and seven thousand. Between 1800 and 1830 they were reduced to only two hundred by warfare with the invading English settlers, by murder, by the effects of alcohol, and the spread of European diseases. After 1830 the two hundred gradually died out, till in 1876 the last of the old Tasmanian race expired.

CHAPTER III

Spanish and Portuguese Explorers lead the Way to the Pacific Ocean

It is remarkable what a bait to the European in discovery have been both spices and strong perfumes, once so popular in cookery and in the toilette. The Romans and Greeks were drawn through Egypt to the Indian trade by the pepper and cinnamon of India and Ceylon, by the sweet-smelling woods and gums of India and Further India—sandalwood, eaglewood, benzoin, storax, dragon's blood from the Calamus palm, rasamala—the resin from a liquid-amber tree of Java. It was to reach pepper-and-spice-producing regions that the Portuguese (and after them the English) were drawn into the exploration of the Guinea coast; and that the Portuguese felt impelled to circumnavigate Africa, so as to gain unfettered access to the commerce of India. The search for an Atlantic route to India and China impelled Spaniards and English, under Genoese and Venetian leadership, to discover Tropical and North America. And having reached India, Ceylon, Sumatra and Malacca, the Portuguese found that the most precious of all spices (cloves and nutmeg) still lay in undiscovered regions to the East—the Maluk or Muluk Islands, as they were called by Arab seamen: a name afterwards corrupted to Moluccas.

When Malacca on the Malay peninsula had been conquered by the Portuguese, the great viceroy Albuquerque dispatched in the same year, 1511, one of his boldest captains—ANTONIO DE ABREU—to search for the Molucca and the Banda Islands, whence the Malay ships brought cloves and nutmegs. De Abreu touched at Java and the Sunda Islands and reached first Amboina, a small island off the south-west coast of Ceram; then passed on northwards till he again anchored off Ternate, one of the smallest of the five small Spice Islands lying close to the west coast of the big island of Jilolo. Here he found the clove trees growing, and probably met Chinese junks trading in cloves: for the Chinese had for several previous centuries been accustomed to travel as far afield as Papuasia in their quest of spices and perfumes. In 1512 de Abreu discovered the little Banda archipelago, lying in the open sea to the south of Ceram, and consisting of twelve islets, all very small, and one of them containing a terrific volcano, Gunong Api—which occasionally becomes active and devastates the neighbourhood of its cone. Just as the original "Moluccas"[1] were five very small islands (Ternate, Tidore, Mare, Mutir, and Makian), off the coast of Jilolo, and were the only places, in those days (besides the not-far-distant island of Bachian), where the right kind of clove tree grew; so the Banda Islands—only 17 square miles in area altogether—were the only home of the proper nutmeg, though inferior nutmegs grew on some of the other islets off the coast of Ceram and the west end of New Guinea.

Cloves nowadays are cultivated on other equatorial islands far away from eastern Malaysia; but in the sixteenth century they were only to be obtained from the Moluccas. The clove tree is a member of the great Myrtle

[1] The geographical term, Moluccas, now includes the very large island of Jilolo, Bachian, Buru, Ceram, &c.

family, and belongs to the genus *Eugenia.* It grows in favourable places to a height of 40 feet, bears a rich evergreen foliage of large oval leaves, and clusters of long, slender crimson flowers growing at the extremity of the twigs. These flowers have their petals concealed in the centre of the calyx opening, but the sepals (false petals or petal-like leaves which often precede the real petals in flowers) stick out in four projections round the mouth of the calyx. These tubular flowers, with their four short sepals at the ends, are in fact the cloves of commerce. They are gathered when ripe, and are a bright crimson in colour, afterwards turning brown or black. The nutmeg (the name is a mixture of English and old French and means musk nut) is the fruit of a tree with the Latin name of Myristica, which has a natural order all to itself, *Myristicaceæ.* It is evergreen, grows to about 50 feet in height in the Banda Islands, and bears male and female flowers without petals, that are green in colour and inconspicuous. The female flowers produce a quince-like downy fruit, which when mature and dry splits and reveals inside a walnut-like nut surrounded by a network of crimson fibre. This fibre is as precious as the actual kernel or nut, for it is the spice known as mace, quite distinct in flavour and use from the actual nutmeg. This last is, of course, the kernel of the hard-shelled nut which is surrounded by the crimson fibre of the mace, and the outer husk of the pear-like fruit.

The Portuguese—to put it vulgarly—soon knew they had got hold of a good thing in these small islands of clove and nutmeg trees. They established themselves more or less as the rulers of the Moluccas, with their headquarters at Ternate. But they treated the Malay subjects badly, and these were soon on the lookout for the arrival of other foreigners whom they could play off against the Portuguese. Yet for some ten years the Portuguese had no rivals in Malaysia. Their conquests and discoveries spread far and wide. They entered into relations with Celebes, reached the Island of Mindanao (the southernmost of the Philippines), and even passed out into the open Pacific, and sighted the Caroline islands of Micronesia. They seem also to have been the first to discover the western promontories of New Guinea, the Island of Timor, and to have had news of a continental territory to the south—Australia—all of which information soon afterwards reached the Spaniards, who put it to practical use.

Among the Portuguese, who thus became acquainted with the Spice Islands of eastern Malaysia, was Fernão de Magalhaẽs—stupidly miscalled, in English literature, MAGELLAN. His earlier story has already been told in a previous volume of this series.[1] Having been very badly treated by the King of Portugal, Magellan and several of his friends and relations passed over into the service of the united kingdoms of Castile and Aragon, which were about to become the great kingdom of Spain. It will be remembered by the reader that, in 1494, the King of Portugal and the King and Queen of Aragon-Castile, to avoid quarrelling about the marvellous discoveries their adventurers were making, had concluded the Treaty of Tordesillas under the auspices of the Pope, a treaty which practically divided between these kingdoms of the Iberian peninsula all the non-Christian world outside Europe and the Turkish Empire. Their boundaries were a meridian of longitude running from pole to pole, and cutting the globe into two divisions. The meridian was fixed at a distance of 1110 miles west of the Cape Verde Islands, and more

[1] *Pioneers in India*, &c.

or less coincident with the fiftieth degree of longitude west of Greenwich. Consequently, in the west it gave Portugal the Brazilian part of the South American continent; while on the other side of the globe the corresponding meridian (130° E. of Greenwich) cut off the Portuguese from entering into possession of all Australasia, and afforded Spain the pretext of attempting to reach Malaysia from the east (across the Pacific), and thus of laying claim to the Spice Islands which might be found to lie outside the Portuguese sphere. [As a matter of fact, when the longitude was correctly calculated, both Philippines and Moluccas lay in the Portuguese domain.] The great Spanish adventurer, Nuñez de Balboa, had in 1513, "from a peak in Darien" near the isthmus of Panama, sighted the Pacific Ocean, which the Spaniards at first called the Southern Sea. The Portuguese realization of the wide ocean which lay to the east of Malaysia, combined with the news that Central America had on the western side of it an ocean at least as vast as the Atlantic, decided Magellan to propose to the new ruler of Spain, the Emperor Charles V, the great project of finding a way round—or a strait through—South America, and the complete fulfilment of the original plan of Columbus—the reaching of the Indies by a western route across the Atlantic. His proposals were accepted, and he was given, in 1518, command over a little fleet of five ships,[1] the largest of which (the *San Antonio*) was only 120 tons in capacity and the smallest 75 tons. He left Spain on September 21, 1519, to search for this passage round or

[1] The *San Antonio* (which deserted the expedition in South America), the *Trinidad* (after a fruitless voyage out into the Pacific and back to the Moluccas, seized and dismantled by the Portuguese), the *Santiago* (lost on the coast of Patagonia), the *Concepcion* (broken up in the Philippines), and the *Victoria*, which ultimately returned to Seville in 1522.

through South America to the Southern Sea. His expedition included 190 Spaniards, and a number of Portuguese, Genoese, and other Italians—including the famous Lombard geographer of those days, ANTONIO PIGAFETTA—several Frenchmen and Flemings, one Englishman (named Andres, a gunner from Bristol), and one or two German gunners or artillerymen. The first account given to the world of this first-recorded circumnavigation of the globe was written by the accomplished Antonio Pigafetta, who accompanied Magellan from mere love of knowledge, and was one of the few who actually returned to Spain after voyaging right round the world.

Magellan explored the east coast of South America for an opening which should lead into the other sea. At first he thought he had found it in the estuary of the Rio de la Plata, but as soon as he noticed the water was fresh he continued southward along the coast of Patagonia (spending five months in that region to rest ships and men, and quelling a dangerous mutiny, till at last he found a likely opening between the mountains of Patagonia and the snowclad peaks of Tierra del Fuego. He had already lost the smallest of his ships on the Patagonian coast, and in the Straits of Magellan the *San Antonio* deserted and sailed back to Spain; but the crews of the others remained faithful to Magellan after their captains had taken anxious counsel together. At length these three little vessels rounded "Cape Deseado"—the desired Cape—and found themselves within sight of a mighty ocean at the end of November, 1520; an ocean which seemed so calm after the stormy Atlantic that Magellan called it the "Pacific Sea".

After emerging into the Pacific Ocean, Magellan's three ships voyaged for ninety-six days without stopping at any land, and the crews went for 110 days (from the Straits of Magellan to the Ladrone Islands) without getting any kind of fresh food. "We ate", wrote Antonio Pigafetta, "biscuit which was no longer biscuit, but powder of biscuits swarming with worms and stinking terribly because it had been befouled by rats. We drank yellow water which had been putrid for many days. We also ate ox hides that covered the top of the mainyard to prevent the mast from chafing the shrouds, which had become exceedingly hard because of its exposure to sun, rain, and wind. These pieces of hide were soaked in sea water for four or five days and then placed for a few minutes on top of glowing charcoal and afterwards eaten." But in their hunger the men often ate sawdust, and as to the rats that were caught, they were sold at a high price. Scurvy soon broke out, and the gums of the men's jaws swelled so that some could not eat at all, and therefore died of starvation—nineteen in all, amongst them a giant Patagonian captured in South America to be carried back to Spain. And thus they sailed some 12,000 miles across the Pacific Ocean. "Truly it was very pacific," wrote Pigafetta, "for during that time we suffered no storm. We saw no land except two desert islands on which were found nothing but birds and trees." The water round them swarmed with sharks. But that they were favoured with such good weather, and sailed a steady 180 to 210 miles a day, they "would all have died of hunger in that exceeding vast sea". But Magellan held on with a tenacity which leaves Columbus behind in resolution, for Columbus reached land on his first voyage after only thirty-six days of anxious expectancy, whereas it was the ninety-seventh day of Magellan's long agony before a land was reached which was likely to be of use as a place of refreshment.

They noted that the skies in this Southern Hemisphere were not so full of stars as in the North, but they also observed the splendid Southern Cross with five bright stars pointing straight towards the west. They passed not far from the Marquezas Islands. Apparently the only land they sighted on their way across the Pacific, except the small islands frequented by birds, was St. Paul Island, of the Paumotu group, and perhaps Malden Island. Magellan's voyage, amongst other things, was remarkable for what he missed quite as much as for what he attained. It is wonderful to think that he sailed across the Pacific from the coast of Chili to Guam, which is well within the Asiatic region, and only sighted land four times, and then only in the form of small and desert islands. His chiefest desire, however, was to get out of stormy latitudes into the peaceful equatorial belt, and to reach as quickly as possible the comparative security of the known, not liking to trust the fate of his crews to unknown lands which might be without good supplies of fresh water and food, and be peopled by savages incapable of understanding them. For it must be remembered that his previous experience had given him a great deal of insight into the islands of Malaysia, and he had managed to obtain from Sumatra before he started on this great voyage an interpreter named Henrique, who spoke Malay as his native tongue.

On the 6th March, 1521, the Spaniards sighted three islands, of which one was higher and larger than the other two. Off this the next day they came to a stop. It was afterwards known as the Island of Guam. The inhabitants, without any fear, boarded the ships and stole whatever they could lay their hands on, even wrenching off and carrying away the small boat that was fastened to the poop of the flagship. Thereupon Magellan in great anger went ashore with forty armed men, burnt many houses and canoes, and killed seven of the natives. He recovered his small boat and the expedition immediately sailed away. Yet so terrible was the craving for fresh food on board that when the sick men, dying of scurvy, realized that the armed party were going on shore, they begged them to bring back the entrails of any man or woman they might kill, the eating of which these poor mad sailors believed would restore them to health!

It is noteworthy that the Spaniards when they landed fought with crossbows and arrows, which were in those days much more effective weapons than the guns of the period. The Micronesian people they met on the Island of Guam they described as going naked, many of the men being bearded and having black hair that reached to the waist. They wore small palm-leaf hats, were as tall as the Spaniards, well-built and of tawny skin, with teeth turned red and black by the chewing of betel. The women, who were good-looking, delicately formed, and much lighter in complexion than the men, had black hair which was worn loose and reached almost to the ground. The women did not work in the fields but stayed at home, weaving mats and baskets from palm leaves. The mats were beautifully made and used to decorate the walls and the floors of their houses. They slept on palm straw, which was soft and fine. Their houses were built of planks and thatched with banana fronds. The food of the people was chiefly coconuts, sweet potatoes, fowls, bananas (really long plantains 1 foot in length), sugar cane, and flying-fish. The chief amusement of both men and women was to plough the seas with their small boats, which were usually painted black, white, or red. Pigafetta describes the outriggers, and says the sails were made of palm leaves.[1] Having no fixed rudder, but only using a long paddle for such a purpose, and the boats being sharp at both ends, they could be sent backwards or forwards without turning round.[2]

At dawn on 16 March, 1521, the expedition sighted high land. This was the Island of Samar, on the eastern side of the Philippine archipelago.

Magellan's first thought was for his sick men, and to give them some chance of recovering he landed them on an uninhabited islet, put up tents there, and had a pig killed to provide fresh meat. Two days afterwards they saw a boat coming towards them and nine men in it. These were very different from the wild-natured barbarians of Guam. They were evidently familiar with the idea of white men and white men's ships, being of course Malays. They were described by Pigafetta as "reasonable men". Presents were exchanged, the Spaniards giving red caps, mirrors, combs, bells, ivory, and cotton cloths of Turkish manufacture. The Philippine Islanders offered fish, a jar of palm wine, a few coconuts, and bunches of long bananas. They promised further supplies of fresh food in a few days, but in the meantime

[1] Magellan first gave to the Ladrone Islands the name of Islands of Sails, on account of the many vessels with sails which he observed in that neighbourhood, showing how firmly established among the Polynesians and Micronesians was the use of the sail in their navigation, a fact which explains the success of their voyages over enormous sea distances.

[2] They were similar to the prahus or praus of Malaysia, which did not turn round, but sailed backwards and forwards, the sharp stem being exactly like the sharp stern. Most of the prahus had outriggers, and in all the leeside of the vessel was flat and perpendicular while the weatherside was rounded. The mast carried a large triangular-shaped sail.

the coconuts seemed to the Spaniards perfectly delicious, and Pigafetta wrote a long description of the tree and its many useful products, and of the nuts with their rich pulp and pleasant-tasting milk.

The name of St. Lazarus, because of the saint's day on which they were first discovered, was given to the islands of this archipelago.[1] The people encountered in the coast regions of these western and southern Philippine Islands do not seem to have been negritos or little negroes like those of the great Island of Luzon, but all more or less of the Malayan-Mongolian stock. They had very black straight hair which fell to the waist; went nearly naked except for cloths round the waist—but some of these cloths were beautifully embroidered; and in the waistbelt the men thrust large daggers ornamented with gold.

The expedition passed on between the islands of Samar, Leyte, and Mindanao, and came to anchor off a small island named Masawa, now not easily identified, but apparently between Leyte and Bohol, arriving there on 7 April. The ruler of this islet, whom they referred to as "the king", received them with some wonderment but great friendliness, and expressed a wish to enter into brotherhood with Magellan. The king understood the Malay spoken by the interpreter on board, for, says Pigafetta, the kings of these districts knew more languages than the common people. He presented Magellan with a basketful of ginger and a large bar of gold, which for some reason or other the great Portuguese would not accept. The next day, Good Friday, the king came on board Magellan's ship, embraced him, and gave him three porcelain jars full of raw rice, two

[1] They were not called the Philippines until 1543, or thereabouts.

very large fish, and other things. He received in exchange a Turkish dress and a fine red cap, while to his courtiers were given knives and mirrors. The king and Magellan made brotherhood together. In order to impress him, Magellan had one of his men put into complete armour, and then placed this man in a group of three men armed with swords and daggers, who forthwith struck him in all parts of his body, but of course did him no harm; "thereby the king was rendered almost speechless". Magellan went on to impress the monarch with the fact that one of these armed men was worth a hundred naked savages, and as there were 200 men in the ships armed with this steel armour from head to foot, the expedition was invincible.

Magellan, and amongst other people Pigafetta, went on shore to return the visit. They were received by the king on the stern deck of a very large prau or native vessel[1] (about 70 feet long). Here pork was brought to them, together with jars filled with palm wine. Although it was Good Friday, they were obliged to sink their religious scruples and feast with the king. Pigafetta then applied himself to writing down a vocabulary in their language, with which feat the natives were greatly astonished. Later on, when it was time for the evening meal, two large porcelain dishes were brought, one containing rice and the other pork and gravy. After this meal was consumed the party of Europeans went to the king's palace, which was raised up high from the ground on huge posts of wood, so that it was necessary to ascend to it by means of ladders. There more food was brought, a roast fish cut in pieces and freshly gathered ginger and palm wine. As it grew dark, lights were

[1] See p. 97.

furnished, a kind of candle made of resin wrapped in palm or banana leaves. All the party went to sleep where they were, and when day dawned Pigafetta and the Spaniards returned to the ship.

He relates that pieces of gold of the size of walnuts and eggs were found by sifting the earth in the island of Masawa. All the dishes of the king were of gold, and also some part of his furniture. The king is described as being a fine-looking man, with glossy black hair hanging down to his shoulders, a covering of silk on his head, two large golden ear-rings, and a cotton cloth embroidered with silk covering him from the waist to the knees. At his side hung a dagger, the haft of which was of gold. Moreover, this king had anticipated American fashions, and had three plugs of gold let into each front tooth, while gold seems also to have been rammed in between the teeth. He was perfumed with storax and benzoin, and his skin was tatued all over. A brother king was apparently chief of the northern part of the great Island of Mindanao, lying to the south. On Easter Sunday Magellan decided to land with his chaplain and have Mass celebrated on shore. He came with fifty men unarmed and dressed in their best clothes. The two kings of Masawa and Mindanao embraced Magellan and were placed with him in the procession. Before the commencement of Mass Magellan sprinkled their bodies with musk water. Apparently at that time all these Malay people of the eastern Philippines were pagans, and had not been converted to Muhammadanism.[1] They were favourably impressed with their first experience of

[1] They told Magellan that they worshipped nothing, but that they believed in a god called Abba, who lived in the sky, and to him they raised their faces and their clasped hands when anxious to appeal to him.

Christianity, and eagerly took part in the service of the mass. They exactly imitated all the Spaniards did, kissing the cross and remaining on their knees with clasped hands at the elevation of the Host.

When Mass was over, Magellan arranged a fencing tournament, at which the kings were greatly pleased.

Magellan, becoming very friendly with the King of Masawa, asked if he had any enemies whom he wished to be destroyed. The king replied that there was indeed one island hostile to his rule.

After a cruise round the islands in the centre of the archipelago—in the course of which they killed a very large fruit-bat, "as big as an eagle", and ate it, finding it to resemble chicken in taste; and also observed the mound-building megapodes (see p. 30)—they reached the important Island of Sebu or Zubu (Cebu). Here the king of the island asked them to pay tribute, and pointed out a ship which had just arrived from Siam to fetch gold and slaves, but which had paid tribute or customs duties to him. But Magellan, through his interpreter, caused the king to be told that he was the captain of so great a monarch that he did not pay tribute to any other prince in the world; that if he wished peace he could have peace, but that otherwise the Spaniards were quite ready for war. The interpreter went on to point out that the employer of Magellan was the great Emperor of the Christians and the King of Spain, a much more powerful monarch than the King of Portugal, though this last had conquered all the coast of India. After consideration, the king decided to make blood brotherhood with Magellan, and even desired to know if he should pay tribute to the Spaniards. Magellan replied, No; it was sufficient that he should give them liberty to trade. Magellan, in his conversations with the notabilities, impressed on them the importance of the Christian religion, promising them if they became Christians they would have perpetual peace with the King of Spain.

Pigafetta accompanied Magellan and his party on shore to visit the King of Sebu. They found this prince in his palace surrounded by many people. He was seated on a palm mat on the ground, an embroidered scarf round his head, and nothing but a cotton cloth about his waist, in order, no doubt, that his elaborately tatued skin might be duly exhibited. He wore, however, a necklace of great value and two large gold ear-rings set with precious stones. In person he was fat and short. At the time the visit took place he was eating turtles' eggs out of porcelain dishes, and had four jars full of palm wine in front of him, covered with sweet-smelling herbs and arranged each with a small reed in the jar, through which he sucked up the palm wine. The Spaniards, whilst joining him in his feast of turtles' eggs and palm wine, renewed their exhortations to him to adopt the Christian religion. He put the question aside for the time whilst he treated them to a concert at which four young girls played on instruments like gongs, "so harmoniously that one would believe they possessed a good musical sense". They were nearly as white skinned as Europeans, and as beautiful, with long black hair. The gongs were made of brass, and apparently came from China. They were, in fact, very like the musical dinner gongs from Japan so much in vogue at the present day.

The king decided to adopt Christianity as his religion, but he complained that some of his chiefs did not wish to follow his example. However, they yielded apparently to Magellan's arguments and agreed to the setting up of a cross. On 14 April, at a ceremonial arranged with great splendour by the Spaniards, the King of Sebu was baptized and given the name of Don Carlos, after the Emperor Charles V. The heir apparent was called Don Fernando, the friendly King of Masawa was named Juan, and all the leading chiefs and notabilities, to the number of 500, were similarly baptized and given Christian names. In the evening the chaplain of the fleet went ashore and baptized the queen[1] and forty of her women. In all, the Spaniards baptized 800 Filipinos. One village on an islet, which refused baptism for its people, was burnt to the ground.

On the following day the queen came with great pomp to hear Mass. Three girls preceded her, carrying other specimens of her tiara hats in their hands. The women who accompanied her were nearly naked, the queen herself being again dressed in black and white, with a large silk scarf crossed with gold stripes. Having made due reverence to the altar she seated herself on a silk embroidered cushion. Magellan then arose, and before the commencement of the Mass sprayed her and her women with rose-water.

In spite of the natives telling Magellan at first that they worshipped nothing but a god in the sky, they seem to have had a number of fetishes to which they paid reverence, especially when pleading for recovery from sickness. These idols were mostly made of wood, were hollow, and were probably representations of wild boars. Magellan incited the people to the destruction of

[1] The queen was young and beautiful, and entirely covered with a white and black cloth. Her mouth and nails were stained very red, while on her head she wore a large hat of palm leaves, like a tiara.

their idols in order that their conversion to Christianity might be better affirmed. This they did, crying out: "Castilla, Castilla!" as they threw the idols and the meat consecrated to them into the flames.

The islet on which a village had been burnt as punishment for its refusing Christianity was called Maktan, and towards the end of April the chief of Maktan sent messengers to Magellan with a present of two goats, and a request that he would send soldiers to assist him in fighting another chief on the islet who had refused allegiance to the King of Spain. Magellan decided to go himself with three boatloads of soldiers. Many of his officers entreated him not to take such a risk, but he persisted, and reached Maktan three hours before dawn with sixty armed men. He then sent messengers to the refractory chief, calling on him to recognize the King of Sebu as his immediate sovereign, and to give in his allegiance to the Crown of Spain and pay the Spaniards tribute. The natives sent back a warlike message. The Spaniards advanced, but found the people had dug pit-holes before their houses in order that they might fall into them. In the village the Spaniards were attacked by about 1500 people, who charged down on them with shouts and cries. The musketeers and the crossbowmen discharged their pieces with little effect on natives who leapt hither and thither incessantly, and covered themselves nimbly with their shields, while at the same time they shot so many arrows and iron-tipped bamboo spears at the Spaniards (besides pointed stakes hardened with fire, stones, and mud) that Magellan and his sixty soldiers despite their armour were overwhelmed. Eight of the soldiers were killed, and Magellan was shot in the leg with a poisoned arrow. [The steel armour of which Magellan boasted seems to have been of little avail.] The order to retreat was given, and as the small party waded back through the water to the boats Magellan was killed by the impetuous assault of the natives, who hurled themselves upon him and practically cut him to pieces. He fought long for his life, and ever and again turned his face seaward, to assure himself that his men were safely retreating to their boats. Some of the Spaniards, it is true, stayed to see what was happening to their captain, but their defence of him seems to have been half-hearted, and as soon as he was down they made the best of their way to the boats.

The King of Sebu is said to have wept on hearing of the death of Magellan (on 27 April, 1521). Nevertheless, this death changed very considerably the attitude of the king and his chiefs towards the Spaniards. It was now realized that the armoured Europeans were mortal like the Filipinos, and could be killed in battle. Therefore a plot was laid to get rid of them altogether, a plot apparently instigated by the Sumatra interpreter already referred to, who was a slave and wished to regain his liberty. By means of fair words, invitations to a banquet, and promises of a present of jewels for the King of Spain, the King of Sebu lured on shore twenty-four Spaniards, including "an astrologer" and the commanders of three of the ships.[1] Pigafetta, fortunately for our records of this voyage, could not go, as he was suffering from the wound of a poisoned arrow in his face. The Spaniards, soon after they landed, were set upon by the natives, and all of them killed except the Malay interpreter. One commander, Juan Serrano, was seen running down to the beach nearly naked and

[1] One of these was the celebrated Duarte Barbosa, commander of the *Trinidad*, whose book on his travels in India and Further India is much quoted by me in *Pioneers in India*, &c.

wounded, and crying out to the Spaniards not to fire any more, as he too would be killed. He then told them how the others had been massacred, and begged that he might be redeemed with merchandise. He made a special appeal to his boon companion, the pilot Joam Carvalho, but the latter would not run the risk of sending any boat on shore, and poor Serrano was left weeping on the strand and probably soon shared the fate of his companions.

Off one of the islands near Sebu the survivors of Magellan's expedition decided to burn the ship *Concepcion*, as too few men were left to work it. There then remained 115 men for the working of the two remaining ships of the squadron, the *Trinidad* and the *Victoria*. These two vessels forthwith sailed to the Island of Panglao (off Bohol) where they noticed that the natives were black-skinned and like negroes. Thence they passed to the large southern island of Mindanao, whose principal chief at once made friends with them. The abundance of gold in the possession of the natives of Mindanao was duly noted. From Mindanao the expedition sailed to the little Kagayan islands in the Sulu Sea, where the people had blowpipes with tiny poisoned arrows, daggers with their hafts adorned with gold and precious stones, and wore armour made of buffalo hide. They were more or less Muhammadans, but called the Spaniards "holy beings". The two ships next visited the long island of Palawan, which seemed to their crews the Land of Promise, because they had suffered great hunger before they found it, and were even on the point of abandoning their ships and going on shore that they might not be consumed with famine. Fortunately the king of this country made peace with them quickly. After slashing himself slightly in the breast with a Spanish knife, and touching the tip of his tongue with it in token of truest peace, he invited them to do the same. His people went naked, but they cultivated the fields carefully. They were well armed with blowpipes and thick wooden arrows tipped with fish bones and bamboo, and poisoned. They possessed very remarkable poultry, large and very tame, which were regarded with such veneration that they were seldom eaten, the cocks being kept for fighting with one another. These Palawan people distilled a wine or spirit from rice, which was very strong. They possessed goats and pigs as well as fowls, and grew quantities of rice, ginger, sweet potatoes, sugar cane, bananas, and different kinds of edible roots. Passing from Palawan to the coast of North Borneo, and stopping off the town of Brunei, the expedition was greeted at one place by a chief who sent to meet the Spanish ships a very beautiful prau, the bow and stern of which were illuminated with gold, while it hoisted a white and blue banner surmounted with peacocks' feathers. This prau contained a band of musicians and eight old men who were chiefs. These came on board the Spanish ships and took seats on a carpet, presenting the Spaniards with a painted wooden jar full of betel paste, jasmine, and orange blossoms, a covering of yellow silk cloth, two cages full of fowls, a couple of goats, three jars of arrack (rice spirit), and bundles of sugar cane. They gave some presents to the other ships, and, after embracing the Spaniards, took their leave. Six days later the king of this district sent three more praus with great pomp, which encircled the ships whilst bands of music were played and drums beaten. Amongst the food given to the Spaniards were "tarts made of eggs and honey". The king and queen of this region—the sultanate of Brunei—were sent green velvet robes, violet velvet chairs, a good many yards of red cloth, writing-books of paper and a gilded writing-case, needlecases, drinking-glasses, and caps.

The Spaniards, being invited to land, dispatched a party on shore, who found elephants awaiting them, on which they rode to the house of the governor of the port, where they slept on beds with cotton mattresses and cotton sheets, and had an excellent supper. The next day elephants were supplied to bring them to the king's palace, where they found 300 foot soldiers with naked swords guarding the king. A brocade curtain was drawn aside from a large window, and through it they could see the Sultan of Brunei seated at a table chewing betel. They were told they could not speak to the king, but they could send their message through his courtiers. One of these would communicate it to the brother of the governor, and this man would send it by means of a speaking-tube through a hole in the wall to another official who was in the king's chamber. They were taught to make three obeisances to the king with their hands clasped above their heads, raising first one foot and then the other, and then kissing their hands towards him.

The king was graciously pleased from a distance to reply to their greetings, that since the King of Spain desired to be his friend he was willing that they should have food and water and permission to trade. After they had returned to the governor's house nine men arrived from the king carrying a splendid repast on large wooden trays. Each tray contained ten or twelve porcelain dishes full of veal, chickens, peacocks, and fish, in all thirty-two different kinds of meat, besides fish and vegetables. After each mouthful of food the visitors drank a small cupful of rice spirit and ate sweetmeats with gold spoons. During the night their sleeping quarters were lit with torches of white wax in tall silver candlesticks, and also with oil lamps, each containing four wicks. Two men sat by each lamp to snuff it continually during the night. They were sent back the next morning on elephants to the seashore, while native vessels conveyed them back to the ship.

The town of Brunei (now a miserable place) was a water city like Venice, the houses being raised on poles rammed into the mud. The king was a Muhammadan, and, as can be seen, his state enjoyed a very large measure of Eastern civilization, derived from traffic with the Arabs, from ancient Indian influence, and from direct trade with China.

A few days later, however, the Spaniards took fright at the approach of a fleet of a hundred praus, cut their cables and hoisted their sails. They were pursued by one or two of the native boats, but they soon beat these off with their guns. In attacking these vessels they captured a number of prisoners, some of whom they released; retaining, however, nineteen Malays (three of them women) for the purpose of taking them to Spain.[1]

As to the Malay junks or ships with which they had now come into contact, Pigafetta writes an interesting description. The hull of the vessel was built of planks fastened together with wooden pegs, the carpentry being very clever and neat; but at a height of about 15 inches above the water level the construction was continued with large bamboos. The masts were of bamboo and the sails were of bark cloth, or palm-leaf matting.

[1] Some of these (including the women) were set free in the Moluccas, others died on the voyage, but a few actually did reach Seville, and with one exception, after being carefully instructed in Christianity and the Spanish language, were sent back to the Philippines in 1527. The exception was a Malay who showed himself so extraordinarily clever about money matters and trade that the Spaniards feared if he returned to the Far East he might be a little too knowing in appraising the value of European trade goods. So he apparently ended his days in Spain.

North Borneo, like the Philippines, had long been semi-civilized by intercourse with China. All well-to-do people possessed porcelain dishes and cups, and the Muhammadan Malays used bronze money impressed with Chinese characters. The Bornean Malays had a curious habit of taking small doses of mercury (quicksilver), not only to cure illnesses, but in the belief that it prevented sickness by purging the body. Pigafetta also relates that the Sultan of Brunei possessed two pearls as large as hens' eggs, so round, however, that they would not stand still on a table. These pearls came from the south-western islands of the Philippine archipelago. They had belonged to the king of the principal island of the Sulu archipelago, whose daughter had married the Sultan of Brunei, and had unwisely boasted of her father's pearls as big as hens' eggs. Her husband determined to get possession of them, by force if necessary, so had assembled a fleet of 500 praus (or, as another variant of the story puts it, 50), and sailing by night he surprised the King of Zolo, or Sulu, and two of his sons, and carried them off to Brunei, where he held them as captives until the pearls were delivered to him.

Pigafetta realized the immense size of the Island of Borneo—the second largest island in the world, only New Guinea being of greater area if Australia be considered a continent—he was informed that it took three months to sail round it in a Malay prau. It was a region that produced camphor,[1] cinnamon, ginger, myrobalans,[1] oranges,

[1] The camphor of Malaysia is a crystalline secretion found in the crevices of the bark of a magnificent tree, the *Dryobalanops aromatica*. The camphor more commonly met with in commerce is derived from the bark of a kind of laurel growing in Japan and Formosa. Myrobalans are the fruit of a tall *Terminalia* tree of the *Combretaceæ* family. They are plum-like in appearance and very astringent. The kernels are eaten, but the rind is used for making ink and very dark dyes.

lemons, water-melons, cucumbers, gourds, and many other vegetables and fruits; buffaloes, oxen, swine, goats, fowls, geese (derived from China), deer, elephants, and horses.

After leaving Brunei the two ships directed their course towards the Sulu archipelago, which lies between North Borneo and Mindanao. They seem to have made little scruple of behaving like pirates towards any Malay prau which could not offer much resistance. In this way they captured a vessel full of coconuts, which was a great resource to them in the way of food. They found a perfect port for repairing ships in Bungei, one of the Sulu Islands. Here they stayed for forty-two days, everyone labouring hard, their greatest fatigue, however, being the journey backwards and forwards to the forest barefoot (probably because their shoes were worn out) to hew timber for the ship's needs. On the island of Bungei they found many wild boars (of the species *Sus longirostris*), with very long heads 2½ feet in length, and with big tusks. There were also huge crocodiles, and on the seashore immense Tridacna clam shells, the actual flesh of one of these clams (a clam is something like an oyster) weighing as much as 44 pounds. Here also they observed the marvellous leaf-insects, which Pigafetta not unnaturally imagined to be a miracle of nature, leaves which became alive and walked about when they fell to the ground. He kept one of these in a box for nine days, and at the end of that time the leaf-insect was still active, though no doubt it soon died, since he believed it fed on nothing but air.[1]

Stopping off the coast of the large island of Mindanao, the southernmost part of the Philippines, they again cap-

[1] These were no doubt examples of the genus *Phyllum*, insects of the *Phasmidæ* family (allied to Mantises). The resemblance to leaves in the *Phylli* is extraordinary, especially in the female insect, even the egg capsules are just like seeds.

tured a Malay vessel (killing several of its seamen) apparently only for the purpose of getting information about the right course to pursue in order to reach the Spice Islands. From these captives they obtained, besides other information, the story that in the southern parts of Mindanao existed a race of *hairy* men who were fierce fighters and used bows and arrows with great effect. They also possessed swords or daggers, and when they were successful in battle they cut out the hearts of their slain enemies and ate them raw, seasoned with the juice of oranges or lemons. These hairy people were called Benaian.

Sailing away from Mindanao the two Spanish ships encountered a furious storm, and in their terror the crews lowered all the sails and offered up fervent prayers to God for their safety. "Immediately our three patron saints of San Nicolau, San Elmo, and Sta. Clara appeared to us like torches of light on the maintop, mizentop, and foretop.[1] We promised a slave each to St. Elmo, San Nicolau, and Sta. Clara, and offered alms to each saint." After this the storm abated and the ship found a welcome refuge in a harbour, where again they captured forcibly Malay seamen to show them the way to the Molucca Islands.

At last, on 8 November, 1521, they reached the five islands known as Maluk or Molucca, and on that date came to an anchor in a harbour of Tidore, where they fired a tremendous salute with their artillery. The next day the king of the island—evidently well used to Europeans and their ways—came off in a prau, and a deputation of Spaniards went in a small boat to meet him. They found

[1] The appearances, of course, were nothing but the displays of electricity which in violent storms show themselves like white globes of flame or torches in the upper parts of the masts and rigging, and are known generally as "corposants" or St. Elmo's Fires.

him seated under a silk awning which sheltered him on all sides, and in front of him squatted one of his sons holding the royal sceptre, and on either side were persons with jars ready to pour water over his hands, while two others held gilded caskets filled with betel paste. The king bade the white men welcome, and said that he had dreamt some time ago that ships were coming to the Molucca Islands from remote parts, and from that assurance he determined to consult the moon, whereupon he had seen the ships coming. He then came on board; all kissed his hand and led him to the stern, where he was honoured with a red velvet chair and given a yellow velvet robe made after the Turkish fashion. The king professed his desire to become the most loyal friend and vassal of the King of Spain, and declared that henceforth his island would no more be called "Tadore" (or Tidore), but Castilla, because of the great love which he bore to the mighty sovereign of Spain.

This Malay chief of Tidore was a Muhammadan, about forty-five years old, well built, of royal presence, and much skilled in astrology. He was clad in a shirt of delicate white muslin, the ends of the sleeves embroidered in gold. Round his waist, and reaching to the ground, was a coloured cloth, while a silk scarf was wrapped round his head, and above it was placed a garland of flowers. He asked for a royal banner and a signature of Charles V, and he would then place his dominions, which included the Island of Ternate, under the direction of Spain. He would also load up the ships with cloves, so that they might return to Spain with good commerce.

Eight months previously a notable personage had died in the Island of Ternate, poisoned by the orders of this same King of Tidore. He was a Portuguese, Francesco Serrão, who had been, curiously enough, a most intimate friend of Magellan, and who was apparently the brother of the João Serrão, or Juan Serrano, the commander of the *Concepcion*, who had been left behind and perhaps killed at Sebu. Francesco Serrão had been sent as captain of a Portuguese ship to the Moluccas in 1511, and had remained in those islands partly on account of disasters having happened to his ship. In course of time he became a very great man, and the Prime Minister, so to speak, of the King of Ternate. He had married a woman from the Island of Java. It was he who had strongly incited Magellan to attempt to reach the Moluccas by way of South America and the Pacific. But Serrano, having excited great jealousy by his powerful influence over the King of Ternate, was poisoned by this same King of Tidore, now so friendly towards the *Trinidad* and the *Victoria*; and soon afterwards the King of Ternate was likewise got rid of by means of poison, and so the monarch of Tidore was the chief person then in the archipelago of the Moluccas.

Whilst remaining at Tidore to load up with cloves, Pigafetta collected some information about the large island of Jilolo lying to the east.[1] He describes it as being inhabited both by Muhammadan Malays (on the coast) and by Papuan heathens (in the interior), and says it was very rich in gold, and that it grew enormous bamboos as thick round as a man's thigh, the segments of which were often filled with water that was very good to drink.

When the King of Tidore heard of their piracies, and of the number of Malay seamen they had captured, he dealt with the question humanely and diplomatically,

[1] He pronounced the name Jailolo. This large island, which in shape is an extraordinary repetition on a smaller scale of the still larger Celebes, is also known as Halmahera.

suggesting that all these prisoners should be returned by him to their island homes, where they could make known the greatness and splendour of the kingdom of Spain. This the Spaniards consented to do, reserving only the people from Brunei, who, as already related, were brought to Seville. As the king was a very zealous Muhammadan, they also killed all the swine on board to please him, and he in return gave them a large number of goats and fowls, besides quantities of vegetable food, including sago derived from the sago palm, which was the principal nourishment of these Molucca Malays.

In the Island of Ternate there arrived presently a Portuguese in a Malay prau, who gave them very interesting information derived from the visit a year previously of a Portuguese ship. The survivors of Magellan's expedition learnt then that the main facts of their voyage had become known to the King of Portugal some time after their departure, and that ships had been sent to the Cape of Good Hope and to other places to prevent their passage. When it was learnt that they had rounded South America and made their way across the Pacific, an attempt was made to dispatch a Portuguese fleet of six ships to the Molucca Islands to capture Magellan's expedition. But this fleet was prevented from accomplishing its purpose through its being detained in the Red Sea by the necessity of fighting a Turkish fleet.

Whilst the two ships stayed at Tidore many festivities took place in connection with the visits of chiefs or kings of the other Molucca Islands. These Malay princes came in their praus, some of which had three tiers of rowers on each side, in all 120 rowers, and they hoisted great banners made of white, yellow, and red parrot feathers. Gongs of bronze and brass were sounded and timed to the rowers' actions. Sometimes the praus would be filled with young girls, female slaves (though not feeling any of the misery of slavery), who were to be presented as household servants to the daughters of chiefs betrothed to this and that heir apparent. The kings of the islands sat on rich carpets, no doubt received by indirect trade from Persia. They wore cloths of gold and silk manufactured in China, and the women were clad in beautiful silk garments from the waist to the knees. They brought with them, amongst other presents for the King of Spain, "two extremely beautiful dead birds". These were as large as thrushes, with a small head and a long beak. They were of a tawny colour, but with beautiful long plumes of a different tint.[1] The natives who brought them called them the Birds of God, and said that they came from the terrestrial Paradise. This was probably the first mention in our European literature of Birds of Paradise.

At last the ships were ready to go, in December, 1521. JUAN DEL CANO (or de Elcano, as it is sometimes written), an officer hitherto scarcely mentioned, had been elected captain of the *Victoria*, and the command of the *Trinidad* had been given to Espinosa, replacing Carvalho, the pilot, who had behaved very badly in regard to the captured natives as well as towards the members of the expedition. [It was Carvalho who refused to stay and ransom poor Juan Serrano.] The *Victoria* set sail on her way towards Timor and the Indian Ocean, when her cruise was suddenly stopped by the news that her consort the *Trinidad* had suddenly developed a dangerous leak. They found the water rushing in as through a pipe, and pumping was

[1] They may have been the Standard-bearer Paradise Bird (*Semioptera*), from the Island of Jilolo, which is fawn colour, with blue and emerald gorget, and large waving plume feathers rising up from the quills of the wings.

useless. The kindly King of Tidore sent down divers, who remained more than half an hour under water, endeavouring to find the leak. Some of these even remained an hour under water (this no doubt was a great exaggeration), and, by wearing their long hair loose, attempted to find the leak by letting it be drawn by the suction of the water towards the place. But it was decided at last that the *Victoria* should start for Spain and the *Trinidad* remain behind for repairs.[1] The *Victoria* therefore left with a crew of forty-seven Europeans and thirteen Malays, chiefly from Borneo.

The *Victoria* on her way to Timor passed the Shulla Islands (Xulla), and heard from their Malay pilots that the inhabitants were naked cannibals. In other islands there were pigmies (negritos); others, again, were more civilized, producing rice, pigs, goats, fowls, sugar cane, and a delicious food made of bananas, almonds, and honey, wrapped in leaves and smoke-dried, then cut into long pieces. Buru Island was noted (though they did not land there) as inhabited by Muhammadan Malays on the coast and cannibal savages in the interior; also the Banda Islands, producing mace and nutmeg. After leaving the vicinity of Buru the *Victoria* encountered a fierce storm, which drove them to seek refuge in a harbour of a lofty island[2] which was inhabited by savage, bestial people, eating human flesh and going naked, except that their

[1] Fifty-three Spaniards remained behind in Tidore with the *Trinidad*, but of these only five returned to Europe. These five included the captain, Gomez Espinosa, already mentioned, and a German gunner, Hans Warge. Many of the Spaniards died in Tidore from various diseases or were killed in quarrels with the natives. The *Trinidad* attempted to sail for Spain back across the Pacific Ocean, but pursued a northern route which took her to the forty-second degree of north latitude, whence she was driven back by storms to some island near New Guinea. Here she was found by the Portuguese, who stripped and abandoned her, conveying the survivors of her crew as prisoners to the Moluccas, where they were treated with considerable harshness.

[2] Called, by Pigafetta, Malina, probably the Island of Ombay.

warriors wore armour made of buffalo hide and goatskins. They dressed their hair (like the New Zealanders) high up on the head, held in position by long reed pins, which they passed from one side to the other. Their beards were wrapped in leaves and thrust into small bamboo tubes. They were the ugliest people Pigafetta had seen, and were armed with bows and arrows of bamboo. Nevertheless they behaved in a friendly way to these Spaniards and sold them quantities of provisions, beeswax, and pepper.

On 26 January, 1522, the *Victoria* reached the Island of Timor, where it laid in a great supply of buffaloes, pigs, and goats. The people, though going almost naked, wore many gold and brass armlets and ear-rings, and bamboo combs in their hair adorned with gold rings.

On 11 February, 1522, the *Victoria* sailed away from Timor into the great Indian Ocean. She was only a little vessel of 85 tons, and she had to buffet her way amidst various storms and high waves across the southern Indian Ocean, as far as the forty-second degree of south latitude before she could beat up north and round the Cape of Good Hope. The sufferings on board were terrible, the ship leaked badly and the pumps were always going, the provision of buffalo meat had putrefied, as they had had no salt to preserve it. There was little other food than rice. After rounding the Cape of Good Hope it took them a further two months before they could land anywhere to obtain fresh provisions, and twenty-one men died of scurvy and starvation during this terrible period. At last, constrained by their despairing condition, they stopped off the Island of Sant Iago, in the Cape Verde archipelago, which for some time had been a settlement of the Portuguese. Here they sent a boat ashore for food, with a concocted story to deceive the Portuguese into believing that the

Victoria was a ship coming from Spanish America and driven out of her course by storms. But on its second voyage to the shore the boat, containing thirteen men, was detained, because, having no money, they offered cloves in payment of the things they purchased. Seeing from a distance that the men had been arrested, the captain of the *Victoria* felt obliged to abandon them to their fate and hastily sailed away.

At last, on 8 September, 1522, the *Victoria*, having sailed into Spain up the Guadalquivir River, dropped anchor at the quay of Seville and discharged all her artillery in crazy joy at this return to the Motherland. On the following day all the survivors of this wonderful expedition—eighteen in number—went in shirts and barefooted, each man holding a candle, to visit the shrines of Santa Maria de la Victoria and of St. Mary of Antiquity in two different churches. As to the thirteen men left behind, they were not so ill treated after all by the Portuguese, but were ultimately dispatched to Seville, so that it may be said of the five ships which started with Magellan in 1519 to reach the Moluccas by way of the Pacific Ocean only one returned to Spain—the *Victoria*, the *Trinidad* having been lost near the Spice Islands; while of the original 265 men (more or less) who left Spain in 1519 only 36 returned to Spain after circumnavigating the globe—18 in the *Victoria*, 13 in Portuguese ships from the Cape Verde Islands, and 5 survivors from the *Trinidad* sent back by the Portuguese from Malaysia.

In spite of all these disasters, however, the cargo of cloves and spices brought back by the *Victoria* sufficed, not only to pay the whole cost of the equipment of the original expedition of five ships, but left a profit of about £200 in value over and above.

This fact, as well as the information (no doubt much exaggerated) about the Philippines and Borneo and the gold to be met with in these islands, made a deep impression on the Court of Spain, and not many years elapsed before further attempts were made to reach Malaysia across the Pacific from Spanish America, the Spaniards being precluded by their agreement with Portugal from adopting the more convenient route round the Cape of Good Hope.

As already related, the Spaniards and Portuguese were out of their reckoning in regard to longitude when they supposed that any part of the Philippines or the Moluccas lay to the east of 130° of E. longitude, and consequently within the domain of Spain. They believed that the Moluccas did come within the Spanish sphere, while the Philippines were, by the same reckoning, Portuguese. After a good deal of wrangling the matter was settled in 1529. A considerable sum of money was paid by Portugal to Spain, the Spanish claim to the Spice Islands was withdrawn, and nothing was said about the Philippines. This archipelago, a few years afterwards, was tacitly recognized as within the Spanish sphere, which also included the lands afterwards to be styled New Guinea.

Borneo thus became part of the Portuguese "sphere of influence" (as it would now be called), though this large island had first been visited by Magellan in Spanish ships. The Portuguese attempted to enter into relations with the then powerful Muhammadan sultanate of North Borneo (Brunei), but (according to the Portuguese chronicler, Barros) their efforts came to nothing through a very curious mischance. Realizing that the Sultan of Brunei was a very powerful prince, a Muhammadan, and therefore much in touch, through Arab and Persian traders, with the civilized world, it was resolved to send him, by the embassy dispatched from Ternate to Brunei in 1528, a selection of really superior and costly presents. Amongst these was a large piece of tapestry illustrating in a most lifelike manner the marriage of Catherine of Aragon (afterwards the unhappy wife of Henry VIII) to Arthur, Prince of Wales—the first link, possibly, in the long history of the relations between the British and North Borneo. But the figures thus portrayed by the needles and wool of industrious Spanish women seemed to the superstitious Malay sultan a work of subtle magic. He believed them to be real persons sent to sleep by the spell of a magician, and that some night they would be released from their enchantment, come to life, and slay him as he slept. So the Portuguese envoy was dismissed, the presents declined, and no political relations entered into between North Borneo and the Portuguese. This was one reason, probably, why the Dutch, not having been preceded by the Portuguese, got no foothold in North Borneo, and therefore left this side of the island open to British administrative enterprise in the first half of the nineteenth century.

Spanish research in the Pacific was resumed five years after the return of Sebastian de Elcano in the *Victoria* in the autumn of 1522. In 1528 two Spanish ships, intending to sail from Mexico to the Philippines, were blown out of their course in a storm and accidentally discovered the Hawaii Islands. They were wrecked there, and such of the crews as were saved from drowning—amongst them were several Spanish women—could not get away from Hawaii, and settled down there for the rest of their lives, marrying the people of the country, and no doubt leaving a strain of Castilian blood in the ruling classes of these cannibal islands.

Hawaii was, however, again visited by Spanish ships in the middle of the sixteenth century; and when, long afterwards, the archipelago was rediscovered by Captain Cook, the people were found to be practising several Spanish customs. The real fact is that Spain knew a good deal about the Oceanic islands in the sixteenth century, but out of jealous dread that her monopoly of the Pacific Ocean might be invaded by other European nations she kept this geographical knowledge, set forth in her charts and logbooks, hidden in her State archives, only to be revealed in the latter part of the eighteenth century, when there was no longer anything to conceal from the adventurous French and English.

In 1542 the Philippines were again visited by Spanish ships under the command of LOPEZ DE VILLALOBOS, who penetrated to the large northern island of Luzon. On his return to Mexico he named this archipelago after Philip, the heir to the Spanish throne. In 1564 an expedition under LOPEZ DE LEGASPI was dispatched from the west coast of Mexico to the Philippines for their conquest and their conversion to Christianity. Four ships conveyed 400 Spanish soldiers and a few friars or missionaries. Between 1565 and his death in 1572 Legaspi had actually achieved the wonderful feat of founding the city of Manila in the large island of Luzon, and making the Spanish power predominant over all this large archipelago. A number of the natives became converted to Christianity, and only the Sulu Islands and Palawan remained Muhammadan.

In 1579 a new portent appeared in the Far East. In the month of November there arrived at the Island of

Ternate, from nowhere, as it seemed, an English ship, the *Golden Hinde*, commanded by FRANCIS DRAKE. This most remarkable English adventurer — then only thirty-four years old—had been purser to a ship trading to the north of Spain when he was only eighteen, and by the age of twenty-two had not only made a voyage to Guinea, but was commanding a ship as captain in an attack on the Spaniards off the coast of Mexico. In 1577 he had navigated the Straits of Magellan in the *Golden Hinde* (originally the *Pelican*, which he renamed thus as a remembrance of the heraldic device of Sir Christopher Hatton and a mark of joy at having safely reached the Pacific Ocean), had sailed up the west coast of South America, attacking and plundering Spanish ships and towns "till his men were satiated with plunder"; and, failing to find another Magellan's Straits in North-west America to take him back to the Atlantic, had boldly sailed from the coast of New Albion (the modern State of Washington) aslant the Pacific Ocean and steered a straight course for the Moluccas.

The Portuguese, of course, were then predominant in the Spice Islands and elsewhere in Malaysia, and with them Drake had no quarrel. He therefore sailed on to Java (after nearly coming to grief by striking a rock off the coast of Celebes), and from Java made his way round the Cape of Good Hope to the Guinea coast, and thence to the Azores and England. He was knighted by Queen Elizabeth on board the *Golden Hinde* at Deptford, after the queen had partaken of a banquet on board the famous ship which had sailed round the world in two years and ten months.

His voyage was a splendid answer to the Spaniards, who believed themselves perfectly safe from interference in the waters of the "great Southern Ocean", and who forbade the rest of the world to trade with America and Australasia. Within eighteen years it was to be followed up by Dutch and British attacks, by way of the Cape of Good Hope, on the Portuguese and Spanish monopoly of intercourse with the East Indies and Malaysia. It is, however, only fair to mention that in the matter of commercial morality the British, French, and Dutch were no more enlightened than the Spaniards. Each sought in turn to make their oversea dependencies regions closed to the trade of other nations than themselves, and even to restrict the commerce of their Asiatic, African, and American colonies to privileged persons or companies.

The Spaniards who sailed to the Moluccas in the two remaining ships of Magellan's squadron had practically got into touch with Papuasia, with the lands of New Guinea and its surrounding islands; and had realized that in this direction there lay a new Negroland, a "New Guinea", in fact. Exactly when the New Guinea coast was reached from the west—whether by ALVARO DE SAAVEDRA the Spaniard in 1528, or in 1511 and 1526 by the Portuguese who had taken possession of the Moluccas—is not known; nor by whom this very appropriate name was first given. Probably it was named "Nueva Guinéa" in 1546 by a Spanish captain—ORTIZ DE RETEZ—who mapped a portion of its northern coast. The impression that this vast island—the biggest in the world—was first called "New Guinea" by Torres when he reached its southern shores in 1607 is incorrect; he, seemingly, was only recognizing a land already named thus for its great superficial resemblance to West Africa. But the Spaniards had heard rumours from the Malay sea captains of a vast land eastward of the Moluccas where there was gold in abundance, besides beautiful birds and curly-haired black people. They jumped to the fantastic conclusion that here lay, not only the Earthly Paradise, but also the Ophir from which Solomon had derived his gold. Mingled with these beliefs was the ever-growing conviction that in this direction must lie a great Southern Continent; and to search for this an expedition was dispatched in 1567 from Callao, the principal port of Peru, under the command of ALVARO DE MENDAÑA DE NEYRA, with the express purpose of discovering the great Antarctic continent and the "Islas de Salomon". Mendaña voyaged for eighty days across the Pacific, more or less through the equatorial belt, and thus discovered and named the Solomon Islands[1] to the east of New Guinea, believing that they might prove to be the Ophir from which Solomon had derived gold. His expedition surveyed the southern portion of the group, giving to three of the large islands the Spanish names, which they still bear, of San Cristoval, Guadalcanal, and Ysabel.

[1] The Solomon Islands are now divided politically between Germany and Britain, Germany having annexed the large island of Bougainville and the smaller Buka on the north, and Great Britain the remainder. The islands are very mountainous and volcanic, and on the largest, Bougainville, one mountain rises to an altitude of over 10,000 feet. In the British Island of Guadalcanal there is an altitude of 8000 feet. The climate is very wet and unhealthy, and vegetation is luxurious, including magnificent forests of sandalwood, ebony, and "lignum vitæ" (a kind of Myrtle—*Metrosideron*). The inhabitants belong mainly to the Melanesian or Negroid stock, and are no doubt closely related to the Papuans of New Guinea. In some of the northern islands, such as Buka, the people often present a striking resemblance in their features, skin colour, and close-growing, woolly hair, to African Negroes. Some tribes in the islands, however, are akin to the Polynesians, and have long, straight hair. They were until quite recently the most ferocious cannibals of any part of the globe. In more remote periods this archipelago was connected with New Guinea, and thence derived the ancestors of its present wild animals, which include numerous Bats of very interesting types, some very large Rats the size of big rabbits, a Cuscus or marsupial Phalanger, and a large Frog about 8 inches long, besides some remarkable Parrots.

JUAN FERNANDEZ was a Spanish pilot who appears to have given some study to the Straits of Magellan. About 1572 he was venturing out some distance into the Pacific Ocean from the coast of South America, and thus discovered the two little islands which have ever since borne his name, and which proved for a time such an important harbourage and resting place for the Dutch and English navigators who flouted the prohibition of Spain to enter the great Southern Ocean. Fernandez conceived the idea that there must be some large extent of land in the southern half of the Pacific Ocean, and he may have sighted Easter Island, or some other Pacific archipelago, and have believed that it was an indication of the coast line of this Terra Australis.

Mendaña de Neyra, who had returned to the coast of Peru in 1570, was very anxious to organize at once another expedition to extend his discoveries. He was not enabled to do so until the year 1595, when he again started from the coast of Peru with a fleet and a number of Spaniards who were to colonize the Solomon Islands. On his way thither he discovered the Marquezas archipelago (which now belongs to France). Sailing along a course which was more or less that of the tenth degree of south latitude, his ship at last reached the little island of Santa Cruz, the northernmost of an archipelago which is now associated with the group of the New Hebrides. Here, for some reason, his expedition came to a stop, and he landed and attempted to establish a portion of his crew as settlers. But the climate, or some other cause of ill health, brought about the death of Mendaña and many of his companions. He had been accompanied on this cruise by his young wife, who played a heroic part in rescuing the remainder of the expedition. After

Mendaña's death, one of his pilots, PEDRO FERNÁNDEZ DE QUIROS (a Portuguese), brought the remains of the Spanish fleet to Manila in the Philippines. Then in one vessel he boldly sailed back across the Pacific to Peru, and thence made his way to Madrid, where he revealed to the Spanish Government the stories gathered from Malays regarding the existence of a great Southern Continent. He obtained permission from the Court to search for this Terra Australis, and for this purpose returned to South America and started on his quest from Callao (Peru) in 1605. The Viceroy of Peru associated with him, practically as admiral in command of the expedition, LUIS VAEZ DE TORRES, as well as a second ship. Directing his voyage across the southern Tropics instead of the northern, de Quiros discovered a small island, which long afterwards was renamed Osnaburg by Cook. A few days afterwards he passed one or more islands of the Tahiti archipelago, which he named "Sagittaria", probably from the month (February, under the zodiacal sign of Sagittarius) in which they were discovered. Sailing on westwards he next reached the group of the New Hebrides. This he believed to be a portion of the coast of the Southern Continent, and he named its largest island[1] Australia del Espiritu Santo, or Australia of the Holy Ghost, this being the first time that the word Australia came into being. He did not pursue his investigations any farther, because his ship's crew mutinied and forced him to sail back again to Mexico.

But his admiral, Luis Vaez de Torres, suddenly abandoned by the ship which had de Quiros on board, was less

[1] Sometimes known as Marina. The name as given by de Quiros seems to have been spelt "Austrialia".

certain about the actual discovery of this continent, so in 1606–7 he pursued a westward course and thus passed through that strait which separates northern Australia from New Guinea, and thence sailed to the Philippines. He was consequently the discoverer of what is now the British province of Papua, and of the important Torres Straits.

For a long time the Spaniards kept these explorations as State secrets, for they were becoming very much alarmed at the progress in oversea exploration of the Dutch and English. The existence, therefore, of Torres Straits, separating the Australian Continent from the huge Island of New Guinea, remained practically unknown to the world of Europe until the voyages of Captain Cook, more than 150 years later. In fact, Cook, when he rediscovered and mapped the strait between North Australia and New Guinea, was not aware that he had been preceded in that direction by Torres. When, however, this fact was made clearly known through the archives of Spain, the name of the bold Spanish seaman was very appropriately (in 1796) given to a strait of water which is one of the most noteworthy passages from the Pacific to the Indian Oceans, and which may some day become of great importance in the world's history.

CHAPTER IV

Dutch Discoveries

In the Malay Archipelago and the Spice Islands both Portuguese and Spanish were attacked by the Dutch, and gradually dispossessed from the end of the sixteenth century onwards. The Dutch had established themselves in the Moluccas in place of the Portuguese between 1604 and 1609, in which year the Portuguese were driven from the Nutmeg Islands of Banda. The Hollanders were followed almost immediately by the English. The merchant adventurers of both nations (who were seamen, soldiers, and pirates at will) soon penetrated to the western peninsulas of New Guinea and ousted the Portuguese from Java, Celebes, and southern Timor, but at first made little or no attempt to pass beyond Malaysia in search of the southern continent. By the conquest of Malacca in 1641 the Dutch had become practically masters of the Malay Archipelago, the Spaniards being confined to the possession of the Philippines (which they administered from the west coast of America across the Pacific),[1] and the Portuguese only lingering on in the islands of Timor and Flores, while the English had been expelled from the Spice Islands

[1] As a matter of fact, the Spanish really only acquired something like mastery over the Philippine Islands at the beginning of the eighteenth century. Up till that time the islands were mostly governed by native chiefs, who paid tribute to Spain, and submitted very willingly to the direction of the Spanish friars or missionary brethren, who acquired considerable influence over the northern part of the Philippine archipelago, where Muhammadanism was not in any way established. The Spaniards never succeeded in finally conquering the whole of the Philippines. This task has only beer achieved by their successors, the people of the United States.

and Java, and merely retained a precarious foothold in Sumatra. Encouraged by these successes to seek for further lands that might be conquered, settled, or traded with, the Dutch began to take up the quest for the Terra Australis as soon as they were established as the masters of the Moluccas and Banda.

In 1615 a bold Dutch navigator, JACOB LE MAIRE (of French extraction), determined, in spite of the prohibition of the Dutch East India Company, to find his way independently to the seas and lands of southern Asia by way of the extremity of South America. He sailed in company with another sea captain, SCHOUTEN, and together they discovered and named Staten Island and the celebrated Cape Horn, the southernmost extremity (a little island) of South America, and since famous as the stormiest cape in the world's seas. From this point they followed closely the coast of South America till they got into equatorial latitudes, and then steered boldly across the Pacific Ocean, either not noticing or actually not seeing the many islands or islets that must have been near their course. Apparently the first land they sighted was the north-east coast of New Guinea, after which they got among the Spice Islands and thus eventually reached Batavia, where they were so severely punished by their fellow countrymen for their splendid adventure that Le Maire ultimately died before he could reach Holland. Previous to this date, however, the Dutch had evidently known something about the Australian Continent[1] (of which it was generally believed that New Guinea was a portion), and they no doubt derived this knowledge from information given to

[1] New Guinea (Nova Guinea) appears duly named on Mercator's first maps of the world, published in 1569. On the other side of a narrow strait (Torres Straits) is a jagged coastline obviously representing North Australia.

them by Malay pilots, and picked up from the Portuguese; for in a work published in 1598 by the Dutch historian, Cornelius Wytfliet, the following passage occurs: "The Terra Australis is the most southern of all lands, and is separated from New Guinea by a narrow strait. . . . It is ascertained by some to be of so great an extent that if it were thoroughly explored it would be regarded as a fifth part of the world." There is a tradition also that in 1606 a Dutch ship, the *Duyfken* or *Little Dove*, which was on its way from Java to the western part of New Guinea, was driven out of her course by a typhoon and sighted the north-east coast of Australia (Cape York Peninsula) as far south as Cape Turnagain. Some of the crew landed, but were repulsed by the savage natives. In the year following the arrival of le Maire at Batavia, a Dutch ship, the *Eendracht*, under the command of a navigator called Hertoge, or Hartog, by a similar cause was blown out of his course and touched the north-west coast of Australia at points now known as Shark Bay and Hartog Island. In 1622–3 the *Leeuwin* (Lioness), another Dutch vessel, penetrated along the west coast of Australia about as far south as Cape Leeuwin. In 1623 an expedition, under a captain named CARTENZ, set out for the Southern Continent and explored and named the Gulf of Carpentaria, in north Australia, the name being derived from Carpentar, who was then the Governor of the Dutch East Indies (the authority says "West" Indies). Between 1622 and 1628 other Dutch expeditions, one of them under PIETER NUYTS, explored the South Australian coast ("Nuytsland") as far as the Eyre Peninsula. But from here to Cape York the east coast of Australia remained absolutely unknown till the coming of Captain Cook.

Abel Janszoon Tasman, the greatest Dutch explorer of Australasia (his middle name was equivalent in English to Johnson), was born about 1603 at Lutjegast, near Groningen, in Friesland, not far from the modern German boundary. He was married twice, first when a young man (the second time when he was twenty-nine years old), and about the age of twenty-one joined the service of the Dutch East India Company and started for Java. He revisited Holland in 1637 and returned to the Malay Archipelago in 1638. Although he had started in life as a common sailor he must have acquired a good education by some means or other, for his journals show him to have been possessed of a singularly beautiful and even handwriting, he was a clever draughtsman (assuming the many sketches in the logbook to be by him), and he had thoroughly mastered the science of navigation, so much so, that soon after his arrival in the East Indies in 1634 he was singled out for work of importance and responsibility. In 1638 he made, in company with another commander, a remarkable voyage of exploration to Japan along the coasts of China, and in 1642 he was selected to command the expedition which was to make such important discoveries in Australasia.

His principal vessel, the *Heemskerk*[1], described as a yacht, was probably of only 150 tons capacity; the second of the two ships, the *Zeehaen* (Seahen) was a third smaller than the *Heemskerk*. With these two small ships he left Batavia (Java) on 14 August, 1642, and sailed right across the Indian Ocean to the Island of Mauritius (the home of

[1] The master of the *Heemskerk* was Captain Yde Tjercxzoon Holman, a Frisian from the Grand duchy of Oldenburg; and the pilot-major, or principal steersman, was a very noteworthy person in the expedition—Frans Jacobszoon Visscher, a native of Flushing, who had made some very remarkable voyages round about Japan, and had resided a good deal in that country.

the Dodo), then occupied by the Dutch, wishing, no doubt, to take as wide a scope as possible for the discovery of the great Southern Continent. From Mauritius he sailed east and south, and did not sight the West Australian coast at all, his course trending so much to the south that instead he crossed the great Australian Bight[1] and first saw land off the west coast of Tasmania, in the vicinity of what is now known as Macquarie Harbour. He at once conferred on this land the name of Anthonij Van Diemen, the Governor-General of the Dutch Indies, and the principal promoter of this exploring expedition. He overlooked the passage to the north (Bass's Strait), and directed his course southwards. On 25 November, 1642, the two ships came to an anchor off the west coast of Tasmania for consultations between the commanders. On the succeeding days they sailed round the south coast of Tasmania, and on 2 December stopped again and sent a pilot in a pinnace with four musketeers and six rowers (all of them well armed) together with another boat commanded by an officer, and containing six more musketeers, to the shore of a large bay (probably Storm Bay) to see if fresh water, vegetables, and timber could be obtained. On the return of these boats the officers reported that they found the land covered with vegetation, but with no signs of cultivation. They brought back with them various wild vegetable products which seemed suited for use as pot-herbs, besides a good supply of fresh water. They reported that they had heard certain human sounds, and noises resembling the music of a trumpet or small gong, but they saw no human beings, though there were notched

[1] In crossing this bight Tasman was clever enough to surmise that they must be passing to the south of the land discovered by Pieter Nuyts in 1627 (the south coast of Australia); and owing to the tremendous swell setting in from the south he felt sure that there was no continent near him in that direction.

trees, the notches having been made with implements of sharpened stone, to form steps enabling persons to climb the trees and take the birds' nests. These notched steps (very wide apart) were so fresh and new that they could only have been cut a few days before. On the ground they saw the footprints of clawed animals and other traces showing that there were beasts in the forest. In the interior numerous trees were observed which had deep holes burnt into them, as if to make of them fireplaces and shelters. They also saw smoke rising in clouds from natives' fires. On 3 December a flagstaff was set up on the shore of Frederick Henry Bay, and possession of this new land was solemnly taken on behalf of the Dutch East India Company.

Then they sailed away from what they believed to be the southernmost extremity of Australia, and on 13 December, 1642, they saw "a large high-lying land bearing south-east . . . at about 16 miles distance". This was the great southern island of New Zealand,[1] but it was encountered by Tasman at its northernmost extremity and close to the North Island. He sailed, in fact, right into the gulf (then named the *Zeehaen's* Bight) between two islands, which finds its outlet to the south in Cook's Strait. He overlooked this outlet and believed the gulf to be only a great indentation. Ultimately he sailed northwards past the west coast of the North Island to its northernmost extremity, which he named Cape Maria Van Diemen. At some distance from this were three

[1] Any sensible person looking at the map of New Zealand would say that this Dominion was divided into two great islands, the North Island and the South Island. But, ridiculously enough, the great South Island is constantly referred to by writers on New Zealand as the Middle Island, the term South Island being applied to a (relatively) very small island just off the extremity of the southern half of the Dominion, while the South Island is called the Middle Island. It should really be known as the South Island and the small island beyond it as Stewart Island.

tiny islets, the size of which he exaggerated. He named them the Three Kings' Islands. On 18 December the two ships came to an anchor about a mile from the shore, off the coast of what is now called Massacre or Golden Bay, not far from the modern settlement of Waitapu. It was sunset, and calm, and as the twilight faded they saw lights on shore and two native boats coming towards them, the men in which began to call to them in rough, "hollow" voices. This people also blew several times on an instrument (probably a conch shell), the sound from which was like that of a Moorish trumpet. The seamen from the ships trumpeted back to them in reply, but when it was dark the native canoes paddled back to the shore. Early the next morning a canoe manned by fifteen natives approached to within a short distance of the ships and called out several times. But the Dutchmen could not understand their language, as it bore no resemblance to the vocabulary of words used in the Solomon Islands, which had been collected through the industry of Anthonij Van Diemen and supplied to Tasman with his other instructions.[1] As far as they could observe, these New Zealanders were of ordinary height, with rough voices and strong bones, the colour of their skin being between brown and yellow. They wore tufts of black hair right on the tops of their heads, tied fast in the manner of the Japanese, but somewhat longer and thicker, each topknot of hair being surmounted by a large white feather. Each of their boats consisted of two long, narrow canoes fastened side by side. Over these twin canoes were placed planks on

[1] In noting this difference of speech Tasman unconsciously laid stress on the great distinction between the Melanesian tongues of the Oceanic Negroids and the Polynesian speech of New Zealand and nearly all the other Pacific islands and archipelagoes south of Fiji and New Caledonia and east of the Ladrones.

which the paddlers sat. The New-Zealanders, though naked from the shoulders to the waist, wore some kind of clothing (in contrast to the nearly always naked Melanesians). This seemed to be made of a stuff something like woven cotton, or else matting.

In spite of offered presents and friendly greetings these two boats would not come alongside the ship. Later on, seven more canoes came off from the shore, one of which was high and pointed in front. With these nine canoes paddling round and round the two ships, and manned by a number of able-bodied armed men, the Dutchmen became a little uneasy, and the skipper of the *Zeehaen* sent out his quartermaster in a small boat with six seamen to advise the officers of the *Heemskerk* not to allow too many natives to come on board, if they wished to do so. But suddenly the little boat of the *Zeehaen* was violently attacked by one of the New Zealand canoes, with the result that one Dutch seamen was knocked overboard, four were killed, while the remainder, thrown into the sea, swam back to their ship. The natives then started for the shore, taking one of the dead bodies with them (which they no doubt afterwards ate in a cannibal feast). None of the shots fired from the *Zeehaen* or *Heemskerk* took effect. The small boat of the *Zeehaen* was recovered, and the two Dutch ships then set sail, despairing of entering into any friendly relations with these people, or getting fresh water at this place. As they sailed out of the bay they saw twenty-two canoes near the shore, of which eleven, swarming with people, were making for the ships. They kept quiet until some of the foremost canoes were within reach of the guns, and then fired one or two shots without doing much damage, though the natives at once turned their canoes back,

c 487

TASMAN'S MEN ATTACKED BY NATIVES OFF THE COAST OF NEW ZEALAND

hoisted a kind of sail, and made with all speed for the shore. "To this murderous spot we have accordingly given the name of Moordenaers Bay."[1]

On this same day, 19 December, 1642, Tasman bestowed on this new country the name of Staten Landt, "in honour of their high mightinesses the States-General of Holland". This name seems really to have been bestowed on account of the much earlier discovery by the Dutch navigator, le Maire, of an island off the south-easternmost extremity of South America (Tierra del Fuego), which Tasman seems to have thought to be the beginning of an Antarctic continent, of which New Zealand was the north-westernmost extremity. But after Tasman's return to Java the Governor-General considered that the two regions were too far separated and distinct to be parts of the same land surface; so he changed the named to Nieuw Zeeland (New Zealand), in honour of the Zeeland (Sea-land) province of south-west Holland.

On 5 January, 1643, they attempted to land on one of the Three Kings' Islands to fill their water casks before directing their course once more across a wide stretch of unknown ocean, but the heavy surf and the rocks made such an attempt too dangerous. The natives, moreover, were very threatening, standing about on the high land armed with long sticks shaped like pikes, and shouting every now and again what seemed to be hostile utterances. So it was decided to do without the fresh water, in the hope that they might reach other islands farther north where it could be obtained. Accordingly, on 6 January the two ships once more set sail across the Pacific Ocean, directing their course as nearly as possible

[1] Murderer's Bay, a name subsequently changed to Massacre Bay, or Golden Bay—from the later discovery of gold in this region.

for the Solomon Islands. On 19 and 20 January they sighted Tropic Bird Island, and two other small islands, which they named Amsterdam and Middelburgh. These were the southernmost islands of the Tonga or Friendly group, probably those which are now known by the names of Tongatabu (Amsterdam, "because of the abundance of refreshments we got there"), Eua (Middelburgh), and Cattow.

"About noon", wrote Tasman on 21 January, "a small canoe with three men in it put off from land and came near our ship. These men were naked, of a brown colour, and slightly above the ordinary stature; two of them had long, thick hair on their heads." The Dutchmen showed white linen to these Polynesians, throwing overboard a piece of 2½ yards. Seeing this, the natives paddled towards it; but as it had sunk to a considerable depth under the water the foremost man in the canoe jumped out and dived for it. He remained under water for a very long time, but at last reappeared with the linen, and when back in the canoe put this several times on the top of his head in sign of gratitude. The natives then came nearer and received from the ships' crews a few more presents, amongst which was a small looking-glass. The Dutchmen then showed them an old coconut and a fowl, and attempted to make enquiries about water, pigs, &c. At last they understood, to a certain extent, and after returning on shore a canoe came back with a white flag, the occupants of which were painted black from the waist to the thighs, and wore necklaces of large leaves. A white flag was fastened to the stern of one of the Dutch boats. The Dutchmen filled a rummer with wine, of which they first drank a little themselves, to show that it was not poison. The Polynesians, however, drank the wine without hesitation, and took the cask back with them on shore. Soon afterwards a great number of canoes came alongside with coconuts, which they bartered for old nails. Other natives swam the whole way from the land to the ships with coconuts for trade. At last an old man came on board one of the Dutch ships who was thought to be a chief. He paid reverence to the Dutchmen by bowing his head down to their feet. They showed him a cup containing fresh water; the native chief implied by signs that plenty of water could be obtained on shore. Meantime other natives had come on board the ship, and exhibited the same shameless thievishness as had angered Magellan. Among other things they stole a pistol and a pair of slippers. The Dutchmen wisely took these articles away from their dishonest visitors without any display of anger. Towards evening twenty canoes came up to the ship, making a great deal of noise and crying out repeatedly: "Wu, wu, wu!" They had brought a present from the king consisting of a pig, a number of coconuts, and some yams. The Dutchmen gave as a return present a common dish and a piece of copper wire.

The next day a quantity of canoes came off with coconuts, yams, bananas, plantains, pigs, and fowls. There also came on board a leper and a bearded woman. The natives were at first frightened by the discharge of the big guns, but soon reassured when they saw that no harm came from this noise. They were entertained with Dutch and German music, at which they were greatly astonished. At last the Dutchmen decided to send a party on shore to get fresh water, and, although the natives seemed to be so friendly, they took the precaution of adding a number of musketeers to defend the watering party. Nothing disagreeable happened, however. Wells were pointed out to them, and they were most hospitably entertained in what seemed to be pleasure houses, where they were invited to sit down on handsome mats. However, the amount of water supplied was perfectly trivial. The next day the chiefs set their men to work to dig larger wells, and the Dutchmen got all the water they wanted. Tasman noted in his journal that the natives here had no knowledge of tobacco or smoking of any kind. Neither men nor women went completely naked (a characteristic feature of the Melanesians), but wore clothing round the waist, which in the case of the women extended to the knees, and was made of the leaves of trees. The women wore their hair shorter than the men, and the latter, as a rule, grew beards about 4 inches long, with very short moustaches, the hair of which was kept clipped. No arms were worn by these people, and all seemed peace and amity in their lives (the "Friendly Isles"). Starting away again on 24 January the two ships passed through the rest of the Tonga Islands, one of which, Nanuka, was named by Tasman the Island of Rotterdam. On one of the islands of the Haapai group the Dutchmen again landed to get fresh water. The party sent to the beach reported on landing that they had seen about seventy persons, apparently the entire male population of the island; they had no arms, and seemed kind and peaceable, and there were many women and children. Nevertheless, these people were very thievish, for they stole everything they could lay hands on—men and women alike. This was a characteristic of nearly all the Pacific islanders when these lands were first discovered, and was a trait which gave rise to many troubles between them and the European explorers, who did not view this practice—not regarded by the natives as being very wrong—with sufficient patience.

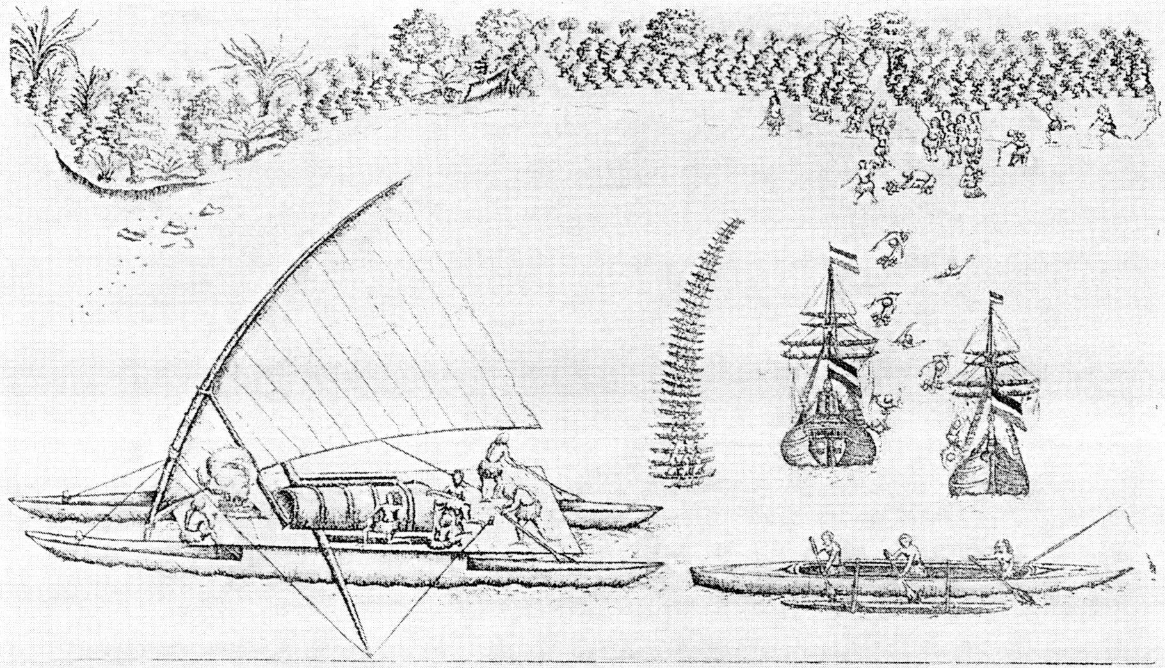

[Double Canoe of the Polynesians] [Simple Outrigger Canoe]

THE TWO DUTCH SHIPS UNDER TASMAN'S COMMAND (THE *HEEMSKERK* AND THE *ZEEHAEN*) AT ANCHOR IN THE TONGA ISLANDS, PACIFIC. NATIVES BRINGING OFF SUPPLIES OF BANANAS

(From a drawing by Tasman)

At the watering place they saw numbers of wild duck swimming, not at all shy or afraid of men. On this island were noticed many enclosures or gardens, with plots elegantly squared and planted with all sorts of fruits and vegetables. There were groves of bananas and other fruit trees, most of them growing so straight that they were a pleasure to look on (to a Dutch eye enamoured of tidiness), while they gave forth a most agreeable odour and fragrance. Though the natives of these Friendly Islands did not seem to have any well-defined religion, they were very superstitious. Tasman noticed one of them take up a water snake which came floating alongside his canoe, lay it on his head with reverence, and put it back on the water. Above all, they had a great dislike to killing flies, though they were so abundant here as to cause considerable trouble. Whilst the Dutchmen were at anchor one of them had the misfortune to kill a fly in the presence of a native chief, who showed himself greatly angered and upset.

On 2 February the voyage was continued, the ships being now well supplied with fresh water and fresh provisions. A period of rough winds followed, and although the outlying islands of the north-eastern part of the Fiji group (which Tasman named after Prince Willem of Orange) were sighted, the weather was too dangerous for any attempt at landing or investigation. Desirous of reaching New Guinea, the course of the vessels was directed to the north-west. It was not until 15 March that they sailed into smooth water and sunshine, after many days of rain, fog, and rough, south-westerly wind. On 22 March they saw land straight ahead of them at four miles distance—about thirty small islands surrounded by reefs. These, and others farther west, were little archipelagos of minute islands to the north of the Solomon group and near the great island of Bougainville. Probably owing to the very stormy, thick, rainy, and misty weather, Tasman's expedition saw nothing of the islands or islets of the Santa Cruz and New Hebrides groups, or the Solomon Islands, very near to which he must have passed.

On 25 March, 1643, the two vessels anchored off one of these islands of Oceanic Negroes. A canoe came alongside with a number of men whose skins were nearly black and who went quite naked. Some of them had their hair cut short, or wore feathers arranged like horns on the top of their heads. One had a ring through his nose. They carried bows and arrows. From another island on the following day came off more of these black people, "with curly hair like that of the Kafirs", but not so woolly, nor were their noses quite so flat as those of true Negroes. They wore white bracelets, probably of pigs' tusks. Their faces were daubed with lime, and a small piece of tree bark was worn on the forehead. For arms they had bows, arrows, and javelins or stabbing spears. At last Tasman got one of the words of his Melanesian vocabularies recognized; it was the word for coconut (*lamas*).

By 1 April the Dutchmen were sailing along the coast of New Mecklenburg (then thought to be part of New Guinea). Already Tasman had recognized islands and capes seen and named by his predecessor, le Maire. Every now and again they anchored to buy coconuts. The people who came off from the shore were black skinned and naked. They seemed already somewhat acquainted with Europeans and their ways and to be afraid of guns. They had little or nothing to sell except the pith of the sago palm. Some of these people at a later date (from the island which we now know as New Hanover) came on board and were rendered very dizzy—"intoxicated"—by the motion of the ships, though they never suffered from seasickness in their own canoes. They brought with them a shark and some small fish.

Turning southwards after rounding New Hanover the expedition sighted the real north coast of New Guinea, ignorant, of course, of the fact that hitherto they had only been following large and small islands now known as the Bismarck Archipelago. Off the north coast of what is now German New Guinea they noted a volcanic island with an active volcano, round which there were clouds of smoke. As they coasted along New Guinea, touching at the islands for fresh water and provisions, they observed that the black Papuan natives could imitate whatever words they heard the Dutchmen pronounce, and were remarkable themselves for the number of "r's" which their own speech contained.

Tasman overlooked the deep indentation of Geelvink Bay, which makes a jagged peninsula of nearly half Dutch New Guinea; and rounding the Island of Waigiu his ships passed through the Spice Islands to the Island of Buru, where he found himself once more within the limits of Dutch influence. The two vessels safely regained Batavia, where their crews were received with much honour and rejoicing. "God be praised and thanked for this happy voyage. Amen", wrote Tasman at the end of his journal on 15 June, 1643.

In the opinion of the Dutch East India Company Tasman's wonderful voyage was too imperfect in its results to merit their complete approbation, though he and his companions received a reward in money for their achievements as "Southland Navigators". But it was realized by the Council of the Dutch East Indies that the actual configuration and extent of the Southland was very little known on the eastern side, though there remained above all things the important fact that a passage well within the South Temperate Zone existed between the Indian and the Pacific Oceans. In 1644 Tasman and Visscher started on another great voyage of discovery for the special purpose of surveying the regions between what was known of New Guinea and what was already placed on the map as Nieuw Holland, or Nieuw Nederland. This region (New Holland) was only what we now call Western Australia, and was thought perhaps to be an independent island. Eastern Australia, which terminated in Tasmania, was called Zuidland or Southland. If there was a still more easterly Australia it was thought to be united with New Zealand under the name of Nieuw Zeeland, and it was conjectured there might also be a separate island to the south, which in that case would be called Nuytsland. Tasman's first expedition had thrown no light on the products of the countries behind these strips of coast line. All these lands in the south might be of great value, or they might be valueless, consequently much more detailed exploration was necessary. The vessels told off for this expedition "for the true and complete discovery of the Southland" consisted of two large schooners or yachts, the *Limmen* and the *Zeemeeuw* (Mew or Seagull), and a much smaller boat, *Bracq*, called a galliot. On 29 January, 1644, these vessels started, "in the name of God" and under the command of Tasman, assisted by Visscher and other officers, including a draughtsman to make maps of the coast and drawings of any remarkable objects or peoples. Directing his course to the little Banda Islands south of the big island of Ceram, so as to commence his new venture from the westernmost limits of New Guinea, Tasman skirted pretty closely the southern coast of that enormous island, sailing eastwards with the express purpose of finding if it was separated from the mainland of New Holland by a strait of water. In fact —knowing nothing of the previous voyage of Torres— he was in search of the celebrated Torres' Straits, and yet, amazing to relate, though he pushed his ships into the beginning of Torres' Straits he allowed himself to be deceived, by the somewhat numerous islands and islets which dot the waters of this not particularly narrow passage, into believing that the gulf before him was landlocked and not worth further investigations. The strait is in reality about 140 miles wide at its narrowest. Nor is it so thickly covered with islands as to be devoid here and there of far sea horizons, suggesting the existence of wider waters beyond. It is therefore very difficult to understand how Tasman can have allowed himself to be so easly misled. It recalls the similar blunder which so long impeded access to Canada, when Jacques Cartier and others overlooked the Cabot Straits between Cape Breton and Newfoundland, and laboriously sailed all the way north of the last-named territory in order to get into the Gulf of St. Lawrence.

The rest of Tasman's voyage, consequently, is not of very great interest to us as regards his pioneering work in Australasia. He made a fairly accurate survey of the Gulf of Carpentaria and of the northern coast of Australia (Arnhem Land), and passing to the west connected this up with the West Australian coast, whence he sailed due north to Java.

The rest of his active life was spent in voyages to

the Philippine Islands and Indo-China. He got into disgrace on one of these expeditions by losing his temper and trying to hang several of the seamen who had disobeyed orders. For this he was punished in various ways, amongst others by being obliged to resign his position as one of the elders of the Church. Eventually, however, his affairs righted themselves, and he retained the respect of his fellow countrymen in Java till the time of his death, which occurred probably in the year 1659, at Batavia. In his will he remembered the poor people of his native village, Lutjegast, in Friesland, and left them out of his property a sum equivalent to about £10 each.

Why the Dutch should have discontinued their explorations of Australasia after the return of Tasman in 1644 is not easily understood, since their appetite for a colonial empire was enormous. But, so far as records go, no further ships were sent for a considerable time in that direction, and the Dutch interested themselves a good deal more either in the settlement of South Africa or attempts to secure a monopoly of the trade with China and Japan. It should be mentioned, however, that in 1696 an expedition was sent to search for a missing East India Company's ship which had sailed twelve years previously from the Cape of Good Hope for Java, and this expedition, under Commander Willem de Vlamingh, in examining the West Australian coast for traces of the ship, made a far more thorough survey of that region than had been effected by the chance visits of Dutchmen in the early part of the seventeenth century. It penetrated as far south as the Swan River (on which the West Australian capital of Perth now stands); and de Vlamingh thus named the river because on it he saw wonderful black swans, thought until then to be such an impossibility that amongst Latin writers a black swan was regarded as a symbol of improbability.

Previous to de Vlamingh's voyage, however, the West Australian coast had been visited by an English ship in 1688, the *Cygnet*, a vessel practically manned by pirates, though they bore the more polite designation of buccaneers, and hailed from the coasts of Tropical America, where they had been plundering the Spaniards. On board this ship was a remarkable pioneer, WILLIAM DAMPIER, who held the post of supercargo, and who spent all his spare time in examining the natural history and native races of the regions he visited as an associate of the pirates.

CHAPTER V

Dampier's Voyages

William Dampier—the surname, like so many in England, is of French origin—was born, the son of a farmer, at East Coker, near Yeovil, in the south of Somersetshire. His attention no doubt was directed to a seafaring life by the constant intercourse which at that time went on between Yeovil and Weymouth; and when Dampier was about seventeen years old, at his own desire he was apprenticed to the master of a ship at Weymouth, with whom he made a voyage to Newfoundland. But the cold experienced in this voyage so disgusted him that he managed to get his indentures cancelled, and in 1671 engaged himself as an able seaman on a great vessel of the East India Company which was leaving England for Java. He soon returned from the Malay Archipelago, however, and enlisted on board a ship of the British navy, in which he took a small part in the naval war with Holland. Then he was sent out to Jamaica as a plantation manager by the lord of the manor of East Coker (the village in which he was born). Except for a brief visit to England in 1678, when his marriage took place, he lived chiefly in the West Indies and on the coast of Central America. He had soon left the work on a plantation to join the buccaneers, or English, French, and Dutch pirates, who were attempting to break down the supremacy of Spain in the waters of the Caribbean Sea

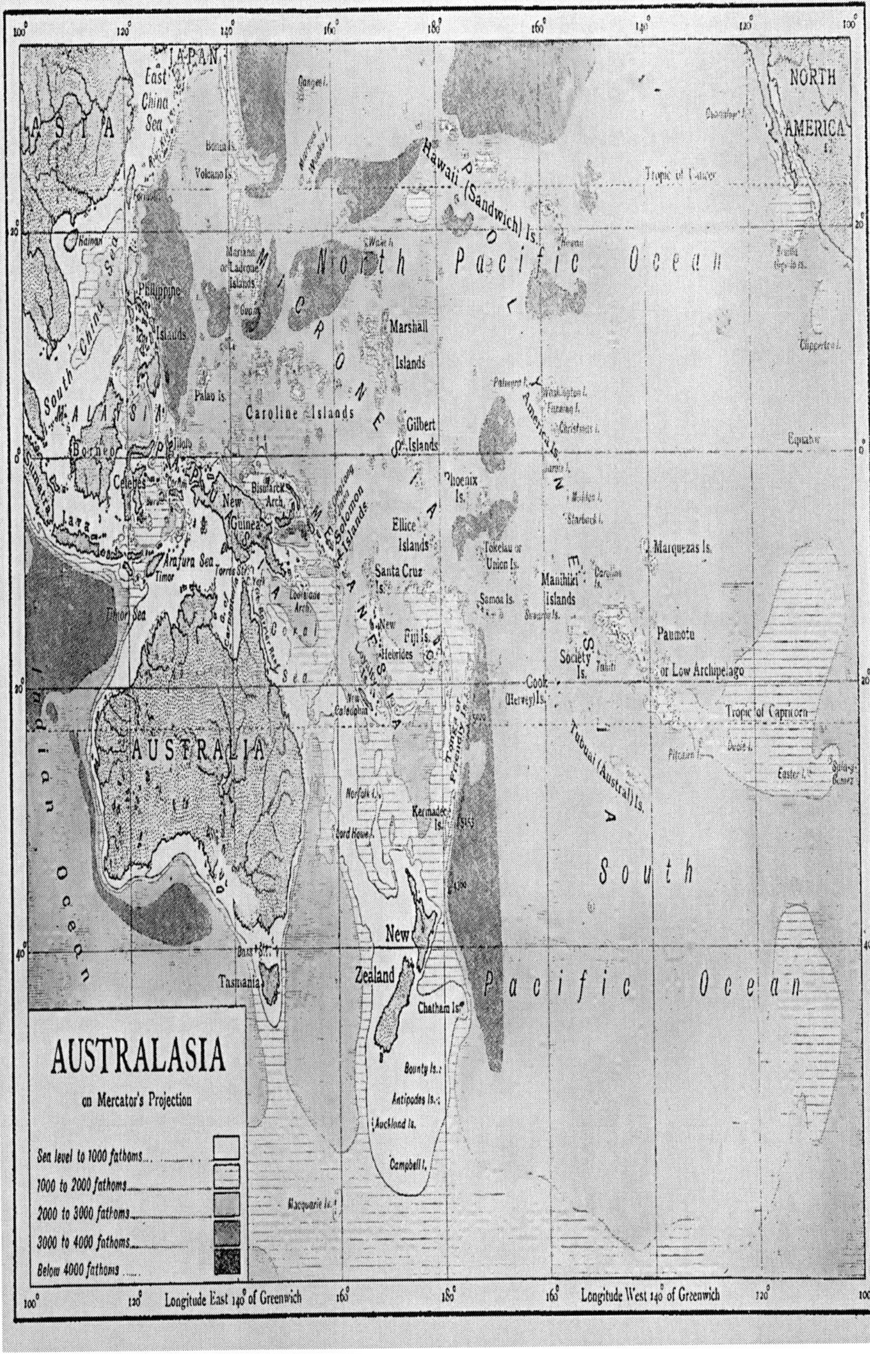
AUSTRALASIA
on Mercator's Projection
Sea level to 1000 fathoms
1000 to 2000 fathoms
2000 to 3000 fathoms
3000 to 4000 fathoms
Below 4000 fathoms
Longitude East 140° of Greenwich
Longitude West 140° of Greenwich
ASIA
JAPAN
East China Sea
NORTH AMERICA
Tropic of Cancer
North Pacific Ocean
South Pacific Ocean
Indian Ocean
Hawaii (Sandwich) Is.
Philippine Islands
Marshall Islands
Caroline Islands
Gilbert Islands
MICRONESIA
MELANESIA
POLYNESIA
MALAYSIA
Borneo
Sumatra
Celebes
Java
New Guinea
Bismarck Arch.
Solomon Islands
Ellice Islands
Phoenix Is.
Santa Cruz Is.
New Hebrides
Fiji Is.
Samoa Is.
Tokelau or Union Is.
Manihiki Islands
Marquezas Is.
Paumotu or Low Archipelago
Society Is.
Cook (Hervey) Is.
Tubuai (Austral) Is.
Tropic of Capricorn
Equator
Arafura Sea
Timor Sea
Coral Sea
AUSTRALIA
Tasmania
New Zealand
Chatham Is.
Kermadec Is.
Bounty Is.
Antipodes Is.
Auckland Is.
Campbell I.
Macquarie Is.
Norfolk I.
Lord Howe I.
New Caledonia
Palau Is.
Bonin Is.
Volcano Is.
Mariana or Ladrone Islands
Guam
Easter I.
Pitcairn I.
Tahiti
Clipperton I.

and Gulf of Mexico. With a party of these buccaneers he estabished himself on the coast of Yucatan to cut logwood, and after his return to and residence in England between 1675–9 he came back to the neighbourhood of what is now British Honduras. Together with a party of buccaneers he crossed the Isthmus of Panama, and, reaching the Pacific littoral, embarked in Indian canoes. And in these they ranged up and down the coast of Central and South America, attacking Spanish towns and shipping. Apparently they must have captured from the Spaniards something more serviceable for ocean traffic than Indian dug-out canoes, because in 1680 they voyaged across the Pacific as far as the lonely island of Juan Fernandez, on which Alexander Selkirk was afterwards stranded by an English buccaneering captain. Some of his adventures in this direction will be described in another volume of the present series dealing with that region. The success of these bold pirates in capturing Spanish treasure ships and seizing Spanish towns on the coasts of Mexico and Peru, and holding them to ransom, was so great that they decided to return in force and renew their operations to the west coast of South America. Thus with bigger ships they passed through the Straits of Magellan and navigated the Pacific Ocean unopposed.

It is interesting to note that on these truly remarkable voyages, which few living seamen would be heroic enough to undertake, their chief means of sustenance were flour (probably from maize) and chocolate mixed with sugar, besides the fish obtained for them by their Indian companions. The buccaneers afterwards recrossed Central America, and rested for a time in the English colony of Virginia. From this region Dampier accompanied a captain, John Cook, in the *Revenge* (a privateer or buccaneering ship), on a voyage to the Pacific. They sailed first to the Cape Verde Islands in the eastern Atlantic.

On one of the easternmost of this still-little-known archipelago Dampier made some most interesting and truthful observations regarding the nesting of flamingoes, though he jumped to a wrong conclusion as to the attitude in which the female flamingo hatches her eggs; but he observes that a dish of flamingoes' tongues is fit for a prince's table, the tongue of this bird being very large and fat. From the Cape Verde Islands they passed on to the Sherboro River (near Sierra Leone), even in those days an English trading settlement. Then, boldly leaving the West African coast, they steered right across the Atlantic to the extremity of South America, helped by a succession of tornadoes to cross the region of equatorial calms till the trade winds blew them over to the Falkland Islands and round Cape Horn. Soon after entering the Pacific Ocean they fell in with other English ships, quite a number of which were now being dispatched round the extremity of South America to the Pacific Ocean, not so much to make discoveries in that direction as to trade with or to plunder the west coast of South America. To all such the Islands of Juan Fernandez[1] were a favourite and safe rendevous for repairs and for obtaining supplies of fresh water. But that the Spaniards became during the seventeenth century perfectly inept in the matter of defending their monopolist pretensions in seas which they attempted to forbid to the rest of the world, they would have occupied and garrisoned at an early date the principal island of the Juan

[1] The largest of these islands was long associated in our minds with Alexander Selkirk and the story of *Robinson Crusoe*, though this wonderful piece of fiction was really concerned with the islands off the delta of the Orinoco River.

Fernandez group.[1] On this island—Mas-a-tierra—goats and pigs had been landed by the Spanish pilot, Juan Fernandez himself, in the sixteenth century. They had increased and multiplied, and furnished excellent mutton and pork for ships that called there. There were only two bays in Mas-a-tierra Island (which was about 36 miles in circumference and of very broad, diversified surface, "high hills and small pleasant valleys") wherein ships might anchor. In the vicinity of each harbour there were rivulets of good fresh water. In course of time the goats multiplied to such an extent that they began to destroy the forests, which still in Dampier's time were a prominent feature in the landscapes, and which included not only good timber trees but an Areca cabbage-palm, the head of which formed an excellent vegetable for seafaring people, badly in need of such an addition to their diet. The sea round about Mas-a-tierra swarmed with fish, and was thronged by seals and sea-lions, which came ashore to breed or to bask in the sun. Dampier states that there were possibly "millions of seals", "either sitting on the shore of the bays or going and coming in the sea round the island". Both seals and sea-lions provided the ships with quantities of train-oil, but the flesh of these aquatic mammals was not liked. [Dampier notes with correctness the abundance of seals along the coasts of North and South America, but their relative absence from the seas washing the East Indies, where indeed they only reappear in the far south along the coasts of Australia and New Zealand.]

From the Juan Fernandez Islands Dampier's ship made

[1] The group consisted of two islands and an islet. The largest of the three was called Mas-a-tierra ("more towards the mainland"), and was 425 miles from the coast of Chile; the next largest was 100 miles farther west and called Mas-a-fuera ("farther away"). The islet near Mas-a-tierra was named Santa Clara. Mas-a-tierra was garrisoned by Spain in 1750.

its way to the Galapagos archipelago, where Dampier duly noted the large, fat, and tame land-lizards—a species of iguana—and, above all, the enormous tortoises "extraordinarily large and fat; so sweet that no pullet eats more pleasantly". A very large tortoise might weigh as much as 200 pounds. He also observed the abundance of turtle of four kinds in the sea round the coasts of this archipelago.[1]

After their stay at the Galapagos Islands Captain John Cook died, and his place was taken by a commander named Davis. Two other English buccaneering ships had joined Dampier's vessel at the Galapagos, and the adventurers spent months which became years in various piratical adventures up and down the west coast of Central and South America from California to Peru. At last a Captain Swan, to whose ship the *Cygnet* Dampier had transferred himself on 25 August, 1685, decided, probably on Dampier's advice, to return to England by way of the East Indies. Accordingly they steered right across the Pacific from Cape Corrientes on the coast of Mexico to Guam in the Ladrone Islands, a passage in which they had been preceded by Francis Drake in 1580 and Sir Thomas Cavendish in 1588. Of course the terrors of this voyage across some seven thousand miles of sea was diminished by this time owing to the frequent passages made by the Spanish ships between Mexico and the Philippine Islands. Apparently this somewhat northern track across the tropical regions of the Pacific Ocean was relatively free from violent tempests, and at the right season of the year provided with continuously favourable

[1] The three species of real turtle belonged two to the genus *Chelone* and one to *Thallassochelys*, viz. the Hawksbill Turtle, the shell of which is the tortoiseshell of commerce; the Green Turtle, which makes turtle soup, and is delicious to eat; and the musky-smelling useless Loggerhead Turtle. The fourth kind was the quite unrelated Leathery Turtle (*Sphargis*), which grows to a great size, 7 to 8 feet long.

winds in one direction or the other. At any rate, the two ships of the expedition, under Captain Swan and Captain Teat (Dampier being with Swan), set out from Cape Corrientes on 31 March, 1686, and reached Guam on 21 May with only three days' provisions left for the ships' crews. The somewhat strict allowance of food and drink on which all were placed was thought by Dampier to have cured him of a dropsy from which he was suffering at the time of his departure from Cape Corrientes. Their sustenance consisted of ten spoonfuls of boiled Indian corn a day, together with a little water for those who were thirsty; but Dampier noticed that some of the seamen did not drink for nine or ten days at a time, and one man went without any liquid for seventeen days, declaring he was not thirsty. For such as these the moisture in the boiled maize seems to have sufficed. But the men had grimly resolved that they would not long grow hungry if Captain Swan's estimate was at fault. It had been decided that, as soon as victuals failed, Captain Swan should be killed and eaten!

Of course the arrival at the Island of Guam (or Guahan, as it was called by the natives) did not mean necessarily that they would at once obtain provisions, because the island, unlike Mas-a-tierra (Juan Fernandez), was strongly fortified and garrisoned by the Spaniards, who kept it, naturally, for the relief and refreshment of Spanish ships alone, those engaged in the transit between the Philippine Islands and the west coast of America. Guam produced in those days rice, pineapples, melons, oranges, limes, bread-fruit, and, above all, coconuts. Upon their first arrival Captain Swan pretended that he and his men were Spaniards. By this means they induced a Spanish priest with three natives of the island to come on board. These they held as hostages, sending word, through them, to the governor of the island of Guam that Captain Swan was badly in want of provisions, was of peaceable intent, and prepared to purchase the same on reasonable terms. Meantime the seamen, including Dampier, landed with little ceremony and brought off quantities of coconuts—as to which Dampier wrote in rapturous terms, noting the delicious liquid preserved in the cavity of the coconut, the flesh of the nut, and the sweet sap drawn from the tree which made either a kind of wine "very sweet and pleasant if it is to be drunk within twenty-four hours after being drawn" and capable of becoming a very alcoholic liquid when fermented. "The kernel", he writes, "is much used in making broth. When the nut is dry they take off the husk, and giving two good blows on the middle of the nut it breaks in two equal parts, letting the water fall on the ground; then with a small iron rasp made for the purpose the kernel or nut is rasped out clean, which being put into a little fresh water, makes it become white as milk. In this milky water they boil a fowl or any other sort of flesh, and it makes very savoury broth. English seamen put this water into boiled rice, which they eat instead of rice-milk, carrying nuts purposely to sea with them. This they learn from the natives."

The Governor of Guam, partly through fear, but also pleased at the presents sent to him by Captain Swan, furnished the two ships with a variety and an abundance of provisions, so that they were able to go on their way to the Philippine Islands, of which Dampier wrote an excellent description, which may be read in his book.[1]

[1] The best edition of Dampier's travels is that edited by John Masefield and published (in 1906) by E. Grant Richards.

The powerful chiefs of the large islands in the Philippine archipelago in those days had not been subdued by the Spaniards, and therefore considered themselves quite free to trade with the English ships. But during the long stay off the island of Mindanao the seamen got out of hand, and mutinied against Captain Swan's projects of founding some establishment for trading purposes in the Philippine Islands. A section of the expedition elected John Read, a young navigator, with Captain Teat as sailing master of the ship, to command them. With Dampier amongst them they then sailed away from Mindanao leaving Swan[1] and thirty-six of his men behind. After cruising about the rest of the Philippine Islands and visiting the coasts of Tonquin, Siam, the Island of Formosa, and southern China, they made for the Island of Timor, intending to pass out that way from the Malay Archipelago into the Indian Ocean, and so return to England by the way of the Cape of Good Hope. On their way thither they anchored before the Dutch fort of Macassar on the remarkable island of Celebes. Here an allusion is made to buffaloes[2] (which they did not see), and to "crockadores" (cockatoos) "as big as a parrot, shaped like it, and with a smaller bill, but as white as milk, with a bunch of feathers on its head like a crown."

[1] Swan was afterwards murdered by the natives.

[2] Dampier also alludes to the wild oxen of the Philippine Islands, which were in reality the very interesting Tamarao buffalo. The only wild buffaloes in Celebes would be the still more interesting Anoa peculiar to that island. Both the Tamarao and the Anoa offer resemblances in the horns and skull to extinct buffaloes once living in northern India. The Anoa is the smallest of the Ox tribe, and the most generalized type of living oxen; that is to say, the type which most resembles antelopes. It is quite a small creature, not much bigger than a very large sheep, and the horns are perfectly straight and directed backwards in a line with the nasal bones of the skull. The Anoa generally shows two white spots on each side of the cheeks, and white markings on the throat and legs (which reappear also in the Tamarao of the Philippine Islands), similar to the white spots and stripes in the Tragelaphine antelopes, like the Bush-buck, Kudu, and Nilghai.

In the month of December, 1687, Dampier, with his companions, had passed the Island of Timor, which he described as long, high, and mountainous, and already a part of the Malay Archipelago specially appropriated by the Portuguese. The commanders of the vessel (Read and Teat) now proposed to "touch at New Holland, a part of Terra Australis Incognita, to see what that country would afford us". After avoiding with great care shoals and reefs, they anchored on 5 January, 1688, two miles from the shore, at the mouth, probably, of King Sound on the north-west coast of Australia; an inlet in which there were numerous islands, at that time somewhat densely inhabited by the aborigines. Dampier must have landed with many of his companions, otherwise he could not have given such a realistic description of this part of Australia and its inhabitants. He describes the land (which he, like the Dutch discoverers who had preceded him, guessed at once to be of continental extent) as having a dry, sandy soil, and being very destitute of water, though it was possible to sink wells and obtain it not far from the surface, yet this part of Tropical Australia produced various kinds of trees growing separately and sparsely, and not in forests. The most prominent tree in the region he visited was a species of Dracæna or tree-lily, which was the biggest seen in that neighbourhood. He at once saw the resemblance between these tree-lilies and the Dragon tree of Tropical Asia, which produced the dark-coloured gum known as dragons' blood. Under the trees grew long, thin grass, but both animals and birds seem to have been scarce; in fact, Dampier and his companions saw no beast, but only the track of one, which suggested the existence of something as big as a "great mastiff dog". This may have been the footprints of a dingo. On the beach there were turtle and also dugongs.[1]

Dampier writes more about the natives of Australia rather than its products or landscapes. He describes them as "the miserablest people in the world", beside whom the Hodmadods (Hottentots) of South Africa were gentlemen. These aboriginal Australians had no houses or skin garments, no domestic animals, and no cultivated forms of vegetable food. They had great bottle noses, pretty full lips and wide mouths, from which the two middle incisor teeth of the upper jaw were wanting, having been extracted from the people of both sexes whilst they were still children. Their faces were long and their heads disproportionately big, with very projecting brows. The eyelids were kept half-closed because of the pest of flies for ever trying to get into their eyes. The head-hair was black, short, and curled, like that of Negroes, and (curiously enough) they had no beards. (This is a strange remark on the part of Dampier, and almost suggests that at this time that broad portion of north-west Australia which he visited was inhabited by a Papuan race from New Guinea, for if there is one thing for which the typical Australian aborigine is noteworthy it is the abundance of the beard in the men. Even the women of middle age frequently grow short whiskers and a tuft of beard at the chin.) The colour of their skins was coal black, like that of the Negroes of Guinea. They were tall, slender people, with somewhat delicate limbs. They had no sort of clothing, but round the waist was tied a girdle of bark, and into this was thrust occasionally a handful of long grass or three or four small green boughs full of leaves. There were no

[1] Called by Dampier *manati*, see pp. 40 and 165.

signs of any houses, the people sleeping on the ground in the open air. But they generally slept round about a fire, and would sometimes stick a few branches in the ground as a shelter from the prevailing wind. From his description they evidently possessed the wooden boomerang and wooden lances or spears, the ends of which were hardened by heat. They seemed to have no boats or even rafts, but they were good swimmers, and were observed swimming from one island to another. Their food seemed to consist almost entirely of fish, which they caught by making weirs of stones across little inlets of the sea, in such a way that the high tides brought the fish up these inlets and left them stranded behind the weirs. They also sought diligently for shellfish along the shore. They were acquainted with the use of fire, and boiled the fish, the clams, the mussels, oysters, and periwinkles which they obtained from the seashore, carefully distributing all the food they thus acquired amongst the old people and the children as well as the able-bodied who procured it. After eating they would lie down and sleep until it was necessary to sally out again at low water and obtain fresh supplies of fish food. Their language seemed to be very guttural.

Dampier and his companions sailed away from north-west Australia to the Cocos or Coconut Islands in the Indian Ocean, which long afterwards were settled by enterprising Scotsmen, and have become a British possession of some little value. From the Cocos Islands they made their way back to Sumatra and the mainland of Indo-China. By this time he had become thoroughly sick of the buccaneers and their piratical ways, and, after making one or two vain attempts to escape, he, with two companions, extorted an unwilling permission from

Captain Read to be left behind on the Nicobar Islands (between Sumatra and the Andamans). One of the seamen who rowed them ashore out of kindliness stole an axe and gave it to the party of three Englishmen, "knowing it was a good commodity with the Indians".[1]

When they landed it was dark, so Dampier lighted a candle and conducted his companions to one of the native houses, where they hung up their hammocks. They were later joined by a Portuguese interpreter and four Achin Malay seamen. "It was a fine, clear moonlight night in which we were left ashore, therefore we walked on the sandy bay to watch when the ship should weigh and be gone, not thinking ourselves secure in our new gotten liberty till then." However, at midnight the pirate vessel sailed away, and Dampier and his companions went peacefully to sleep. The next day they bought from their native landlord a canoe for the axe, and, putting their chests and clothes in it, decided to go to the south of the island and wait there till the monsoon had shifted and the wind was favourable for a passage across to the north end of Sumatra. But no sooner was their canoe launched, with all their goods and men in it, than it

[1] The after career of the *Cygnet* and her crew, with her two captains, Read and Teat, was sufficiently remarkable to be briefly sketched. Some more of her men left her at the Philippines and entered the Royal Navy, wherein at least one of them rose to a very honourable command. Captain Teat, and thirty to forty stout seamen, quitted the *Cygnet* on the Coromandel coast and made their way to Agra, where they entered the bodyguard of the Mughal emperor. Read, joined by some more adventurers, took the *Cygnet*, over to Madagaskar, where, in alliance with a Sakalava chief, he played the pirate successfully. Wearying of this, he and some of his men turned slavers, and joined a ship which had come from New York to convey slaves from Madagaskar and East Africa to America. Read and his men went to New York, and quite possibly became the ancestors of excellent citizens of the United States. Other adventurers then proposed patching up the old *Cygnet*, whose bottom was honeycombed with the attacks of the Teredo boring worm, and sailing her back to England. They were obliged, however, to abandon her in St. Augustine's Bay (Southern Madagaskar), where she foundered.

capsized and the party were obliged to save their lives by swimming. Their boxes and clothes were also saved, and Dampier applied himself most assiduously to the drying of his precious journal and drawings. During the next three days the Achinese seamen of their party (who had been members of the crew of a native vessel seized by the pirates) had arranged outriggers to the canoe, fitted her with a good mast, and made a substantial sail of mats. Their canoe thus steadied, they put off once more to sea, and so sailed southwards to another island. Here, through an unfortunate accident, they caused the natives to think that they came as enemies. By a bold manœuvre, organized by Dampier, friendship was concluded with them and "all very joyfully accepted of a peace. This became universal over all the islands, to the great joy of the inhabitants. . . . Gladness appeared in their countenances, and now we could go out and fish again without fear of being taken. This peace was not more welcome to them than to us. . . . They again brought their mellory to us, which we bought for old rags." The loaves of mellory, of which Dampier writes so much and so gratefully, for it was sometimes the only sustenance he had in these adventures, were derived from the local bread-fruit, either identical with the species of the Pacific islands or belonging to an allied kind of *Artocarpus*[1].

"On 15 May, 1688, about four o'clock in the afternoon, we left Nicobar Island, directing our course towards Achin, being eight men of us in company, namely, three Englishmen, four Malayans (Achinese), and a mongrel

[1] Several plants and animals which are found in Austro-Malaysia and the Western Pacific islands, but not in India or Further India, make their appearance in the Nicobars; amongst others the Megapode gallinaceous birds.

Portuguese." Their vessel, the Nicobar canoe, was about the size (he writes) of a London wherry, coming to a sharp point at either end, rather narrower than a wherry, and so thin and light that when empty four men could launch her or pull her ashore. She would have easily capsized but for the outriggers made of strong poles and lashed fast and firm on each side of the vessel. The gunwale of the little vessel was not more than 3 inches above the water when she was loaded.

In the middle of their passage from Nicobar to Achin a terrible storm arose, with a violent wind. The sea rose higher and higher, but at first did them no damage, for the steersman kept the little vessel at right angles to the great waves and the crew baled incessantly. What they feared most was that the violence of the ups and downs would smash the outriggers; there would then be no hope for them, as the canoe would promptly capsize. The evening of 18 May was very dismal, the sky looked black, being covered with dark clouds, the wind blew hard and the seas ran high and roared in a white foam about the canoe. The still darker night was coming on, no land was in sight, and it seemed as though their little ark must be swallowed up by each great wave in succession. "What was worst of all, none of us thought ourselves prepared for another world. I have been in many imminent dangers before now, but the worst of them all was but a play game in comparison to this." In the middle of the night heavy rain fell, which not only lessened the wind but gave the wretched crew fresh water to drink. Then again arose a fresh hurricane. It was again abated by another torrential downpour, so that in addition to other miseries the occupants of the canoe had not one dry patch in their clothing and were chilled extremely.

At length the day appeared, but with such dark, black clouds near the horizon that it brought little comfort. However, the weather began to improve, and on the second day after this violent storm they landed safely at the mouth of a river in Achin. "The gentlemen of Sumatra were extraordinarily kind to us", providing the fever-stricken party with everything that they had need of—young buffaloes, goats, coconuts, plantains, fowls, eggs, fish, and rice. They were afterwards conveyed to the town of Achin and put up at the English factory there. The Portuguese and one of the English companions of Dampier died of the fever which afflicted all the party, and which made Dampier himself so ill that he was long in recovering his strength. After spending nearly three years with the English traders in different parts of Sumatra and the Malay Peninsula, he managed to smuggle himself on board a British East Indiaman, and thus returned, after many adventures, round the Cape of Good Hope to England.

He brought back with him to England, as the only asset of property acquired after his tremendous adventures, a "painted prince" named Jeoly. This was a man born on the little island of Meangis (north of Jilolo), whom Dampier had purchased at the fort of Benkulen, an English factory on the south-west coast of Sumatra, where he (Dampier) had served for five months as a gunner. Jeoly claimed to be the son of the chief of his island, and was most remarkably tatued, or, as Dampier phrases it, "painted", all over his body, the decoration being made by minute punctures of the skin into which was rubbed the powdered gum of a tree. Jeoly and his relations had been driven in their canoes by a strong wind on to the coast of Mindanao (Philippine Islands), where they were sold as slaves, and, having been bought by an Englishman, were transferred to Benkulen in Sumatra. Here Dampier made the acquaintance of this man, whom he seems to have treated with great kindness when he was ill. At his own request he acquired a right over Jeoly by purchase. When he reached England with Jeoly, whom he had managed to convey away on the ship which had given him a return passage, he supported himself for some time by exhibiting Jeoly at country fairs as a painted prince. It is sad to relate, however, that, either because of his necessity or for profit, he sold the faithful Jeoly to another master, and then took up a sea life again. Jeoly—no doubt catching cold by being constantly exhibited without clothes at English fairs—died at Oxford about 1696.

Meantime Dampier was steadily working away at his journals, and in 1697 he published his first book on his truly remarkable adventures and his circumnavigation of the globe. It met with a well-merited success, being, indeed, superior to any work of travel published up to that time in the English tongue; and apparently the excellence of his book obtained for him a small position in the service of the Customs House in London. Having by these means got into touch with the Admiralty, he proposed that he should be put in command of an expedition to explore the coasts of New Holland (Australia), and on this voyage, commanding the *Roebuck*, he started on 14 January, 1699.

After touching at Brazil, which was almost obligatory as part of the sailing voyage to the Cape of Good Hope, he sailed on a direct course from South Africa to the west coast of Australia, which he reached at the place christened by himself Sharks Bay. The land everwhere appeared generally low, flat, and even, but with steep cliffs to the sea—a desolate coast, without trees, shrubs, or grass. After coming to an anchor in what is now called Dampier Bay he went on shore with his men, carrying pickaxes and shovels to dig for water, and axes to cut wood. They found no water, but the soil was less sterile than had seemed at a distance, a reddish sand in which grew grasses, plants, and shrubs. The grass grew in great tufts as big as a bushel basket, and intermixed with much heather. The low trees or shrubs were evidently some kind of Eucalyptus, with reddish timber and strong-scented leaves. In the brackish water of the coast lagoons there were quantities of water-fowl, pelicans, cormorants, ducks, curlews, various kinds of oyster-catcher and plover, and gulls. On the land were a few singing birds, some of them no bigger than wrens, all singing with a great variety of fine, shrill notes. Eagles soared in the blue heaven and apparently preyed on the few beasts and reptiles which were to be seen in the neighbourhood. Amongst these was a sort of racoon, "different from those of America in that it had very short forelegs but powerful hind limbs on which it jumped". This was probably one of the smaller species of kangaru. Then there was a lizard (described wrongly as an iguana) with a large and ugly head, and a very short, thick tail, which seemed another head at the other end of the animal, but without mouth or eyes. These were speckled black and yellow like toads, with scales and knobs on their backs similar to those of crocodiles. They were very slow in motion, but when a man came near them they would stand still and hiss, and not endeavour to get away.[1]

[1] These were, perhaps, the Moloch lizards (*Moloch horridus*).

There was no river, lake, or pond of fresh water to be seen here, but the sea water along the coast abounded with fish, and especially with sharks and rays. On the beach were many kinds of shellfish—mussels, periwinkles, limpets, cockles, oysters—both edible and of the kind which produces pearls. The shore was lined thick with many other sorts of strange and beautiful shells, most finely spotted with red, black, or yellow. There were also green turtle weighing about 200 pounds each, two of which the party caught when they were stranded on shore by the ebbing tide, and which were a most welcome sustenance to the crew, though he speaks of their meat as only being indifferently good. On the other hand, his seamen ate most heartily of the sharks. One of these was 11 feet long, and its maw, or stomach, was like a leather sack, very thick, and so tough that a sharp knife could scarcely cut it. In this they found the head and bones of a "hippopotamus",[1] the hairy lips of which were still sound and not putrefied, the jaw also firm, out of which they plucked a great many teeth, two of them very large, as big as a man's thumb, small at one end, and a little crooked.

[1] It was not, of course, a hippopotamus, this creature never having penetrated, even in bygone ages, farther eastwards than India, but a dugong. The dugong is a near relation of the manati, which frequents the tropical rivers and estuaries of West Africa, the West Indies, and South America. The place of the manati is taken in the waters of the Pacific and Indian Oceans by the dugong, which differs from the manati chiefly in having retained in the upper jaw two of the incisor teeth. The manati has only molars, and no front teeth. These incisors of the male dugong develop sometimes into tusks of considerable size—an inferior kind of ivory in the commerce of the Pacific Ocean. The manati, the dugong, and the extinct rhytina of Kamchatka are surviving members of the Sirenian order of aquatic mammals, creatures distantly related to the Ungulate or Hoofed mammals, which adopted an existence in the water ages ago, and gradually lost their hind limbs from disuse. The Sirenians feed only on vegetable food, and the two surviving members of this order, the manati and the dugong, live chiefly on seaweed and the shore vegetation at the mouths of rivers. The manati frequents the coasts of the Atlantic and the dugong those of the Indian Ocean and the Pacific.

During Dampier's stay in the vicinity of Shark's Bay (in or about which he anchored at three separate places searching in vain for fresh water) his company were well refreshed with the flesh of kangarus, turtle, shark, ducks, and plovers. Pursuing his course farther he explored the waters of Freycinet Harbour and realized that the great promontory to the west of it was really an island (Dirk Hartog's Island), but finding no means of getting on shore to search for water (owing to the dangers of the shoals and the rocks) he sailed northwards, and was impressed by the noise made by the whales (blowing through their nostrils, or even uttering sounds more vocal) at night-time, and by the beautiful sea snakes during the day. Of these they saw two different kinds, one was yellow, about the bigness of a woman's wrist, and 4 feet long, with a flat tail, and the other much smaller and shorter, and spotted black and yellow.

About the twentieth degree of south latitude they found themselves sailing through an archipelago of islands, since named after Dampier. Here again they landed in their eager search after fresh water, but were once more disappointed. The islands were dry, rocky, and barren, of a general rusty-yellow colour, yet supporting a fair amount of vegetation, shrubs like rosemary, and others with blue and yellow flowers, creeping peas and beans, some with beautiful deep-red flowers. On these islands, besides the ordinary sea birds, they beheld large flocks of white parrots (cockatoos). They also enjoyed the abundance of small oysters, which were delicious eating. Here and there smoke rose from the islands, showing that they were inhabited by man, and this was the characteristic of the distant mainland. But it was not until the vessel had sailed as far north as the eighteenth degree of south latitude that Dampier was able to approach near enough to the shore to land on it in his search for water. Here at last they came into contact with the Australian aborigines. As they neared the shore they saw three tall, black, naked men, who fled at their approach. These they pursued with amicable intentions till they reached something which looked like a human settlement and was marked as such by its "haycocks" or shelters, which were possibly adaptations of tall anthills. But they found no water here, so they returned to the sea-shore and there dug into the sand. The natives followed them at a distance, making threatening noises and gestures. In the afternoon Dampier made another attempt to get into touch with the people, and one of his seamen, an active young man named Alexander Beal, outran them. They turned and fought him with their wooden lances and wounded him. In order to save his life Dampier was obliged to come to his rescue and shoot one of the natives with his gun, after which the rest ran away, carrying off their wounded companions. Amongst these natives was one who by his appearance and carriage seemed to be a chief amongst them. He was a brisk young man, not very tall, or even as good-looking as some of the others, but more active and courageous. He alone was painted, and his face was decorated with a circle of white paste round his eyes, a white streak down his forehead and nose, while white patterns were painted on his breast and arms. He and his people had unpleasant looks, and seemed to Dampier more savage than any human race he had ever met with. They were rendered additionally ugly by their blinking eyes, due to the flies which gathered round the eyelids in teasing numbers. Their skins were black and the hair bushy and frizzled. It was found that at their camps, when they did not use the shelter of anthills, they would stick three or four leafy boughs into the ground against the prevailing wind blowing off the sea. Near these they made their fireplaces, and thus obtained shelter and warmth during the night. At each fireplace were great heaps of the shells of oysters, mussels, cockles, &c., the chief sustenance of these savages. Unlike the natives whom Dampier had encountered farther north, in his first glimpse of Australia, these people seemed to live entirely on shellfish, and made no weirs to catch fish at the ebbing of the tide.

From this place they obtained only four hogsheads of brackish water by digging wells in the sand, while engaged in which work they were pestered with the flies, whose attentions they felt far more than the blazing sun. Indeed, by inference, we may gather that Dampier experienced on the tropical coast of West Australia the same immunity from sunstroke as is characteristic of other parts of Australia.

The land of this region (which would be the southern part of the vast Kimberley district) was level, and although terribly waterless by no means devoid of vegetation, being more or less covered with flowering shrubs and bushes and bright with red, white, blue, and yellow flowers, most of them belonging to some kind of pea or bean, which also bore ripened seeds in pods. He notes the number of "rocks" in the vast plains, 5 or 6 feet high, round at the top, like a haycock, red, or in some cases white. These were obviously the anthills built by a termite or "white ant". Farther inland beyond these plains was a thin forest, and along the creeks of the seashore grew a few dwarf mangrove trees. Animals were scarce and consisted chiefly of lizards, snakes, and a few marsupial mammals (probably kangarus) and wandering dingoes "like hungry wolves". As to birds, there were "crows just like ours in England" (see p. 41), small hawks and kites, turtle-doves, and a variety of small birds about the size of larks.

In despair of finding fresh water in this inhospitable country, Dampier directed his course towards the Island of Timor. On their way thither they saw more sea snakes, some of which were all black, whilst another large one had a red head. At last, "to our great joy", they saw the tops of the high mountains of Timor peeping above the clouds, and came to an anchor on the south side of the island about 200 yards from the shore.[1] The land by the sea was full of tall, straight-bodied trees like pines (Casuarinas), but they were again balked, for the approach to land which

[1] An admirable description of the Island of Timor is given by Dampier, much of which might be applicable to this region at the present day. This large island (some 12,500 square miles in area, 300 miles long, and an average 40 miles broad) lies, as he remarks, nearly north-east and south-west, and consequently somewhat out of the general direction of the other Sunda Islands in the long string between Java on the west and Wetar on the east. Of all the islands of the Malay Archipelago (except the New Guinea group) it is the one which approaches nearest to the Australian continent. On its southern side are tremendously high mountains rising to a culminating altitude of more than 12,000 feet close to the seashore. But a great deal of the actual coast-line is obstructed for the access of mariners, especially on the south, by an obstinate fringe of mangroves. The mangrove is a tree which grows out of the mud and shallow sea water, supporting itself by innumerable roots. It is practically impossible for anyone to make their way by land through the mangrove swamps. Beyond the mangroves, before the land rises into mountains, is a stretch of sandy country sparsely clothed with a tree which Dampier describes as a pine, which was more probably the Casuarina. The mountains form an almost continuous chain running through the middle of Timor from one extremity to the other, without outlying mountains of great height in the southern districts. The indigenous inhabitants of Timor are mainly of Papuan or Negroid stock, with a considerable intermixture of Mongolian Malay. As in Dampier's time, so at the present day, the island was practically divided between the Portuguese and the Dutch. What first drew the attention of Portuguese navigators to this out-of-the-way island of the Malay Archipelago is not known to us. They found their way to Timor in 1520, being followed soon afterwards by the ships of Magellan's expedition. The Portuguese have stuck to Timor through all the changing circumstances of their history, even after the Dutch had turned them out of all the other Malay islands. They now are admitted by Holland and the rest of Europe to be the rulers over nearly two-thirds of the island..

might yield fresh water was hindered by a long mangrove creek. Much of the south coast of Timor proved "barricaded with mangroves", though beyond the land appeared pleasant enough to the eye, the sides and tops of lofty mountains covered with large forests and meadows, and obvious plantations in which they could see coconut palms growing. The weary mariners, suffering terribly from scurvy, were obliged to turn the ship about and sail to the west end of the island in order to get on its north coast.

Here they found themselves approaching a Dutch fort—Concordia—and a Dutch ship came to meet them, greatly surprised at the arrival of Englishmen from such a direction, especially as they had found their way between the islands at the south-west extremity of Timor. The discourse between the two parties was in French, as there was no one on board the English ship who could speak Dutch. The Hollanders proved most inhospitable, as they suspected Dampier and his men of being pirates. Grudgingly they were allowed to obtain water from the Dutch fort at Kupang. Passing round the north coast (stopping here and there to get fresh water, buffalo meat, and cockatoos) they reached the region of the Portuguese settlements. Here they were much more hospitably treated than they had been by the Dutch, and the Deputy-Governor of Lifau sent them a most welcome present of young buffaloes, goats, kids, coconuts, ripe mangoes, and jack-fruit. The only pure-blooded Portuguese at this place were a priest and a lieutenant; the rest were mostly Christianized natives of Timor, "copper coloured, with black, lank hair". The Portuguese lieutenant was named Alexis Mendoza. Dampier was informed that at the east end of Timor (Dilli) there was a good harbour and a large Portuguese town where he could get plenty refreshments for his men and pitch for his ship, the Governor of the place (Capitão Môr) being a very courteous gentlemen and glad to entertain English ships. For some reason he turned back to the west and camped on the coast in a region called Babao, near the Dutch settlement of Kupang. Here he obtained the pitch with which he caulked the planks of his leaking ship, and cleaned the sides of weed and shells, giving them afterwards a coating of lime. Every now and again his men went inland and hunted buffaloes, afterwards roasting, smoking, or drying the flesh. The Dutch visited them here to find out what they were doing. After some misunderstandings Dampier went to dine with the Governors of the Dutch fort of Concordia in Kupang Bay. Here he found plenty of very good victuals well dressed, the linen being white and clean, the dishes and all plate being fine china. Nowhere on this voyage did he meet with better entertainment or so much decency and order. With their meals they drank wine, beer, or rum and water. The Dutch Governor had formed an interesting collection of beautiful shells. Still, their treatment by the Dutch was grudging. They were denied stores, and though offered fresh provisions, realized that these would be much dearer than the things they could obtain at little cost to themselves by hunting.

From Timor Dampier sailed between the islands of Ombai and Wetar or Vetta and past the small island of Gunong Api,[1] which consists mainly of one huge, active volcano, sloping up from the sea towards the top, where it is divided into two peaks, between which issued more smoke than Dampier had ever seen from any other volcano. Most of this island was burnt up and desolate from the devastating effect of the streams of red-hot lava. Thence

[1] Quite distinct from the Gunong Api of the Banda Islands.

he sailed through the Banda Sea till on New Year's Day, 1700, he first descried the coast of New Guinea, probably the country of Baaik, the southern part of that extraordinary western projection of New Guinea—the Arfak Peninsula—which is nearly cut into two large islands by M'Clure Inlet and Geelvink Bay. Here, nearly opposite the big island of Ceram, his men landed to obtain fresh water. The country was mountainous and well clothed with magnificent forests, which appeared very green. The seamen brought back with them from the shore a variety of wild fruits which they found in the forest, and "a stately land fowl of a sky colour", with white and red spots on the wings, and on the crown a large bunch of long feathers. The bill was like that of a pigeon, but the red legs and feet resembled those of fowls. The men had also discovered the nest of this bird with one egg in it as large as that of a hen. It was the now well-known Victoria Crowned Pigeon, sometimes styled the Goura. Some 150 years afterwards it was rediscovered in what is now British New Guinea, and named after Queen Victoria. From this point Dampier seems to have shaped his course to a small island off M'Clure Inlet, which he calls by its Malay name of Pulo Sabuda. Here he saw more of these large Goura pigeons and enormous fruit-bats (of the genus *Pteropus*), the bodies of which were as big as those of rabbits, while in a general way they looked exactly what their name implies "flying foxes", with a stretch of wing from tip to tip measuring 4 feet. The inhabitants of this island were of two distinct types—the Malayan, with tawny skin and long, lank, black hair, and "curl-pated New Guinea negroes", many of which were slaves to the people of Malayan type. The Malays possessed large sailing boats with which they visited the coasts of New

Guinea, where they obtained Papuan slaves, parrots, and Paradise-birds, which they carried over to the Dutch settlements in Ceram and exchanged for European trade goods.

After stopping at Pulo Sabuda Dampier rounded the north-western promontory of New Guinea, calling at some of the small islands for wood and water and shell-fish, some of which were "cockles" weighing 10 pounds each, and other huge bivalves, clams, weighing 78 pounds. At most of these islands they saw the same large fruit-bats. One of these islands off Waigiu (in what is still called the Dampier Strait) he named after King William III. After that he continued to sail round the north coast of New Guinea, past islands which he knew to have been previously discovered by the Dutch.

At last he reached the vicinity of the two great islands now known as New Mecklenburg and New Pomerania. He took them to be one island, to which he gave the name of Nova Britannia (New Britain), a name which it bore down to the days of Captain Cook, who christened the northern portion, which was found to be a separate island, New Ireland. Dampier, landing on the northern coast of New Ireland (now New Mecklenburg), described it as high and mountainous, adorned with tall, flourishing trees, possessing many plantations and patches of cleared land. The natives, however, flung stones at them with their slings, so Dampier renounced any attempt to obtain water there. For this purpose he called at Gerrit Denys Island, one of an archipelago lying to the north of New Ireland, and here the natives were more friendly. The island was thickly populated, the people being very black, strong, and stout-limbed. Their hair was short and curly; besides being clipped into different patterns, it was dyed or bleached a variety of colours, red, white, or yellow, besides its original black. These people had broad, round faces, with big, bottle noses, yet looked agreeable enough until they disfigured themselves by tatuing[1] and by wearing things through the septum of the nostrils as big as a man's thumb and 4 inches long. Sometimes these objects were passed actually through the cheeks, and not through the nostrils. They also made holes in their ears into which they thrust pieces of bone or wood. They were very dexterous with their canoes; which were fitted with outriggers on one side. The bow and the stern rose high and were carved into extraordinary painted devices resembling birds, fish, or a man's hand. Dampier, noticing these people had no knowledge of metal utensils, and knowing nothing of their stone weapons, wondered how they could carve this work so elaborately. Their speech was clear and distinct, and for a sign of friendship they would hold up the bow of a tree full of leaves. Continuing his circumnavigation of "Nova Britannia", Dampier discovered and named the entrance to St. George's Channel, but he believed it to be only a deep indentation, and did not realize it was a passage between New Ireland and New Britain. Calling at Port Montague, off the south coast of New Britain, where the land was mountainous, woody, full of rich valleys and pleasant water brooks, Dampier found this part of the great island abounded in food—coconuts, yams,[2] ginger; hogs, pigeons, and fish. The natives proved to be friendly. The men were finely decked with feathers of various colours. The women wore nothing but a bunch of small green leaves. Pigs swarmed in their villages and ran wild in the woods.

[1] Really marking their faces and bodies with huge blobs of skin or scars.
[2] Probably the Taro, the tuberous root of a species of Arum.

c 487

DAMPIER AND HIS CREW WATCHING A VOLCANIC ERUPTION

Reaching the western extremity of New Britain, Dampier sailed through the strait which still bears his name, into the sea of the Bismarck Archipelago. Off this part of the New Guinea coast there are several small islands which still contain active volcanoes. One of these amazed the crew of Dampier's ship by vomiting fire and smoke with dreadful noises and explosions all through the night at intervals of about half a minute. These convulsions were alternately slight and tremendous, and when they were severe great volumes of flame rose into the sky above the crater, while red-hot streams of lava could be seen running down to the seashore. Why Dampier should have turned to the north and rounded New Britain, instead of pursuing his course southwards to discover the connection—if any—between New Guinea and Australia, it is difficult to understand. Perhaps he thought that the indentation of Huon Gulf indicated the eastern extremity of New Guinea; but even then one would have thought that he would have sailed in that direction in order to circumnavigate this island, and so regain the Malay Archipelago or the coast of Australia. But instead of this he contented himself with once more sailing past the north of New Guinea, till he regained the known regions about Ceram.

He landed on that large island and noticed how it abounded in strange or beautiful birds: cassowaries, pigeons, parrots, and cockatoos. One of the seamen killed two hornbills. From Ceram they made their way back to Timor, calling again at the Dutch settlements. He then thought of revisiting the coast of Australia, but owing to contrary winds made his way instead to Java, from which he voyaged back to the Cape of Good Hope and so towards England. But when off the island of

Ascension their ship sprang a leak and they were obliged to abandon it. To their great thankfulness they found a spring of fresh water on the high mountain of Ascension, while plenty of turtle visited the beach. There was also an abundance of goats running wild, and there were edible land-crabs. The hollow rocks afforded a convenient lodging in the mild and equable climate, and before they had spent more than a week on this refuge there arrived a British ship which gave them a passage back to England.

On his return to England he was charged by his officers and men with cruelty, and was found guilty of this charge by a court of enquiry, who decided he was not a fit person to command a king's ship, and fined him all his pay. There must have been some truth in these charges, and friction between him and his men was probably the reason why Dampier ceased his explorations after rounding New Britain. But he soon afterwards obtained the command of a ship belonging to a company of merchants, and in this he made his way back to the Pacific Ocean round Cape Horn. This ship was little else than a pirate vessel, which, under the guise of privateering in the French wars, was sent out to prey on foreign commerce off the west coast of South America. They met with varying fortunes after calling at the island of Juan Fernandez, and Dampier quarrelled with his officers and men, some of whom deserted him. Dampier eventually made his way back across the Pacific Ocean to the Dutch East Indies, where he was imprisoned for some months. But in 1707 he got back to England and attempted to vindicate himself from the further charges brought against him by members of his crew, who had reached England after deserting him. In 1708 he obtained a position as pilot on another privateer, and this voyage stands out in history from the interesting fact that the captain under whom he sailed (Woodes-Rogers) called at the island of Juan Fernandez, and there took away the celebrated Alexander Selkirk, who had been landed on that island more than four years previously, and had lived there, like Robinson Crusoe, in solitude.

The two privateers, on one of which Dampier made this voyage, were very successful in preying on Spanish shipping and plundering the rich towns on the west coast of South America, so that when Dampier returned to England, in 1711, he probably obtained, as an advance of his share in the profits, enough money on which to subsist for the remainder of his life, which terminated in London in 1715.

For the age in which he lived he was—as his most recent biographer (Mr. John Masefield) points out—a very remarkable man. Although his life was spent amongst pirates, semi-savage mahogany cutters, drunken and ignorant sailors, he was temperate and refined, with a passionate love of the wild nature around him, never failing to observe the flowers, the fish, the birds, or the beasts of the strange countries he visited. His descriptions of native manners and customs are remarkably accurate, and he has been the first to record the existence of many a strange beast and bird, such as the Mountain Tapir of Tropical America (which he thought was a kind of hippopotamus) and the Victoria Crowned Pigeon of New Guinea.

CHAPTER VI

James Cook's First Voyage

In 1740 a naval commander, George Anson, was dispatched to the Pacific to take part in that ocean in the naval war against Spain. Apparently, after rounding the extremity of South America, he was content at first to proceed up the coast of Peru and plunder the Spanish towns on the western coast of Tropical Africa. He then sailed across the Pacific with his Spanish prizes by way of the Spanish route to the Philippines, making no new discoveries on his way, but passing through the Malay Archipelago to the Cape of Good Hope. Twenty-two years afterwards a British fleet, conveying 6000 soldiers, sailed across the Indian Ocean and took possession of Manila, but failed to conquer the Philippine archipelago, owing to the bravery of the small Spanish garrison of 600 men. But when this war drew to a close, Vice-Admiral John Byron (the grandfather of Lord Byron, the poet) was sent out in the *Dolphin* in 1764 to explore the Pacific Ocean and make some search for the Great Southern Continent. This journey, however, like that of Lord Anson's, resulted in no gain to geographical knowledge, for he simply sailed by the northern tropical route from Mexico to the Ladrone Islands, and then came back along much the same course to South America and the Atlantic. After his return his ship, the *Dolphin*, together with a vessel called the *Swallow*, were once more dispatched to the

Pacific Ocean through the Straits of Magellan, but this time under the command of Captain SAMUEL WALLIS.

The Tahiti archipelago, which was to play such an important part as a basis for Cook's discoveries in the Pacific, had apparently been seen by the Spanish navigator de Quiros, as early as 1606, and named "Sagittaria". It was rediscovered in 1767 by Wallis on this voyage of H.M.S. *Dolphin*. Wallis named Tahiti Island "King George III Island", and stayed on its coasts for a month. On his north-westward journey he discovered the Marshall Islands. In the following year there arrived at Tahiti the great Bougainville, the first French explorer of the Pacific Ocean.

France, through her enterprising Norman and Breton seamen, was not slow to interest herself in Far Eastern discoveries, and in 1528 defied the Papal bull and worried the Portuguese in Malaysia, just as she followed up Spaniards and Portuguese along the east coast of the Americas. Early in the sixteenth century her mariners, following the Portuguese, had rounded the Cape of Good Hope and adventured themselves in the Indian Ocean to snatch a small share in the trade which was so jealously monopolized by the Spaniards and Portuguese. It is even said (see p. 57) that the first hint of the existence of a Great Southern Continent is due to a French navigator, le Testu, who returned in 1532 from the eastern seas with stories of a Greater Java which lay to the south of the islands of the Malay Archipelago.

But for various reasons the French slackened in their exploration of the Indian Ocean in the second half of the sixteenth century. Their interest in this direction was only revived under the great ministers of Henry IV and Louis XIII. In the first half of the seventeenth century the French laid the foundation of their future claims to Madagascar and the Mascarene Islands, and founded repeatedly chartered companies to deal with the trade of the Indian Ocean. But none of their adventurers seem to have penetrated to the Spice Islands or the Pacific until the eighteenth century. Their colonial ambitions in Africa and Asia were awakened in a great measure through the most remarkable of their kings, Louis XIV. With far-sighted ambition this monarch strove to acquire special interests for France in Abyssinia (in which direction he failed), in Siam, and Cochin China; and he took advantage of his occasional alliances or friendship with the Spanish monarch to send explorers and men of science to examine the wonderful regions of South America, under the jealous rule of Spain and Portugal. One of these explorers was Frézier (Fraser), of Scottish descent, and the work which he published on his return, dealing with the southern extremity of South America, drew attention to the unoccupied Falkland Islands, known to the French as Malouines, and the Spaniards as Malvinas. This hint attracted the notice of a very remarkable Frenchman, Louis Antoine de Bougainville, who had served in the French Embassy in London, and had also been an officer of the French army in Canada. In 1765 he persuaded the merchants of St. Malo, in Brittany, to fit out an expedition which should colonize the Falkland Islands. But, this archipelago being claimed by Spain, it was handed over to the Spanish authorities by Bougainville, who afterwards proceeded in command of a ship called the *Boudeuse* (the Sulker) to navigate the Straits of Magellan and explore the Pacific Ocean. In his westward course he touched at the Tuamotu Islands, and rediscovered the Island of Tahiti, which he called Cythère (the Island of Venus). Sailing westwards, he was probably the first explorer to discover the Samoa group, named by him the Navigators' Islands, from the bold seamanship of its Polynesian people. From Samoa he passed on to the New Hebrides, and, then directing his course due west, with the deliberate intention of searching for the Great Southern Continent, he was stopped in this search by encountering the Great Barrier Reef, which guards so much of the approach to the north-east coast of Australia from south latitude 23° to 15°. Turning off, therefore, to the north-west, he encountered and named the Louisiade archipelago of islands and islets, which is off the south-easternmost extremity of New Guinea. Instead, however, of venturing through the Torres Straits (the existence of which was then a geographical secret in possession of Spain), he turned northwards to the Solomon Islands,[1] and thence sailed past the coasts of the large island of New Ireland (now known as New Mecklenburg), and so on along the north coast of New Guinea. Rounding this great island, and directing his course southward, he arrived at the island of Buru, between the Moluccas and Celebes. Here he found himself within the sphere of Dutch influence, and after calling in at Batavia, the capital of Java, he made his way back, round the Cape of Good Hope, to St. Malo, only having lost seven out of a crew of two hundred men in this remarkable sea journey round the world.

Thus, before Cook set out on his famous journey in 1768, the position of European knowledge in regard to the Pacific Ocean and the continent and islands of Australasia was as follows: The outline of the Australian continent had been roughly traced by the Dutch (who

[1] The largest and nearly the most northern of the group is named after him.

called the land New Holland) from Cape York westwards to the southernmost point of Tasmania (which was not known to be an island); a portion of the west coast of New Zealand (the North Island and a small part of the South) had been placed on the map by Tasman, but it was not known whether this land of high mountains consisted of one or more large islands, or whether it might not even be another peninsula of a mighty southern continent; Tasman had discovered the small Tonga Islands; New Guinea was known in regard to its western and eastern extremities and a part of its north coast, but, owing to secrecy having been kept as to the existence of Torres Straits, it was also thought to be an outlying part of New Holland (Australia); New Britain and New Ireland (now Neu Pommern and New Mecklenburg) had been explored by Dampier in 1700; the Solomon Islands, Santa Cruz, and the islands of the New Hebrides group had been rediscovered by Bougainville, who had also first visited and named the Louisiade archipelago to the south-east of New Guinea. [The Solomons and the New Hebrides had been known for two centuries to the Spanish Government, and for a shorter period to Dutch navigators]. Easter Island—the easternmost of the Polynesian islands, not much more than 2000 miles from the coast of South America—had been seen by the English pirate, Captain Davis, in 1685, but was only definitely known and named, after its discovery by the Dutch navigator, Roggeveen,[1] on Easter Sunday in 1722; and was considered by some geographers in Holland and France to be an outlying point of the great southern continent: which, if this were the case, would be almost as large as Asia, and would

[1] Admiral Roggeveen is also thought to have first realized the separate, insular character of New Britain in 1723.

occupy quite half the space actually covered by the Pacific Ocean. The existence of Tahiti was fully known, inasmuch as it was pitched upon by the British astronomers as being the best place in that region of the globe from which to observe the transit of Venus. The existence of the Marquezas Islands had long been established by Spanish navigators, but it is doubtful whether, before Cook started, news had been received of the sighting of the Tuamotu archipelago of islets by Bougainville, or of the Samoa group (Navigators' Islands). Most of the largest and most important of the Pacific islands remained practically or completely undiscovered. These were the Hawaii archipelago (see pp. 121–2), the Fiji Islands, the southern islands of the New Hebrides, the large island of New Caledonia, the Loyalty Islands, the groups of the Gilbert, Phœnix, and Ellice Islands, the Hervey or Cook Islands, the Tubuai or Austral Islands, besides the whole east coast and Alpine range of New Zealand, and the little Norfolk Island midway between New Zealand and New Caledonia. Finally, there were the undecided questions of the supposed connection of New Guinea with the north coast of the Australian continent, and the existence of a vast southern continent occupying much of the area of the Pacific Ocean in the South Temperate Zone. The whole of these blanks in Australasian geography were filled up and more or less accurately mapped, the vexed questions were set at rest and solved, by the great JAMES COOK in the two voyages of discovery which he made in the years 1768–71, 1772–5, and 1776–9.

Captain JAMES COOK, who will certainly be regarded in universal history as the foremost hero of Australasian discovery, was born on 27 October, 1728, at the little Yorkshire village of Marton, in the Cleveland district of northern Yorkshire, in a two-roomed wattle-and-clay cottage. He was the son of a farm labourer, also named James Cook and said to have been of Scottish origin. In time Cook's father rose to the position of a farm bailiff. The great James Cook, his second son, was sent to school when he was eight years old, and received the elements of a good education, especially in arithmetic. At the age of sixteen or seventeen he was bound apprentice to a grocer and haberdasher, or, more correctly, a general-store dealer, a man, in fact, who kept the principal shop in the pretty little village of Staithes, in a hollow of the cliffs 10 miles north of Whitby. This move brought Cook into close relations with a sea-faring life, as most of the customers of the shop were fishermen and smugglers. In fact, his place of business was only 300 yards from the sea waves (which now entirely cover the site of the original shop).

Evidently he did not like his work as shop apprentice, and longed to become a sailor, with the result that he was transferred as an apprentice to the employment of a coal merchant who owned or employed sailing ships to carry coals to and from Whitby. Earlier accounts of Cook's boyhood assert that he ran away to sea from the grocer-haberdasher's shop, stealing a shilling from the till as something to sustain his enterprise. There certainly was trouble about a shilling in his relations with the general-storekeeper, but it seems to have been that he saw—prophetically enough—a new South Sea shilling[1] in the till, and, fascinated with its appearance,

[1] The original South Sea Company, which became so notorious through its connection with the first great speculative mania in England in 1720, came into existence in 1711 (partly promoted, it may be, by Dampier and Daniel Defoe), for the purpose of trading with the "South Sea", viz. the Pacific Ocean, and chiefly the west coast of South America and the vaguely known islands of Oceania. It received in course of

changed it for an ordinary shilling of his own. The new bright shilling was found in his box, but his explanations apparently convinced his employer of his innocence. However, by some friendly arrangement he seems to have been relieved of his apprenticeship to the general-store dealer of Staithes, and was transferred to the employment of a Mr. John Walker, whom he served as apprentice on his ships for about three years. In between his voyages he lived at Mr. Walker's house, where he was treated very kindly and where the housekeeper gave him a table and candles in a quiet corner so that he might read and study in peace. From apprentice he became an able seaman, and at last, in the year 1752 (always working hard to acquire the science of navigation and to educate himself in every way), he became mate of a collier vessel. He was now twenty-four years of age. Three years afterwards—in 1755—Cook, as mate of the collier *Friendship*, found himself in the Thames on the eve of the outbreak of war between Britain and France, and determined to join the Royal Navy, which he did first as an able seaman; but, his qualities being soon discovered, he was not long afterwards rated as master's mate on board H.M.S. *Eagle*. Between 1755 and 1762 he was employed mainly in American waters, and distinguished himself there, not only by his gallantry in action and his many hairbreadth escapes, but by his careful surveying work round the coasts of Newfoundland.

In 1762 he returned to England and married. His

time certain concessions from Spain, such as the sole right to supply Negro slaves to the Pacific coast of Spanish America, and from the British Government the exclusive monopoly of British trade with the "South Seas". Although fraudulently speculative, it did not smash in 1720, but continued an uncertain existence till 1807. Amongst other privileges it received permission to coin the silver it brought back from Peru into shillings, and these were the "South Sea" shillings—coined mostly in 1723—so often referred to in the history of the eighteenth century.

married life lasted for sixteen years, but it is computed that of that sixteen he spent only about four and a half in his wife's society, chiefly at a house in Shadwell, in the eastern part of London, which he bought for her. Nevertheless they were fond of one another, and a family of six children was born to them in course of time.[1]

Between the time of his marriage and 1768 he began to make himself noteworthy by his publications of sailing directions and his work as a mathematician and astronomer; for he found the opportunity of observing a solar eclipse off the coast of North America, and described it very lucidly. Consequently, when at the instance of the Committee of the Royal Society, who were desirous that the transit of Venus across the disk of the sun should be carefully observed by competent persons from some central part of the Pacific Ocean, the British Admiralty decided to appoint James Cook to take charge of this expedition, and at the same time to make a determined search in the Central and Southern Pacific for the supposed vast southern continent, stretching from the south tropic to the South Pole. Cook, therefore, was given a commission as a lieutenant-commander, and appointed to H.M.S. *Endeavour*.[2] The *Endeavour* was a sailing vessel of only 368 tons burden, which had been con structeed at Whitby and purchased by the Admiralty.

The Government entrusted to the Royal Society the sum of £4000, to spend on equipping this vessel and paying her officers and crew. Cook apparently received

[1] All of whom died young, from illnesses or accidents. Mrs. Cook, the widow, lived to the age of ninety-three, and died in 1835.

[2] Originally the Royal Society had suggested a Mr. Dalrymple, a sort of merchant-adventurer, who had traded a good deal in the Malay Archipelago, and who had formed and promulgated theories about the immense size of the Australian continent, but apparently Dalrymple knew very little about astronomy, and the Admiralty wisely refused to allow him to command the king's ship.

a clear salary of £120 a year, in addition to a special gratuity of £105 for his astronomical work, and a sustenance allowance for himself and his assistant astronomer, Mr. Green, of £120. He was also paid by the Admiralty a small "command" allowance of five shillings a day.

Next in importance to Captain Cook in the history of this remarkable voyage will rank (Sir) JOSEPH BANKS, described by the Royal Society as a gentleman of large fortune, and said in other correspondence of the period to have an estate bringing in £6000 a year. He was born in London in 1743, the son of a wealthy physician who had become a Member of Parliament for Peterborough. Educated at Oxford, he early conceived an intense interest in botany and zoology; and having in 1764 inherited all his father's property, he soon afterwards made at his own expense a scientific expedition to Newfoundland and Labrador, where he made a famous collection of insects and plants.

A neighbouring landowner, Lord Sandwich, had become head of the Admiralty, and Banks obtained through him leave to join Cook's expedition. He then laid out about £10,000 on all the stores and other preparations necessary for the conduct of an elaborate enquiry into the natural history of the lands and seas through which the expedition was to pass, and he engaged a Swedish naturalist, a pupil of Linnæus—Dr. Daniel Solander—to accompany him, besides four draughtsmen to make pictures, and nine servants to do all the rough work of natural-history collecting, &c.

The diary which Mr.—afterwards Sir Joseph—Banks kept on this voyage, between August, 1768, and July, 1771, is almost as interesting and remarkable as the diary kept on H.M.S. *Beagle* by his greater successor in the same studies, Charles Darwin. This journal of Sir Joseph Banks really served to give the substance of greatest interest to the volumes published on the First Voyage of Cook, which were edited by Dr. Hawksworth; and although Hawksworth in his introduction laid stress on the important part played in the narrative by the incorporation of Banks's journals (most generously placed at his disposal), nevertheless the mass of the reading public has been too apt to ascribe to Captain James Cook observations and descriptions which were entirely the work of Banks. Though Cook's mighty achievements as a navigator, and as one who laid the foundations of the British Empire in Australasia and British Columbia, can never be lessened by the results of any research into the history of his voyages, it is only fair to point out that the records of his first great adventure would not have achieved their world-wide popularity but for Banks's co-operation and his munificent expenditure on the expedition. Banks, in fact, was a man born out of due time. His was a nineteenth-century mind which made its appearance in the middle of the eighteenth century, just as Shakespeare was an intelligence of the twentieth century which made its appearance three hundred years before its appropriate period. In order not to interrupt the course of the narrative it might be as well to give in a footnote final information as to Sir Joseph Banks's career.[1]

[1] The really scientific results of his expedition, largely the work of Solander, consisted of "five folio books of neat manuscript" (wrote the late Sir Joseph D. Hooker, the greatest botanist of the nineteenth century, who died at the end of 1911), and seven hundred engraved copperplates which are said still to repose in the hands of the trustees of the British Museum never published to the world up to the present day. The cause of this inexcusable negligence is not given, but the matter is one which calls for urgent enquiry. In 1772, when Cook's Second Expedition was in course of preparation,

The ship *Endeavour* sailed from Plymouth on 26 August, 1768, with a crew of officers, naturalists, seamen, and servants, of ninety-four in all, with provisions for eighteen months, and an armament of guns which would be quite sufficient to keep at bay any attack by savages. Captain Cook, from the first, was resolved to combat resolutely that foe of seamen-adventurers—scurvy—the disease which is constantly alluded to in the earlier pages of this book, and which I have described elsewhere as so seriously impeding the first attempts of colonization on the part of the French in Canada. In this resolve he was backed up by Banks, who had made special enquiries on the subject of anti-scorbutics. An attempt was made to convey fresh cabbage from England to the Pacific, and casks of this vegetable

Banks proposed once more to accompany the great navigator, and made such elaborate preparations for this purpose that he was obliged to embarrass his estate for the purpose of raising the necessary money. But the Board of Admiralty, which in those days regarded natural science with contempt, put so many vexatious obstacles in his way, amongst others, that Banks's principal assistant was not a member of the Church of England!—that Banks at the last moment withdrew and went off instead with Solander on a scientific expedition to Iceland. Once again he handed over his journal and observations to other people, who made free use of it in their works on Iceland. In 1778 he was chosen President of the Royal Society, and until the day of his death in 1820 he was a true friend to science and discovery. He practically founded Kew Gardens as the great botanical gardens of the metropolis, he threw himself enthusiastically into what may be called economic botany, and was the first person who advocated the use of indiarubber in various industries, and the cultivation of rubber-bearing trees and plants. He proposed the cultivation of tea in India, and established botanical gardens in Jamaica, St. Vincent, Ceylon, and Calcutta, besides taking an immense and practical interest in British horticulture. He had much to do with the dispatch of Mungo Park, Clapperton, and other travellers to explore Africa; in fact, the full indebtedness of the world of science, and of the British Empire in particular, to Sir Joseph Banks is not yet fully known, and certainly not yet sufficiently appreciated. All young students should make a point of reading the biographical preface to the *Journal of the Right Hon. Sir Joseph Banks* by an equally great man, Sir Joseph Hooker, born just about the time that Banks died, and a son of one of Banks's friends.

To a great extent Banks was admired and appreciated by the political world of his day, but probably more because he was a wealthy landed proprietor who was enthusiastic for science than because of his own scientific achievements and deeds of great daring on behalf of science. He was made a baronet in 1781 and a Knight of the Bath in 1795, and finally a member of the Privy Council in 1797.

lasted out for nearly a year. The leaves and the heart of the cabbage were preserved between layers of salt. But the greatest benefit in checking scurvy was derived from lemon juice, of which Banks himself took nearly 6 ounces a day. The juice of oranges and lemons mixed with a little brandy had been evaporated till it was very thick, and this essence was enclosed in small casks before the *Endeavour* left England. The expedition also took with it treacle, turpentine, and "wort" (the unfermented infusion of malt), with which they were to brew some kind of beer.

The *Endeavour's* course towards the Pacific was via Brazil (where she was mistaken by the Portuguese for a privateer or pirate and received very badly) and the extremity of South America. Off the coast of Patagonia Banks noticed "shoals of red lobsters", as Dampier had done in the southern Pacific. These "sea crayfish", or Langoustes as they really were (allied to the excellent Langouste of the Mediterranean[1]), frequently astonished the pioneers of the Pacific and south Indian Oceans by their immense numbers which passed in shoals swimming on the surface, very often proving a godsend to the crew by providing them with fresh and savoury food. Unlike the lobster, which is only red when it is boiled, these Langoustes (probably of the genera *Iasus* or *Panulirus*) were naturally of a bright crimson or scarlet colour.

Cook, Banks, and some of the seamen landed on Staten Island at the extremity of the curly tail of South America. The Dutch had thought in the previous century that Staten Island was a northern promontory of a vast Antarctic continent, of which New Zealand might be another projection (which was why Tasman had first called New Zealand

[1] The real lobster is limited in its range to the northern Atlantic.

"Staten Island"). Banks was very anxious to examine its flora, and found far more flowering plants at this season of Antarctic summer than he thought possible of existence in such a cold bleak country; yet, in the very searching for natural-history specimens, he and the rest of the party were caught in a snowstorm and nearly frozen to death. Two negro servants who had drunk too much grog and had lain down to rest were killed by the cold.

After rounding Cape Horn, in January, 1769, the *Endeavour* had sailed as far to the south as the sixtieth degree of south latitude. On her course north-westwards into the Pacific the ship was brought to a standstill occasionally whilst Mr. Banks went out in a boat to shoot sea birds, principally albatrosses. These were thought by Cook to be larger than those of the Atlantic Ocean. One of them measured 10 feet 2 inches from the tip of one wing to that of the other. Their bodies, after being carefully skinned, were soaked in salt water, parboiled also in sea water, and finally stood in a very little fresh water (the phrase "very little" shows how necessary it was in those days to be avaricious of the store of fresh water). After this they were served up to table with a savoury sauce, and the dish was universally commended. It was in any case a grateful variation from the constant round of salt beef and salt pork. Another inhabitant of these south Pacific seas which aroused great interest was a large octopus or cuttlefish, apparently just killed by albatrosses, and floating in a mangled condition upon the water. Banks noticed that it was very different from the cuttlefishes found in European seas, for its immense arms were furnished, instead of suckers, with a double row of very sharp talons which resembled the claws of a cat, and like them were retractable into a sheath, from which they could be thrust out at pleasure. "Of this cuttlefish we made one of the best soups we had ever tasted."

On 24 March, 1769, they noticed a log of wood passing by the ship, and the sea, which was rough, became suddenly as smooth as a millpond, so that they were probably passing by the vicinity of some undiscovered island.

On 4 April, 1769, land was sighted and was discovered to be an island of an oval form, with a lagoon in the middle, which occupied much the larger part of it. The border of land circumscribing the lagoon was in many places low and narrow, consisting chiefly of a reef or beach of rocks; in other words, it was one of the coralline atolls described on p. 21, and as usual possessed coconut palms. It was inhabited by tall, copper-coloured natives, with long, black hair, whose heads seemed to be remarkably large, probably because of some cap or headdress. Eleven of them walked along the beach abreast of the ship, with poles or pikes in their hands which reached twice as high as themselves. As they so walked they were without clothing; but after the ship had drawn off from the island it was seen that they covered themselves with some light-coloured material. To Cook and his mariners, who for a long time had seen nothing but water and sky, except the cold hills of Tierra del Fuego, these coconut groves of Lagoon Island in tropical latitudes seemed a terrestrial paradise.

The following day they passed another atoll, shaped exactly like a bow, the arc and cord being land, and the space between them water, that part answering to the arc of the bow being about 200 yards wide, 12 or more miles long, and fairly well covered with trees, while the straight, low beach answering to the bowstring was a long strip of coral rocks, through which there were openings connecting the lagoon with the sea. This island, like similar

c 487

CAPTAIN COOK'S ARRIVAL AT TAHITI (1769)

ones which they sailed by in the succeeding days, was inhabited by Polynesians of the usual type, brown-skinned, naked, tall, well-made, and with abundance of black hair; but in some cases this bushed out from the head, showing that the people were not without some Melanesian blood. They seemed to be armed with wooden weapons, one of them a slender pole with a knob at the end, and another a paddle, which might be used for striking or stabbing or for navigating a canoe. The canoes these people had possessed sails.

Passing by Osnaburg Island, already discovered by Captain Wallis, Cook reached Tahiti (which at once struck them in its difference from the atoll islands by being high and mountainous) on 12 April, 1769. Before even he could get near the shore his ship was surrounded by canoes, in which there were bunches of bananas and branches of a tree, which it was the custom of these people to wave as a token of peace and amity. By signs they expressed the wish that these branches should be stuck amongst the rigging of the ship as a sign that they would be received with friendliness. This having been done, the canoes approached the ship close enough to hand their cargoes of coconuts, bananas, and other fruit on board, where it was eagerly purchased by the sailors, being extremely acceptable after their long privation from such additions to their diet. The next day the ship came to an anchor in Port Royal Bay (Matavai). Here the first thing that attracted their attention, when the natives came off to trade, was the bread-fruit.[1]

Before anyone from the *Endeavour* was allowed to land at Tahiti, Cook wisely drew up rules to guide the relations of the seamen and officers with the natives, in order as far

[1] See pp. 64 and 160.

as possible to avoid provoking quarrels with them, or enabling the latter to acquire weapons which might be turned against the white men. Landing himself, with Banks and Dr. Solander, a party of armed seamen, and a native of Tahiti, who had come off to the ship and constituted himself their guide, he noticed that the Polynesian people were so awestruck that the first who approached them almost came creeping on his hands and knees. Leafy boughs having been offered in token of peace, the Englishmen likewise broke off green branches and held them in their hands, and, the whole party having marched to a place where there was a freshwater spring and where the ground was clean and bare, green boughs were dropped by both sides in a regular heap, and after that relations between them became much less formal, especially after Cook's party had distributed beads and other small presents. They walked for about 5 miles through groves of trees loaded with coconuts and breadfruit, and offering the most grateful shade. Under the trees were the houses of the natives, most of them being only a roof without walls, and the whole scene realizing "the poetical fables of Arcadia".

The next day canoes came out to the *Endeavour* evidently filled with people of superior rank. Two of these chiefs came on board and selected Cook and Banks to be their special friends, carrying out this ceremony by taking off most of their clothing and putting it about the shoulders of the Englishmen. Return presents were given to them, and after a long row in the boats of the *Endeavour* the notabilities of that ship accompanying their Tahitian friends landed and went to a house of much greater length and size than any they had yet seen. Here was found a chief by the name of Tutaha, who presented them with a cock and hen and pieces of perfumed bark cloth. In other houses they met the women, who received them with such extravagant demonstrations of affection that they were embarrassed. Soon afterwards another chief gave them a meal, which they ate with the greatest heartiness. It consisted of fish, bread-fruit, coconut, and bananas, cooked after the native fashion. They were enjoying this meal, though perhaps not quite so much the affectionate attentions of the native ladies (who kept plying them with coconut milk), when suddenly two of the officers complained that their pockets had been picked—a complaint, one would think, under the circumstances, they might have waived on such an occasion. However, Dr. Solander lost an opera glass, and Mr. Monkhouse, a surgeon, his snuff box.

Complaint was at once made to the chief, and Banks somewhat aggressively jumped to his feet and struck the butt end of his gun on the ground. Immediately all the natives fled in a panic, with the exception of two or three chiefs and their wives. The principal personage amongst these at once took Mr. Banks by the hand and led him to a large quantity of cloth which lay at the other end of the house, offering it to him piece by piece, and intimating by signs that if that would atone for the wrong which had been done he might take all he saw. But this compensation was refused, and eventually the chief, after being absent for some time, returned with the missing snuff box and the case of the opera glass. This, however, upon being opened, was found to be empty. Whereupon the chief, catching Mr. Banks by the hand, led him rapidly along the shore for a mile or more, till he reached a house from which a woman came out and gave him a piece of cloth, which he hastily took from her and continued to press forward. Banks had been followed by Dr. Solander and Surgeon Monkhouse, and at last the whole party came to a place where they were received by a woman to whom the chief presented the piece of cloth and to whom the Englishmen gave a few beads. The beads and cloth being deposited on the floor, the woman went out, and in about half an hour she returned with the opera glass, and expressing the same joy as was now shown by the chief. She also returned the beads and the cloth, refusing to accept them.

The next day the chiefs came off to the ship with pigs, bread-fruit, and other provisions, for which they received suitable return presents of hatchets and linen. Cook then established an encampment on shore, but their pleasant relations with the natives were temporarily spoilt by the petulance of a midshipman named Monkhouse (not to be confused with the surgeon of that name) commanding one of the landing parties. A Tahitian had snatched away the musket of one of the marines. Whereupon this midshipman ordered his men to fire into the thickest of the crowd, afterwards pursuing the thief and shooting him dead. However, thanks to the chiefs Tuburai, Tamaide, and Tutaha, peace was made and intercourse soon resumed without much restraint. The body of the man who had been shot in the encampment was found to be wrapped in cloth and placed on a bier supported by stakes under a roof, where it would be allowed to decay with a terrible stench until at last it was nothing but a dry skeleton.

Charming as life was in many respects on this Pacific island there was one pest which at times proved almost unendurable—apparently none other than the common house fly, which existed in such enormous numbers that it was an incessant torment during daylight. If one of the draughtsmen attached to the expedition attempted to make a water-colour study of any object, the flies would settle on his paper so thickly that no part of its surface could be seen, and eat the colour up as fast as he could lay it on. [It will be remembered that Tasman noted the same plague of flies in the Tonga archipelago.]

The principal personage of Tahiti seemed to be a queen, whose name was Oberea, about forty years of age, almost white-skinned, but now very stout, though with evidence of great beauty at an earlier age. There were several men chiefs of importance in the main island, and something like an aristocracy. This "nobility" had faces of a more Caucasian character and a taller stature than the common people, who were many of them in the position of serfs.

The Tahitians believed in numerous gods, one of which was supreme over the rest. They also had priests called *tahawa*, who were the "wise men" of the land, possessing more knowledge of navigation, astronomy, and medicine than the others. They believed vaguely in a life after death, and their dead were disposed of usually (in all but cases of worthless slaves) in the following manner (I quote from Banks):—

"I found the shed under which the body lay, close by the house in which the man resided when he was alive, some other houses being not more than 10 yards distant. The shed was about 15 feet long, and 11 broad, and of a proportionate height: one end was wholly open, and the other end and the two sides, were partly enclosed with a kind of wicker work. The bier on which the corpse was deposited, was a frame of wood . . . with a matted bottom, and supported by four posts, at the height of about 5 feet from the ground. The body was covered first with a mat, and then with white cloth; by the side of it lay a wooden mace, one of their weapons of war, and near the head of it, which lay next to the close end of the shed, lay two coconut shells, such as are sometimes used to carry water in; at the other end a bunch of green leaves, with some dried twigs, all tied together, were stuck in the ground, by which lay a stone about as big as a coconut: near these lay one of the young plantain trees, which are used for emblems of peace, and close by it a stone axe. At the open end of the shed also hung, in several strings, a great number of palm nuts, and without the shed, was stuck upright in the ground, the stem of a plantain tree about 5 feet high, upon the top of which was placed a coconut shell full of fresh water; against the side of one of the posts hung a small bag, containing a few pieces of bread-fruit ready roasted."

The emotions of the Tahitians were easily excited. Both men and women readily gave way to tears, and would fly into hysterical rages in which they struck their heads several times with sharks' teeth, so that a profusion of blood often followed. A woman who acted thus owing to some trifling affair which had piqued her, after her bleeding was over looked up with a smile, ceased her loud, doleful talking, collected the pieces of blood-stained cloth with which she had dabbed her head and neck, and threw them into the sea. Then she plunged herself into a river, washed her whole body, and returned to the encampment as gay and cheerful as if nothing had happened.

Cook was greatly struck with the stature of the men and with the beautiful shape of their bodies. One man coming from a small outlying island measured nearly 6 feet 4 inches. The women of the better class were in general taller than English women. On the other hand, those of the more serf-like people were not only below the average stature of Europeans but even quite dwarf-like. Occasionally albinos made their appearance with skins of a dead white, red eyes, and white hair. As to their tatuing, the Tahitians pricked the skin, so as just to fetch blood, with a small instrument something in the form of a hoe, with a blade made of bone or shell scraped very thin, and from ¼ inch to 1½ inches wide. The edge of this was cut into sharp teeth, and when about to be used the teeth of the hoe were dipped into a black paste made from the soot from an oily nut—a nut which the natives burnt in lieu of candles. Having been dipped into this mixture and pressed into the skin, the top of the hoe would be struck a smart blow with a stick, so that it punctured the skin and left behind an indelible black stain. The operation was painful and it took some days before the wounds were healed.

Cook expatiates on the personal cleanliness of the Tahitians, who constantly washed the whole of the body in running water perhaps three times a day. After every meal their mouth and hands were washed, and their clothes as well as their persons were kept without spot or stain, "so that in a large company of these people nothing is suffered but heat, which, perhaps, is more than can be said of the politest assembly in Europe". For in Cook's day—and, indeed, for nearly one hundred years later—civilized Europeans (to say nothing of the working classes, who were most uncleanly) very seldom washed their bodies. Tahitian clothing consisted of bark cloth or matting of different kinds. The bark cloth would not bear wetting, so it was only worn in dry weather and exchanged for matting when it came on to rain. None of the materials of their dress were sewn. Their clothes consisted of long strips of bark cloth or matting, which would be draped about the body, principally round the waist. Large pieces were worn loosely over the shoulders in the manner of a cloak, or allowed to fall about the limbs like loose trousers. In the heat of the day clothing was mostly reduced to a scanty petticoat for the women and a sash for the men. To shade their faces from the sun they sometimes wore bonnets made of matting or coconut fronds. These they would plait together in a few minutes. The women also wore little turbans of cloth, and sometimes a very elaborate dress made of plaited human hair. Of this material Sir Joseph Banks brought away with him pieces that were over a mile in length, apparently without a knot. They would wind these strips of hair (like silk) round and round the head, and thus produce a very pretty effect. Amongst these threads they stuck flowers of various kinds. The men would thrust the pinkish tail-feathers of the Tropic-bird upright into the bunch of hair on the top of their head, or wear whimsical garlands of flowers or scarlet seeds, or wigs made of dogs' hair, or men's hair, or coconut matting. Ear-rings made of shells, stones, berries, seeds, or small pearls were also worn.

The only domestic animals of Tahiti were pigs, dogs, and fowls, but the natives also ate wild ducks, which were plentiful. Cannibalism did not exist in this archipelago, though there were traces of it in the religious customs.

Their manner of executing and cooking dogs, which they bred for eating, was as follows: The man who performed the double office of butcher and cook killed the dog by holding his hand over the dog's mouth and nose. In about a quarter of an hour the animal was stifled. Whilst this was being done someone else was digging a hole in the ground about a foot deep, in which the fire was kindled. On top of the fire were placed stones to be heated. The dog was then singed by being held over the fire, and scraped with a shell. Thus all the hair was taken off. The entrails were removed, and the body was cut up with a sharp shell. The entrails, after being carefully washed in sea water, were put into coconut shells, together with all the blood which had been collected from the body. When the oven in the ground had been sufficiently heated the fire was taken out, and some of the stones which were not hot enough to burn anything were placed at the bottom and covered with green leaves. The cut-up dog, together with its entrails, was then placed on these leaves, and other leaves were laid on top. The hole was afterwards covered with the remainder of the hot stones, on which earth was heaped. In about four hours this oven was opened, and the dog's meat taken out, "excellently baked, so that we all agreed he made a very good dish". The dogs which were bred in Tahiti for food were kept wholly on a vegetable diet—bread-fruit, coconuts, and yams.

The principal vegetable foods of the natives of the island of Tahiti were bread-fruit, coconuts, bananas of thirteen sorts, and the long banana which is known by the name of plantain; then there were a fruit not unlike an apple, which when ripe was very pleasant; another resembling a nectarine, and called *ahiya*; sweet potatoes, *dioscorea* yams, koko or taro yams (an aroid); a fruit known by the name of *jambu*, and reckoned most delicious; sugar cane; a root called by the inhabitants *pea*; a plant called *ethe*, of which the root only was eaten; a fruit like a large kidney-bean, grown in a pod and tasting like a chestnut after being roasted, called by the natives *ahi*; the fruits of the pandanus; the *morinda* fruit; a kind of bracken fern, of which not only the root but the leaves were sometimes eaten; and a plant called *theve*, which had an edible root. There was also in the island the paper-mulberry tree (the range of which extends from China to Polynesia), and several fig trees, some of which, with their enormously extended aerial roots and branches, covered an area of 60 square feet. This mulberry and most of the figs provided bast which was made into cloth.

Bread-fruit was sometimes turned into a delicious dish by mixing its farinaceous pulp with coconut milk, with pounded bananas, or with a paste made of the *mahi* fruit. This *mahi* was gathered just before it became ripe, and, being laid in heaps, was closely covered with leaves. In this state it fermented and became disagreeably sweet. After pulling out the core from the rotten fruit the rest was thrown into a hole neatly lined with grass. The hole having been covered with stones, the fruit then underwent fermentation and became sour. After that it was wrapped up in leaves and baked, and, both cooked and uncooked, would keep for weeks. It was eaten hot or cold, and the natives seldom made a meal without it, though its taste to Europeans was "as disagreeable as that of a pickled olive". Salt water was the universal sauce to their food, no meal being eaten without it, so much so that the natives who lived at a great distance from the seacoast had to keep sea water in segments of bamboos like tubes. A kind of butter was also made of coconut kernels flavoured with salt water, which at first tasted to the Europeans nauseous and rancid, but afterwards grew so much in favour with them that they preferred it to the sauces they had brought out from England.

The Tahitians possessed no narcotic like opium, betel, or tobacco, and at first Cook thought that they knew no intoxicant. But he afterwards found that they were able to get drunk on the juice of a plant called *ava ava* (the well-known *kava* pepper vine, referred to on p. 64). But the vice of drunkenness was almost confined to the chiefs and the nobility, and was forbidden to the women.

Banks gives the following interesting description of how a Tahitian gentleman would eat a meal:—

"He sits down under the shade of a tree, or on the shady side of his house, and a large quantity of leaves, either of the bread-fruit or banana, are neatly spread before him upon the ground as a tablecloth. A basket is then set by him that contains his provision, which, if fish and flesh, is ready dressed and wrapped up in leaves, and two coconut shells, one full of salt water and the other of fresh. His attendants, who are not few, seat themselves round him, and when all is ready he begins washing his hands and his mouth thoroughly with the fresh water, and this he repeats almost continually throughout the whole meal; he then takes part of his provision out of the basket, which generally consists of a small fish or two, two or three bread-fruits, fourteen or fifteen ripe bananas, or six or seven 'apples'. He first takes half a bread-fruit, peels off the rind, and takes out the core with his nails; of this he puts as much into his mouth as it can hold, and while he chews it takes the fish out of the leaves and breaks one of them into the salt water, placing the other, and what remains of the bread-fruit, upon the leaves that have been spread before him. When this is done he takes up a small piece of the fish that has been broken into the salt water, with all the fingers of one hand, and sucks it into his mouth, so as to get with it as much of the salt water as possible: in the same manner he takes the rest by different morsels, and between them, at least very frequently, takes a small sup of the salt water, either out of the coconut shell or the palm of his hand: in the meantime one of his attendants has prepared a young coconut, by peeling off the outer rind with his teeth, an operation which to a European appears very surprising, but it depends so much upon sleight that many of us were able to do it before we left the island. . . . The master, when he chooses to drink, takes the coconut thus prepared and, boring a hole through the shell with his finger, or breaking it with a stone, he sucks out the liquor. When he has eaten his bread-fruit and fish he begins with his plantains, one of which makes but a mouthful, though it be as big as a black pudding; if instead of plantains he has 'apples', he never tastes them till they have been pared. To do this a shell is picked up from the ground, where they are always in plenty, and tossed to him by an attendant: he immediately begins to cut or scrape off the rind, but so awkwardly that great part of the fruit is wasted. If, instead of fish, he has flesh, he must have something like a knife to divide it; and for this purpose a piece of bamboo is tossed to him, of which he makes the necessary implement by splitting it transversely with his nail. While all this has been doing, some of his attendants have been employed in beating bread-fruit with a stone pestle upon a block of wood; by being beaten in this manner, and sprinkled from time to time with water, it is reduced to the consistence of a soft paste, and is then put into a vessel somewhat like a butcher's tray, and either made up alone or mixed with banana or *mahi* sauce, according to the taste of the master, by pouring water upon it by degrees and squeezing it often through the hand. Under this operation it acquires the consistence of a thick custard, and, a large coconut shell full of it being set before him, he sips it as we should do a jelly if we had no spoon to take it from the glass. The meal is then finished by again washing his hands and his mouth, after which the coconut shells are cleaned, and everything that is left is replaced in the basket."

The Tahitian dances were often of an elaborate character; but some of them of an immodest nature. The people were very fond of music, and had a great sense of rhythm. Their musical instruments were chiefly drums and flutes.

The Tahiti drum was made of a hollow block of wood, solid at one end and covered at the other with sharks' skin. This was beaten by the hand and not with a stick. The flutes upon which the people played had only two stops, and therefore could not sound more than four notes by half-tones. They were not applied to the mouth, but were blown into from one nostril whilst the other was stopped with the performer's thumb. Nevertheless, to the music of these instruments four people would sing in concert, keeping very good time. They also had an expedient for bringing flutes that were played together into unison by rolling a leaf over the end of the shortest, like a sliding tube, moved up or down till they were certain that the playing was in tune, a fact of which they judged with much nicety of ear. They were very fond of singing couplets, especially after dark, to amuse themselves before going to sleep. Their language was a melodious Polynesian dialect, but, being deficient in several consonants, the native rendering of the names of officers and men of the *Endeavour* was quaintly imperfect. Cook was called Toot. The sailing-master, Mr. Molineux, had a name which they did not attempt to pronounce, so in preference they called him Boba, from his Christian name, Bob (Robert). Gore was turned into Toarro; Solander became Torano; Banks, Tapane; and Petersgill, Petrodero.

The Tahitian houses of the better sort were usually built, on a raised clay platform, of bamboo poles and palm thatch or matting. The furniture inside was very simple—little else than mats on the floor. No pottery was required, coconut shells and calabashes taking its place. The houses, when necessary, were lit up at night-time by the kernels of an oily nut, which they stuck on a wooden skewer one over the other. These candles burnt a considerable time, and gave a very tolerable light.

These Polynesians of Tahiti, as elsewhere in Oceania, were still living in the "Stone Age" when Cook visited them, but they had already learnt the value of iron from the previous visits of Bougainville and Wallis, and were very keen to obtain iron from the crew of the *Endeavour*. Previous to their intercourse with Europeans, fish hooks were made of mother-of-pearl, or some other hard shell, filed into shape with pieces of coral, drilled with holes by sharp-pointed stones, fixed into the end of a piece of bamboo, which was then rotated between the hands. Coral rock made excellent files for this and other industries. Their axes and adzes were derived chiefly from basaltic volcanic stone. The skin of a sting-ray[1] with its

[1] The sting-ray is so often referred to by Pacific voyagers that some description of it is necessary. This fish—probably of the genus *Urogymnus* or *Pteroplatea*—belongs to the family of the *Trygonidæ*, the whip-tailed or sting-tailed rays, so called because the thin, pliable tail is armed with a series of bony spines, as much as 8 or 9 inches long, which have proved very useful to primitive man on the Pacific and Indian Ocean coasts (where the sting-rays are often stranded) as a ready-made lancehead or dagger

THE ISLAND OF TAHITI AND ITS EXTRAORDINARY DOUBLE CANOES: AS SEEN BY CAPTAIN COOK

rough tubercles, and used with coral sand, made a fricative for polishing or rubbing down stone surfaces. With their stone axes they were able to fell trees, and, what is more, to split the trunk into planks from 3 to 4 inches thick, the whole length and breadth of the tree, though some of these trees were 8 feet thick and 40 feet long. They would smooth planks very expeditiously with their adzes, and take off a thin shaving from a plank without missing a stroke.

Their small canoes for short excursions were flat-bottomed and with upright sides, but the *pahi*, used for long voyages, was bowed and with a sharp keel. The flat-bottomed boats, called *ivaha*, were sometimes united at a distance of about 3 feet by a strong pole of wood laid across them and lashed to the gunwales. On the fore part of these double canoes a stage or platform was raised, rather wider than the boat itself, and upon this stage would stand the fighting men, whose missile weapons were slings and spears. Below these stages sat the men who paddled the canoe, and who furnished reinforcements to replace those who were wounded. Some of the fighting canoes were 40 feet long, and their sterns might be as much as 18 feet above the surface of the water. The *pahi*, or long-distance boat, was sometimes as much as 60-feet long, but very narrow. If intended for warfare it would be fitted with a stage or platform, or for long-distance journeys contain a house. It was steadied with one outrigger projecting 6 to 10 feet, and might have one or even two masts carrying sails that were made of matting.

After discovering and exploring the rest of the Society

point. The skin of some species of sting-ray is covered with bony tubercles. The rays or skates are distantly related to sharks, but are specially remarkable for being broad and flat—occasionally broader than they are long—owing to the immense development of the fin flaps at the sides.

Islands to the north-west of Tahiti, which is an outlying member of the group, Cook directed the course of the *Endeavour* southwards in search of land; but finding none, except the minute inhabited island of Oheteroa (where the people were lusty and well made and clothed in beautiful bark-cloths painted in stripes of different patterns and colours, and armed with wooden weapons, sometimes pointed with the sharp bone of the sting-ray), he turned his course more to the west, and after sailing from 15 August, 1769, to 6 October, land was sighted on the latter date and became the subject of much eager conversation, it being believed that at last they had found "the unknown Southern land" (Terra Australis Incognita).[1]

On Sunday, 8 October, 1769, the ship was at anchor in Poverty Bay, off the east coast of the North Island of New Zealand; and Captain Cook, accompanied by (Sir Joseph) Banks and Dr. Solander, and a party of marines, landed—the first amongst Europeans—on the shores of New Zealand. Their reception from the natives was not a friendly one. When they had got some distance from the boat, four men armed with long wooden lances rushed out of the woods and attempted to attack the seamen who were left in the boat. The coxswain of the small pinnace was obliged to fire in the air to scare them. This, however, did not deter the Maoris, who renewed their attack, and at last one of them was shot dead. At this the other three stood motionless, as if petrified with astonishment; but as soon as they recovered their senses they seized the body of their dead companion to drag it after them, but

[1] About the same day the *Endeavour* was seen approaching New Zealand from the east and was taken by the natives to be a monstrous bird with beautiful white wings. When she came to an anchor and a boat was let down into the sea it was taken to be a fledgling whose wings were not grown. When, however, the boat was seen to contain people, the Maoris decided these must be gods, and probably evil gods.

abandoned it at last in a panic flight. Cook and his party returned to the ship, and heard the natives on shore discussing in loud voices what had happened. The next morning Cook, accompanied by Banks, Solander, and the interpreter, Tupia, landed and advanced slowly and quietly towards a party of fifty natives who were seated on the ground, every man of whom at their approach produced either a long wooden pike or a small axe of green jade, about a foot long and thick enough to weigh 4 or 5 pounds. The interpreter, Tupia, called to them aloud in the language of Tahiti, but they only answered by flourishing their weapons. Then a musket was fired wide, so as to scare them whilst the party retreated. A body of marines was landed, and marched with a union jack carried before them to a little bank. The officers once more approached the Maoris, and it was with great pleasure they perceived that their Tahiti interpreter was actually understood when he spoke, he and the Maoris only speaking different dialects of the same language. (This was a very remarkable fact, that the Maoris could understand the speech of other Polynesian natives from 1000 to 2000 miles distant, for the two peoples must have been separated in time by about six or seven hundred years.)

The New Zealanders were told that all the white men wanted was provisions and water, and that they would give them iron in exchange. The properties of iron were then explained to them. The Maoris replied they were willing to trade, but declined to lay by their arms, and insisted on the white men coming into their midst. However, after some further exchange of shouted messages to and fro, one of the Maoris put down his weapons, stripped off his clothing, and swam over the intervening river, and with great bravery (considering all the circumstances of the case) walked into the midst of the white men, and was soon followed by other Maoris to the number of twenty or thirty. Some of them were armed. To all were given presents of iron and beads. But they set very little value on either, particularly of iron, of which they had not the least idea. In exchange they gave a few birds' feathers, which they considered ornaments. They then offered to exchange their weapons for those of the white men, and, when the latter refused, made attempts to snatch them from the hands of the officers and soldiers. They were plainly told that if they did not desist the white men would be obliged to kill them. However, a few minutes afterwards, one of the officers happening to turn his back on the Maoris, one of them snatched away his hanger (sword), and, retiring to a little distance, waved it above his head with a shout of exultation. The rest of the savages now became extremely insolent, and called to their friends across the river to join them. The invitation being accepted, it was necessary for the white men to defend themselves. Thereupon Banks fired at the Maori, who was still waving the hanger above his head. The gun was loaded with small shot, which peppered the man at a distance of about 15 yards. He still continued to flourish the sword about, but began slowly to retreat to a greater distance. Whereupon the midshipman named Monkhouse, who figures prominently in Cook's narrative as a person very ready to fire on natives, and who was responsible for the death of the first Tahitian (see p. 196), fired at the Maori with ball cartridge and killed him. The main body of New Zealanders, who in their advance had halted on a rock in the middle of the river when the first gun was fired, began to return to the other shore, while two of those still remaining on the side where the white men were snatched the weapon of green jade (see p. 215) from the dead man, and another endeavoured to secure the naval officer's sword. This was prevented by Mr. Monkhouse. Once again the whole body of Maoris attempted to cross the river and attack the Englishmen, but they were met by a discharge of small shot, whereupon they recrossed the river and retired slowly up country, whilst Cook and his men returned in their boats to the *Endeavour*.

This river was probably the little Ormond River, which flows into Poverty Bay. Near the sea it was salt, so that Cook and his party, unable to furnish their ship with fresh water, made an expedition in boats round the head of the bay to search for fresh water. On their way they saw two canoes coming in from the sea, one under sail and the other worked with paddles. It was decided to intercept these canoes and seize the people in them, so that they might be conveyed to the ship, given presents, and, as it were, forcibly made friends with, and then return on shore to open up negotiations with their fellow countrymen. The two canoes, however, escaped the cordon of boats by desperate paddling. A musket was fired over their heads. Upon the discharge of the piece the men of one of the canoes ceased paddling, stripped off their garments, and actually tackled the boat that came up to seize them, fighting, with their paddles, stones, and other weapons which they had, so vigorously that Cook's party was obliged to fire on them in their own defence. Four, unhappily, were killed, and the other three—boys or youths—leaped into the sea. With great difficulty they were seized and hauled into the boats.

On reaching the ship they had already regained their composure, and evinced a most intense curiosity as to everything they saw, taking especial pleasure in eating bread and salt pork. During the night, however, they gave way to sadness, and sighed very loudly, but Tupia, the invaluable interpreter from Tahiti, came and talked to them so soothingly that they regained their cheerfulness, and to pass the time sang a song with a degree of taste that surprised the crew. The tune was solemn and slow, like that of a psalm, and contained many notes and semitones. The names of these three young Maoris are recorded as Taurangi, Koikerange, and Maragovete. Next morning, after eating another enormous meal, and having been dressed in European clothes and adorned with bracelets, anklets, and necklaces, they were taken on shore by Cook and his party, but evinced great fear when they found they were to be landed at the mouth of the little river, since at that spot the natives were the enemies of their own tribe. However, amongst the large party of Maoris which began to advance on the landing party the boys discerned a relation. Eventually peace was made between the white men and the Maoris, and the boys probably returned to their relations.

As the result of this turn in events a canoe came off from Poverty Bay before the *Endeavour* left the vicinity, others from the neighbourhood followed, and soon there were fifty Maoris on board, who sold everything they had, even the clothes from their backs and the paddles from their boats. Cook sailed southwards at first as far as the point which he named Cape Turnagain. The rumours of his kindly treatment of Maoris on board the *Endeavour* having fortunately spread in all directions, whenever the *Endeavour* came to an anchor canoes would come off to visit the ship and to bring produce for trade, and although one or two disagreeable incidents occurred, such as when the natives attempted to kidnap a Polynesian boy on board for the purpose of eating him—for their cannibalism began to be patent to Cook and his officers—the relations between the Englishmen and the Maoris became so friendly that frequent excursions were made on shore, the houses of chiefs were visited, and meals were taken with them.

The food of these New Zealanders consisted mainly of fish, with which they ate, as a kind of bread, the roots of a bracken fern. These roots were scorched over a fire, beaten with a stick till the bark fell off, and what remained was a soft substance, somewhat clammy and sweet, though not unpleasing to the taste, but very fibrous and stringy. The natives, being tidy in their eating, kept baskets by them into which they spat out the fibrous refuse of the bracken-fern roots. They had no domestic animals except dogs, which were very small and ugly. (The black, bear-like skins which Cook saw being worn occasionally were probably skins of sea-lions or seals.) But they had plantations of sweet potatoes, taro yams, and gourds. The surroundings of their houses were kept scrupulously clean, and there were regular places in which all litter, offal, and refuse was piled up in regular dunghills. The women were not so good-looking as the men, and made themselves uglier by painting their faces with red ochre and oil, an adornment which was very disagreeable to Europeans, because they found out the favourite salutation of the New Zealanders to be that of rubbing noses, so that any attempts to get into friendly relations resulted in most of the officers having their faces smeared with greasy red paint. As a rule, the men confined their decorations to the elaborate tatuing, which has since become so famous, yet there were some who liked to cover their faces, bodies, and clothing with red ochre, and went about carrying pieces of this earth with which to renew the colouring wherever it was removed by contact. Each woman wore a girdle made of sweet-smelling grasses and leaves, and over this a petticoat of roughly plaited *Phormium* fibre.

They found the country luxuriantly clothed with forest and everywhere a beautiful verdure. The species of trees in the woods were unknown to them. They specially noticed here and there cabbage-palms, which they cut down for the cabbages.[1]

The woods abounded in birds of great variety, some of them exquisitely beautiful, but all quite unknown to the Europeans.

Amongst the food supplies of the natives were observed occasionally "lobsters" (which were probably langoustes, see p. 190), besides various wild birds, which the Maoris either roasted by fastening them upon a small stick stuck into the ground and inclined towards the open fire, or baked by putting them into the ground with hot stones. Like the other Polynesians, these Maoris were given to displaying their sorrow, either for the death of a relation or for some matter of mere personal pique, not only by shedding quantities of tears and singing mournful songs, but by cutting their arms, faces, chests, and thighs with sharp-edged shells, so that in the middle of their paroxysm of grief their bodies were covered with blood. Many of the natives met with were scarred from head to foot with old "grief marks".

Some of the promontories stretching out into the sea were noteworthy for the fortified villages, called by the natives *eppah* or *pah*. "The best engineer in Europe could not have chosen a situation better adapted to enable

[1] There is only one kind of palm in New Zealand (the North Island) and that is of the peculiar genus *Rhopalostylis* of which there are two species. Most palms produce a "cabbage"—which is simply the mass of undeveloped fronds, the heart of the tree.

a small number to defend themselves against a greater. The steepness of the cliffs renders it wholly inaccessible from the water, which encloses it on three sides; and, to the land, it is fortified by a ditch and a bank raised on the inside: from the top of the bank to the bottom of the ditch is 22 feet; the ditch on the outside is 14 feet deep, and its breadth is in proportion. The whole seemed to have been executed with great judgment; and there had been a row of pickets or palisades, both on the top of the bank and along the brink of the ditch on the outside; those on the outside had been driven very deep into the ground, and were inclined towards the ditch, so as to project over it; but of these the thickest posts only were left, and upon them there were evident marks of fire, so that the place had probably been taken and destroyed by an enemy."

The weakness of these forts as regards standing a siege was that in none of them did there seem to have been wells sunk or any provision made for storing water in large quantities. And although always built near a stream, the besieged would be obliged every now and then to elude the vigilance of their enemies at night-time and renew their supplies of water by fetching it up to the fort from the stream below. But otherwise these forts were provisioned with quantities of fern roots and dried fish. The people's only weapons seemed to be lances, pikes, and halberds of wood, pointed sometimes with jade[1] or bone, and heavy jade clubs and axes; but

[1] Jade, which is so often referred to (though sometimes miscalled "green talc") in the works of early Pacific explorers, is a beautiful green stone of several quite distinct species. The Jade of New Zealand is either a fibrous silicate called nephrite or a green serpentine silicate. The Maoris called these green stones *poenamu* or *poünamu*, and because Jade of both kinds was specially abundant in the South Island this was called Tarai-poenamu=the Land of Jade.

they had no bows and arrows or slings, and very few weapons that they could throw.

On 20 November, 1769, Cook discovered a river at the head of a great inlet, which he named the Thames, and in this region of the North Island he noticed the splendid kauri pines.[1] One of these he judged to be 89 feet from the root to the first branch, and perhaps 200 feet high altogether. Its girth near the ground was nearly 20 feet. In the most northern part of the North Island they met with the paper-mulberry tree growing in the native plantations, and here they frequently found a kind of celery, which was eagerly gathered by the seamen as a vegetable addition to their diet.

In December, 1769, they rounded the northernmost promontory of New Zealand, which Cook at once identified with Cape Maria Van Diemen of Tasman's discovery, and perhaps realized then for the first time that the Terra Australis along which he had been coasting was none other than the New Zealand discovered by Tasman. The natives in this northernmost part gave a very interesting description, through Tupia the interpreter (when asked if they knew of any other land besides New Zealand), and said that far away to the north-west there was a country of great extent, which they called Ulimaroa, and which had been reached by some of their people in a very large canoe after a month's sail. The most striking feature to them in this distant land was that its inhabitants possessed and ate pigs, and they called these pigs by the widespread name, *bua*. It is probable that the land to which they alluded was Fiji; for though New Caledonia answers better to the description, the

[1] See pp. 35 and 42.

people possessed no pigs when this large island was first visited by Cook.

After rounding Cape Maria Van Diemen, the *Endeavour* sailed southwards along the west coast of the North Island and sighted Mount Egmont, which is 8340 feet high. The appearance of this mountain rising straight up from the sea coast was superb, and even although it was the middle of the New Zealand summer its summit was covered with snow. They next entered the broad gulf between the Taranaki Peninsula and the South Island. The ship came to an anchor in Queen Charlotte Sound. On the waters of this beautiful inlet they saw floating the dead body of a woman. Landing shortly afterwards, and getting into friendly relations with a small family of Maoris, they enquired about the dead body of the woman, and were told that it was one of their relations who had died a natural death, and, according to their custom, they had tied a stone to the body and had thrown it into the sea.

"This family when we came on shore, was employed in dressing some provisions: the body of a dog was at this time buried in their oven, and many provision baskets stood near it. Having cast our eyes carelessly into one of these as we passed it, we saw two bones pretty cleanly picked, which did not seem to be the bones of a dog, and which, upon a nearer examination, we discovered to be those of a human body. At this sight we were struck with horror, though it was only a confirmation of what we had heard many times since we arrived upon this coast. As we could have no doubt but the bones were human, neither could be have any doubt but that the flesh which covered them had been eaten. They were found in a provision basket; the flesh that remained appeared manifestly to have been dressed by fire, and in the gristles at the end were the marks of the teeth which had gnawed them. To put an end, however, to conjecture, founded upon circumstances and appearances, we directed Tupia to ask what bones they were; and the Indians, without the least hesitation, answered: 'the bones of a man'. They were then asked what was become of the flesh, and they replied that they had eaten it. 'But,' said Tupia, 'why did you not eat the body of the woman which we saw floating upon the water?' 'The woman', said they, 'died of disease; besides, she was our relation, and we eat only the bodies of our enemies who are killed in battle.'"

Upon enquiry who the man was whose bones had been found, they told the party from the *Endeavour* that about five days before a boat belonging to their enemies came into the bay with many persons on board, and that this man was one of seven whom they had killed. "Though stronger evidence of this horrible practice prevailing among the inhabitants of this coast will scarcely be required, we have still stronger to give. One of us asked if they had any human bones with the flesh remaining upon them, and upon their answering us that all had been eaten, we affected to disbelieve that the bones were human, and said that they were the bones of a dog; upon which one of the Indians[1] with some eagerness took hold of his own forearm, and, thrusting it towards us, said that the bone which Mr. Banks held in his hand had belonged to that part of a human body. At the same time, to convince us that the flesh

[1] The natives of all these Australasian and Pacific islands were styled "Indians" in Cook's day—following the silly fashion started by Columbus. This practice lasted even to the early part of the nineteenth century and in some of the explorations of the Niger and Fernando Po in West Africa the natives are referred to as Indians.

had been eaten, he took hold of his own arm with his teeth and made show of eating. He also bit and gnawed the bone which Mr. Banks had taken, drawing it through his mouth, and showing, by signs, that it had afforded a delicious repast."

Elsewhere along this coast human bones with the flesh on were often offered to Cook and his men for sale.[1]

On 30 January, 1770, on the shores of Queen Charlotte Sound, Lieutenant James Cook hoisted the British flag and took possession of the two great islands of New Zealand in the name of His Majesty, King George III—of the two islands, for they had already learnt from the natives the existence of Cook's Strait, which separated the North Island from the South, and which would lead them back into the eastern sea. The principal person to give this information was an old man named Topaa. He was asked if he had ever seen such a vessel before as the *Endeavour*, and whether white men had ever visited the land in the memory of the people. Topaa replied in the negative, but added that his ancestors had told him that there had once arrived (probably on the North Island) four men who had come in a small vessel from a distant country—Ulimaroa—but upon the four men landing they were all killed. This additional reference to Ulimaroa—which was either Fiji or the New Hebrides—is very interesting, as it would show that it has been possible for natives, probably of Melanesian

[1] On one of his visits to New Zealand of his second voyage, Cook, to be quite certain of the cannibalism of the New Zealanders, steeled himself to seeing them cook and eat the flesh of a young man who had been killed on the beach (apparently for that purpose). Many of the seamen with him who witnessed this disgusting spectacle were literally sick at the sight, but the person most affected was Oedidi, a youth from Tahiti, who had come with Cook as an interpreter, and who nearly went out of his mind with disgust, horror, and rage, extending his indignation to the white men who had allowed such a spectacle to take place in order to satisfy their curiosity.

type, to reach New Zealand in bygone times, and, this being the case, it would explain why succeeding French expeditions thought that in the Southern Island they detected a negroid type of New Zealander, altogether uglier and inferior in physique to the Polynesian Maori. It seems possible that the Polynesian Maoris were preceded by a dark-skinned race, who destroyed most of the Moas and other large flightless birds which had apparently become nearly or quite extinct before the Maori colonization took place.

Passing through the passage afterwards to be named Cook's Strait, the *Endeavour* turned to the north and once more sighted Cape Turnagain, besides meeting Maori canoes, the occupants of which recognized the *Endeavour* and entered into friendly relations. From Turnagain they sailed southwards in the early part of 1770, and after zigzagging about in search of other islands which might lie to the eastward of New Zealand, they at length reached South Cape, the southernmost extremity of the Dominion, the promontory of Stewart Island. They overlooked the passage between South Island and Stewart Island, which was afterwards discovered by Captain FOVEAUX. Rounding this, and following as well as they could the distant glimpses of the coast, they reached the west coast of the great South Island at Dusky Bay. Continuing their circumnavigation northwards they became gradually aware that behind the hills of the coast was a ridge of mountains "of a stupendous height, covered with snow in places". Cook had, in fact, discovered the Southern Alps, the remarkable snowy range of Southern New Zealand, of which the loftiest peak, rising to an altitude of 12,349 feet, has been named after him. At length, on 27 March, they were back again at Queen Charlotte Sound, having completely circumnavigated New Zealand.

Before passing on with Cook to the discovery of eastern Australia, it may be of interest to give here his first impressions of the Maoris or indigenes of New Zealand—though the name of Maori did not come into use till the early nineteenth century. The men were tall and sometimes handsome (except for their frightful face-tatuing), with the features of white men and a skin colour not much darker. They usually wore short beards. The women were generally much shorter in stature than the men, with darker skins and more negroid features. [Even at the present day some of the Maori women are very negroid in appearance. This was also the case with both men and women of some of the tribes in the great South Island; and it would really seem that New Zealand had at one time received a colonization from the direction of Melanesia.]

The food of the Maoris has already been described in its main elements—sweet potatoes, gourds, fern roots, and the flesh of human beings, dogs, and wood-birds. Cook also mentions that they ate penguins, albatrosses, and seals. They had no intoxicating drink, and water was their only beverage. The Maoris seemed to Cook singularly free of disease and to enjoy perfect and uninterrupted health. The expedition never saw a single person who appeared to have any bodily complaint or to suffer from any eruption of the skin. Their wounds healed with remarkable facility, and in all large assemblages of people were noticed the number of old men, who, by the loss of their hair and teeth, appeared to be very ancient, but who were not decrepit, and though not equal to the young in muscular strength, exhibited great liveliness of disposition.

The Maori dress was of several kinds. The roughest was made from the leaves of the Phormium[1]. These leaves were split into three or four slips, which, when dried, were plaited into a material midway between knitting and cloth, with the unwoven ends hanging out as a fringe. Two or three pieces of this would serve as a complete dress, one of them being tied over the shoulders with a string and reaching down to the knees. At the end of this upper garment was fastened a bodkin of bone, which served the purpose of raising a corner to the shoulder or any other part of the dress. The second piece of cloth was wrapped round the waist and reached nearly to the ground, but both sexes wore a belt or girdle, which they scarcely ever removed. The finer cloths were made from the fibre obtained by macerating the Phormium leaves, and were roughly woven in a frame about 5 feet long and 4 broad, somewhat after the fashion of matting. This beautiful, glistening, silky cloth was ornamented with borders of different colours done with stitching, something like the old English wool-work. Some of the chiefs wore dresses made entirely of dogs' skin, but, this fur being very valuable, it was more often cut into strips and sewn on to their clothes as an adornment. Cloaks of sealskin were worn in the south. In both islands the men and women trimmed their garments with birds' feathers, especially those of parrots,

[1] *Phormium tenax*, New Zealand "flax", which is so important a feature in the resources and development of New Zealand in earlier days, was an aloe-like plant with stiff, sword-shaped leaves like those of a flag in growth. From the centre of the mass of flag-like leaves rises a tall flower column, perhaps 10 feet high, bearing numerous orange-red tubular flowers like those of an aloe. Phormium, indeed, belongs to the Lily and Aloe order.

A VIEW OF DUSKY BAY, ON THE GREAT SOUTH ISLAND OF NEW ZEALAND, WITH A MAORI FAMILY:
AS SEEN BY CAPTAIN COOK

penguins, and albatrosses. Dogs' teeth were collected and strung into necklaces. The women wore bracelets and anklets made of the bones of birds or of shells, while the men preferred pieces of green jade or whalebone. Besides boring their ears and wearing ornaments in the lobes, or decorating them with the down of the albatross, which was as white as snow, they often bored the septum or gristle of the nose between the nostrils and thrust feathers through the hole. The chiefs would carry a staff of distinction, generally the rib of a whale as white as snow, much carved, and ornamented with dogs' hair and with feathers; or a stick about 6 feet long, adorned in the same manner and inlaid with mother-of-pearl. Chiefs and warriors also carried a great jade club, called *patu-patu*. It was fastened to the wrist by a strong strap, lest it should be wrenched from the owner in fight, but the chiefs sometimes wore this handsome weapon stuck into the girdle round their waists.

The Maoris were of course, like all the Polynesians, completely in the Stone Age when first visited by Cook, and ignored the use of any metal. Their adzes and axes were made of a hard basaltic stone; and a jasper-like stone was very useful in its small fragments for making a sharp, hard borer. These fragments were chipped off a block as flints might be. They were used in finishing their nicest work until they were blunt, and then they were thrown away. With these splinters of jasper they were able in no time to drill a hole through a piece of glass. Their canoes were long and narrow, and the largest sort would carry as many as 100 armed men. One such war canoe was 68 feet long, 5 feet broad, and 3½ feet deep, with a sharp keel. It consisted of three lengths hollowed out to a thickness of about

2 inches, and fastened together with strong plaiting. Each side consisted of one entire plank, 63 feet long and nearly 1 foot broad. Both the prow and the stern were decorated with wonderful pieces of carved wood. Some of the canoes, however, were only dug-outs, trunks hollowed by fire and axes. The Maoris were experts at sailing of the simpler kind, but their canoes could only go before the wind. The sail was made of netting or mats set up between two poles that were fixed upright upon each gunwale and served both as masts and yards.

CHAPTER VII

New South Wales

On 31 March, 1770, the *Endeavour* sailed from Cape Farewell on the north coast of the South Island of New Zealand, and on 19 April sighted the coast of what Cook still knew as "New Holland", which was, of course, the south-eastern extremity of Australia near Cape Howe. Cook then sailed along the coast to the northward, seeing smoke in several places, by which he knew the country to be inhabited. A camel-like mountain was called Mount Dromedary, a peaked hill, which resembled a square dovehouse with a dome at the top, was called Pigeonhouse, names which seem to have disappeared from the map of Australia. An attempt to land near the place now called Sutherland[1] was defeated by the heavy surf which lashed the white cliffs, while the natives on the beach, whose presence had attracted them, ran away. They were therefore obliged to guess at the landscape from a distance, and even then they observed that although there were numerous trees there was no underwood.

At last a bay—the celebrated Botany Bay, as it was subsequently named—opened before the *Endeavour*. The astonished natives appeared again on the beach, gazing

[1] Sutherland—really Cape Sutherland, at the entrance to Port Hacking—was named after Forby Sutherland, an English seaman, who died and was buried near here, the first white man, probably, and certainly the first Englishman, to lie in the soil of Australia. He was buried near the watering place.

at the ship as she slowly made her way into sheltered waters. They were absolutely naked, but their faces were dusted over with a white powder, and their bodies were painted in stripes of the same colour, which, passing obliquely over their breasts and backs, appeared like the belts worn crosswise in those days by British soldiers. Similar streaks were drawn round their legs and thighs like broad garters. They were armed with long wooden pikes, and "a wooden weapon shaped somewhat like a scimitar". This was the celebrated boomerang, the curved or crooked flat piece of wood which was one of Man's earliest weapons. Hurled by a practised hand it will whirl through the air, and unless it strikes the object aimed at with its sharp, flat edge, it returns almost to the spot from which it has been thrown. The boomerang has been in use at one time or another from West Africa to east Australia, and was once used in ancient Egypt. Reproduced in metal it is the origin of the throwing-knife of North Central Africa.

On Saturday, 28 April, 1770, the *Endeavour* anchored in Botany Bay, abreast of a small village consisting of six or eight houses. As the sailors were preparing to hoist out the boat they saw an old man, followed by three children, come out of the forest carrying firewood, and each of the children had also its little burden. Other children came out to meet them, and all alike gazed at the ship without either fear or surprise. The women set to work to kindle a fire, and four canoes came in from fishing. The men landed, and, having hauled up their boats, began to dress their dinner, to all appearance wholly unconcerned about this wonderful arrival, though the *Endeavour* was anchored within half a mile of them. As soon, however, as Cook and his party landed, two men of the native Australians came down to dispute their landing, whilst the others ran away. Each of these men was armed with a wooden lance about 10 feet long, and a short stick. They called out to the white men in a very loud tone in a hard, dissonant language, which neither the Englishmen nor Tupia, their Polynesian interpreter, understood in the least. They brandished their weapons and seemed resolved to defend their coast to the uttermost, though they were but two and the white men forty in number. Unwilling to provoke hostilities, Cook ordered the boat to lie upon her oars, and commenced to parley by signs, and to bespeak the goodwill of these stark-naked savages, throwing them at the same time nails, beads, and other trifles, which they took up and seemed to be well pleased with.

These overtures were of no use, however. As soon as the boat neared the shore the men again opposed the landing. A musket, consequently, was fired in the air, and upon hearing the report the younger of the two men dropped a bundle of lances, then in an instant snatched them up again and threw a stone, upon which a musket was fired with small shot, which struck the elder man in the legs. He immediately ran to one of the houses, which was distant about 100 yards, but only to return with a shield for his defence. As soon as he came up he threw a wooden lance, and his comrade another. Fortunately none of the white men was struck. A third musket with small shot was then fired at them, another lance was thrown, and at last the Australians ran away sufficiently far into the woods to make it prudent for the white men to venture into the village. Amongst these huts they found the children, who had hidden themselves behind a shield and some bark. They were left in their retreat, but beads, ribbons, and pieces of cloth and other presents were thrown into the huts to secure the goodwill of the inhabitants. Some of the lances lying about were taken away. They were from 6 to 15 feet long, and all of them had four prongs, each of which was armed with fish bone, and very sharp. They were in reality a kind of fish harpoon. The canoes are described as having been the worst that Cook had ever seen, between 12 and 14 feet long, and simply made (as already described in Chapter II) out of the bark of a tree removed in a single piece, tied at each end, and the middle kept open by sticks used as thwarts from gunwale to gunwale.

Crossing over to the north side of the bay, fresh water was found trickling down from the top of the rocks. None of the presents left in the huts were taken, nor were the natives inclined to enter into friendly relations. The face of the country round about Botany Bay was finely diversified by woods and grassy lawns. The trees were tall and straight, and standing at such a distance from each other that the whole country (wrote Cook) might be cultivated without cutting down one of them. Between the trees the ground was covered with grass, of which there was great abundance, growing in tufts about as big as could be well grasped in the hand. They had a transient view of an animal about as big as a rabbit, and came upon traces of what was really a kangaru, together with the footsteps of a beast like a wolf (a dingo or native dog), and the tracks of a polecat or weasel (the small white-spotted native "cats" or dasyures). The branches over their heads abounded with birds of exquisite beauty, particularly parrakeets and cockatoos, which flew in flocks of several scores together. Many of the trees had been barked, and one or two had been felled by some blunt instrument.

c 487

CAPTAIN COOK AT BOTANY BAY

Those that were standing, especially such as yielded gum, had had steps cut into their trunks, about 3 feet distant from each other, so that the natives could climb them. Some of the trees bore fruit that in colour and shape resembled a cherry; the juice had an agreeable tartness, but little flavour. About the head of the bay they traversed natural lawns which seemed to Cook the finest meadows in the world.

On the beach there was an abundance of mussels and oysters, some of which latter had been already roasted by the natives, and were eaten by Cook and his party. Banks shot a number of quails resembling those of England. One of the midshipmen accompanying a party sent to get into touch with the natives (who did nothing but run away whenever they were approached) strayed from his companions and suddenly found himself in the presence of a very old man and woman and some little children. They showed no signs of fear, and did not attempt to run away. The midshipman gave them a parrot which he had just killed, but they refused to accept it. All these people seemed a dark chocolate brown in colour. Both men and women were grey-headed. The hair of the men was long and ragged, while the women's hair was cropped short.

On the north shore of the bay there were no trees, and the ground resembled an English moor, its surface being covered with a thin scrub of plants about as high as the knees.

On Sunday, 6 May, 1770, the *Endeavour* sailed out of Botany Bay (as the place had been named, on account the abundance of wild flowers), and as she passed northwards Cook noticed a harbour which seemed to promise great things, and named it Port Jackson. This was the celebrated harbour of SYDNEY, one of the most remarkable inlets of the sea for beauty, extent, and the variety and number of deep and sheltered anchorages, to be found anywhere in the world. As the *Endeavour* sailed northwards the land gradually increased in height, so that it became actually mountainous, with a pleasing variety of hills and plains all clothed with woods. Cook sighted the large islands off the pleasant town of Brisbane (the capital of Queensland), and named one of them Cape Moreton. The coast of Queensland (as long afterwards it came to be called) was less hilly than that of New South Wales. Rounding the great promontory of Sandy Cape, the *Endeavour* anchored in what was then and there called Bustard Bay, from the killing and eating of a fine large bustard as big as a turkey.[1] "We all agreed that this was the best bird we had eaten since we left England." The landing parties found innumerable oysters—some of them pearl-producing, others hammer-shaped—on the mud banks under the mangroves. Upon these mangroves also were swarms of small green caterpillars, the bodies of which were thick-set with hairs. "They were ranged upon the leaves side by side, like a file of soldiers, to the number of twenty or thirty: when we touched them we found that the hair of their bodies had the quality of a nettle, and gave us an acute though less durable pain." Among the shoals and sandbanks were many water birds, especially the large black-and-white pelicans, but the country inland was not so attractive as the region round Botany Bay, being dry and sandy, though the sides of the hills were covered sparsely with trees, most of them eucalypti, yielding a yellow gum. The natives seen in

[1] Australia, like the drier parts of Africa or Asia, possesses several examples of the bustard family, though in the case of Australia there are at most two or three species of the one Asiatic genus, *Eupodotis*.

the distance from time to time were few in numbers, and seemed to lead an even more barbarous life than those of New South Wales, to be without houses as well as clothes, and to sleep in the open air. But they made use of fire, and even constructed rough drinking vessels out of bark, and made bark beds, and shelters against which they slept.

The *Endeavour* again came to an anchor in the vicinity of Keppel Bay (near Rockhampton). The water had become very shallow, and they had to stop to find a channel. Banks took advantage of this halt to fish from the cabin windows with hook and line, and in this way managed to catch some of the crabs which swarmed over the sea bottom. One of these was an exceedingly beautiful creature, adorned with the finest blue that can be imagined, with a white under side, and so exquisitely polished that its blue and white resembled old china. Another crab was marked with vivid ultramarine upon his joints and toes, and had on his back three large brown spóts of singular appearance. A landing was made in Shoalwater Bay, and they found the ground covered with a kind of grass, the seeds of which were very sharp and bearded backwards, so that when they stuck into the clothes they worked inwards by means of the beard till they got at the flesh.[1] There were also clouds of mosquitoes which tormented the landing party with their bites. As usual the trees seemed to be mainly gums of the eucalyptus type. On the branches of some of these were large ant nests made of clay, as big as a bushel. There were also an incredible number of butterflies: for the space of 3 or 4 acres the air would be so crowded with them that millions must have been visible in every direction, while the branches and twigs

[1] The terrible *Spinifex* grass so characteristic of Australia.

of the trees were covered with those that were not in flight. They also found a small fish (the *Periophthalmus* or mud-skipper) "about the size of a minnow", with two very strong breast-fins, in places that were quite dry, where it might have been left by the tide. It did not seem to feel the want of water, but leapt about by means of the breast-fins as nimbly as a frog. Even when found in the water it leapt out and pursued its way upon dry ground, and in shallow water it liked to progress by leaping from stone to stone above the surface.

On the islands off this coast of northern Queensland they noted that the natives were provided with outrigger canoes, showing that Melanesian or Polynesian influence had once reached this part.

All this was a dangerous coast where the sea in many parts concealed shoals which suddenly projected from the shore and rocks that rose abruptly, like a pyramid, from the bottom to within a few inches of the surface. For more than 1300 miles the navigation of the *Endeavour* had been a source of the utmost anxiety to Cook and to her sailing-master. Anxiety was to be followed by actual misfortune near Cape Tribulation, a point which lies to the north of a very mountainous part of the north Queensland coast region, where the peaks rise to altitudes of nearly 6000 feet. On this coast the water shallowed suddenly, the ship struck, and remained immovable, except for the heaving of the surge which beat her against the rocks on which she lay. In a few moments everyone was on deck with countenances fully expressing the horror of their situation. The rock was evidently of coral, which is the most fatal kind owing to its hardness and sharpness. Against these pinnacles the bottom of the ship was being rubbed away by the rising and falling of the swell. The sails were at once taken in, and it was found that the *Endeavour* had been lifted over a ledge of the rock by the surge and lay in a hollow inside it, in about 18 to 24 feet of water. For hours they strove by means of anchors and cables to warp her off the rock into deeper water and so get her out to sea; but she was immovable, and yet all this time continued to beat with great violence against the rock, so that it was with the utmost difficulty her crew could keep upon their legs. To add to their distress of mind they saw by the light of the moon the shifting boards from the bottom of the vessel floating around her, and at last her false keel, so that every moment the time was coming nearer in which the sea would rush into the ship and swallow her up. Land was actually about 24 miles distant. However, the wind gradually died away. Had it continued, the ship must inevitably have gone to pieces, and Cook and all his party would probably never have been heard of again; for the boats were insufficient to carry them all at once on shore, and even if they had reached the land it is doubtful whether they could have survived, for their northward march along the Cape York Peninsula would have been dogged by hostile natives, who would in the end have succeeded in killing and eating them. Even supposing they had reached Torres Straits and managed by means of native canoes to cross over to New Guinea, a similar fate awaited them there, for that part of New Guinea was then quite out of touch with the Dutch possessions.

However, the wind and swell having died down, everything that they could possibly throw overboard was thrown out of the ship (now heeling over dangerously to starboard). The pumps were incessantly at work keeping at bay the appalling inrush of the sea through the cracks and holes made by the injuries to the ship's sides and bottom.

At last with the rise of the tide the *Endeavour* righted herself so that she rode on an even keel and was apparently floating off. But even then they dreaded that when she was free of the rocks she might founder with the inrush of water through the leaks. "We well knew that our boats were not capable of carrying us all on shore, and that when the dreadful crisis should arrive, as all command and subordination would be at an end, a contest for preference would probably ensue that would increase the horrors even of shipwreck and terminate in the destruction of all of us at the hands of each other. . . . To those only who have waited in such a state of suspense, death has approached in all its terrors; and as the dreadful moment that was to determine our fate came on, everyone saw his own sensations pictured in the countenances of his companions."

However, the capstan and windlass were manned with as many hands as could be spared from the pumps, and the ship floating about twenty minutes after ten o'clock, a great effort was made, and she was warped and heaved into deep water. It was some comfort to find that she did not now admit more water than she had done upon the rock; and though, by the gaining of the leak upon the pumps, there was no less than 3 feet 9 inches of water in the hold, yet the men did not relinquish their labour, and held the water, as it were, at bay. "But having now endured excessive fatigue of body and agitation of mind for more than four-and-twenty hours, and having but little hope of succeeding at last, they began to flag: none of them could work at the pump more than five or six minutes together, and then, being totally exhausted, they threw themselves down upon the deck, though a stream of water was running over it from the pumps between 3 and 4 inches deep; when those who succeeded them had worked their spell, and were exhausted in their turn, they threw themselves down in the same manner, and the others started up again, and renewed their labour; thus relieving each other, till an accident was very near putting an end to their efforts at once. The planking which lines the inside of the ship's bottom is called the ceiling, and between this and the outside planking there is a space of about 18 inches: the man who till this time had attended the well to take the depth of water, had taken it only to the ceiling, and gave the measure accordingly; but he being now relieved, the person who came in his stead reckoned the depth to the outside planking, by which it appeared in a few minutes to have gained upon the pumps 18 inches, the difference between the planking without and within. Upon this, even the bravest was upon the point of giving up his labour with his hope, and in a few minutes everything would have been involved in all the confusion of despair. But this accident, however dreadful in its first consequences, was eventually the cause of our preservation: the mistake was soon detected, and the sudden joy which every man felt upon finding his situation better than his fears had suggested, operated like a charm, and seemed to possess him with a strong belief that scarcely any real danger remained."

The men now renewed their efforts with such alacrity and spirit, that before eight o'clock in the morning the leak no longer gained upon them, but the pumps gained considerably upon the leak. They cut most of their cables with the consequent loss of anchors, but got once more under sail and stood for the land.

It would, however, have been impossible to continue indefinitely the frightful labour of pumping out the sea water as fast as it poured in through the leaks, and the expedition would only have received a miserable respite but for the ingenious suggestion made by the same reckless midshipman, Monkhouse, who had been so ready to open fire on boisterous natives. He approached his commander, and proposed an expedient he had once seen used on board a merchant ship, which sprung a leak that admitted more than 4 feet of water an hour, and yet by this expedient had been brought safely from North America to London.[1] To midshipman Monkhouse, therefore, the care of the expedient, which is called "fothering" the ship, was immediately committed, four or five of the people being appointed to assist him, and he performed it in this manner: "He took the lower studding sail, and having mixed together a large quantity of oakham and wool, chopped pretty small, he stitched it down in handfuls upon the sail, as lightly as possible, and over this he spread the dung of our sheep and other filth. When the sail was thus prepared, it was hauled under the ship's bottom by ropes, which kept it extended, and when it came under the leak, the suction which carried in the water, carried in with it the oakham and wool from the surface of the sail, which in other parts the water was not sufficiently agitated to wash off. By the success of this expedient our leak was so far reduced that, instead of gaining upon three pumps, it was easily kept under by one. This was a new source of confidence and comfort; the people could scarcely have expressed more joy if they had been already in port." Cook goes on to observe in his journal that even when everything looked at its worst both officers and crew

[1] Admiral Sir W. J. L. Wharton, who edited Cook's original journal, points out that the idea seems equally to have emanated from Captain Cook, its carrying out being merely entrusted to Monkhouse because he was familiar with the process.

exhibited perfect possession of mind, and that everyone exerted himself to the uttermost, "with a quiet and patient perseverance, equally distant from the tumultuous violence of terror, and the gloomy inactivity of despair".

Sailing away with this device, which reduced the leaking of the ship to only about 15 inches of water an hour, easily kept at bay by the pumps, Cook passed close to two small islands, which at one time had seemed almost unattainable, and which out of gratitude he called Hope Islands. "In all the joy of our unexpected deliverance we had not forgotten that there was nothing but a lock of wool between us and destruction." At last they managed to reach the right kind of harbour at the place where the great town of Cooktown now stands. Here the ship was run up against a steep part of the shore, the stores, provisions, and the men were all transferred to the beach, where a camp was made and tents were put up for the sick; for, in addition to their other troubles, scurvy had broken out. Amongst other people thus affected was Tupia, the invaluable Polynesian interpreter, who, however, no sooner got on shore than he caught plenty of fresh fish and obtained herbs which cured his scurvy. Banks explored the country in all directions. There were many traces of the natives, but none of these people were visible. In his walks he met with vast flocks of pigeons and crows[1], and the pigeons (the plumage of which was exceedingly beautiful) proved most welcome as stores of fresh food.

On examining the main leak of the ship it was found that the coral rocks had pierced through four planks even into the timbers of her construction. There was not a

[1] These crows, so often referred to by Cook and the early Australian explorers, were not true crows of the sub-family Corvinæ (crows, ravens, or jackdaws), but belonged to genera like *Corcorax* and *Gymnorhina*, more nearly related to choughs and shrikes.

splinter to be seen, but all was as smooth as though it had been cut by sharp instruments. The vessel would have been inevitably swamped but that a portion of the leak was filled up by fragments of rock broken off the spikes of coral.

On shore, palms yielding "cabbages" were found, which proved to be a grateful supply of vegetable food, and they even met with clumps of wild bananas yielding small fruit with nice-tasting pulp, but full of hard black seeds. "As I was walking this morning at a little distance from the ship", wrote Cook in his journal, "I saw myself one of the animals which had been so often described. It was of a light mouse colour, and in size and shape very much resembled a greyhound. It had a long tail also. . . . I should have taken it for a wild dog if instead of running it had not leapt like a hare or bird." It was, in fact, a kangaru. They also saw two animals like dogs (dingoes), of a straw colour. There were very large fruit-eating bats, "as big as a partridge", with wide-stretching black wings.

At last, after they had been many days on shore, they succeeded in getting into touch with the natives, who were more amenable to reason than the savages farther south. Their skin was dark chocolate, the hair was black, in some cases lank and in others curly, but never woolly like the Papuans. Their bodies were painted with streaks of red and white, the features of their faces were agreeable, and their voices were soft and tuneful. One of them wore the bone of a bird 5 or 6 inches long thrust through the gristle between the nostrils. However, the kindness shown them led these people on to acts of great presumption. They began to pester the party on land with requests for food, and, when this was denied them, gave way to transports of rage, and finally, seizing brands from a fire, set light to the dry grass. Having in this way nearly succeeded in destroying the camp, it was necessary to shoot at them with muskets. With great difficulty peace was made, which was perhaps fortunate, for the seamen, straying out in all directions in search of food, encountered parties of native Australians who might otherwise have killed them had they not been reassured as to the intentions of the white men. In one such instance a seaman found himself alone in a little camp of four natives, who had kindled a fire and were broiling a bird over it together with part of a kangaru. The seaman, being unarmed, was very much alarmed, but had the presence of mind to assume a placid demeanour. He sat down with the people and offered them his knife, but after examining it they returned it to him politely. They examined his hands and face and clothes with the greatest attention, and then made signs that he could go away if he wished, a leave which he hastened to take. It was invariably found, however, that presents given to these people, whether cloth, beads, trinkets, or iron, were thrown away as useless lumber. The expedition also obtained a specimen of phalanger, a marsupial often misnamed the Australian opossum.[1] These phalangers or cuscuses had already been sent home to European collections from the Dutch East Indies, and had been described and named by Buffon, the great eighteenth-century French zoologist. Among the birds seen at *Endeavour* Harbour, where the ship was laid up for repairs, and where the chief fresh food of the crew was the green turtle, were Australian crows, kites, hawks, black cockatoos and white cockatoos, many beautiful parrots and parrakeets, a variety of pigeons, tree-ducks

[1] See pp. 38, 39.

(noted for their whistling cry), geese, and curlews. On the islands off the coast which they touched at as they sailed northwards there were large Monitor lizards; and the nests of great eagles could be seen, mostly built on the ground. In their passage northward they were again and again within a few yards of destruction amongst the shoals, the coral reefs, the sudden storms, and the holes of unfathomable water. The dangers of navigating the unknown parts of the vast Pacific Ocean were greatly increased by having a crazy ship and by being short of provisions, "yet the first adventures of a first discoverer made us cheerfully encounter every danger".

On Tuesday, 21 August, 1770, Cook rounded Cape York and realized that he was quitting the shores of Australia and had found a passage between that island continent and New Guinea—the straits through which the Spaniard, Torres, had sailed in 1607, the existence of which had been entirely overlooked or forgotten. Cook, believing that he had at last found a passage into the Indian Ocean, landed on a little islet, climbed its highest hill, and hoisted the British flag, taking possession of the whole eastern coast of Australia (by the name of "New South Wales") on behalf of His Majesty King George III, "with all the bays, harbours, rivers, and islands situated upon it".

No clue is given in Cook's journals to his reason for giving the very inappropriate name of New South Wales to the eastern side of the Australian continent.

Almost unconsciously they rounded the northernmost extremity of Australia, feeling their way between islands, sandbanks, and shoals. On 23 August, 1770, they saw an open sea to the westward and realized that they were passing Tasman's Gulf of Carpentaria, and that they had discovered (in reality, rediscovered) the important strait between New Guinea and Australia, proving that the last-named (which they knew as "New Holland"), though continental in size, was in reality a separate island, and not connected with New Guinea.

New South Wales and much of Queensland was found by Cook to be fairly well watered, with innumerable small brooks and springs, but no great rivers. Access to the coast was much obstructed by the dense mangrove thickets. Eucalyptus was the most prominent type of tree in the forests. Cook observed two sorts of this "gum tree", with its "narrow leaves not much unlike those of a willow", and its gum of a deep-red colour. The pine trees[1] he mentions were probably species of *Araucaria* and *Frenela* (miscalled *Callitris*). They found three different kinds of palm[2], that which grew in the southern part of New South Wales had fan-shaped fronds, and the heart of the palm (namely, the undeveloped fronds—the cabbage, as it was called by the mariners in those days, who depended on it so much for vegetable food) was exceedingly sweet to the taste. The nuts which it bore in great abundance were

[1] The *Conifers* or "pines" (they are not of the actual pine or fir family of the northern hemisphere) of Australia belong chiefly to the following types (I am informed by Doctor Otto Stapf of Kew Gardens): *Frenela*, resembling the South African *Callitris*; *Araucaria* (Monkey-puzzle trees); *Podocarpus* (related to the yews); *Phyllocladus* (often miscalled a "spruce" fir); *Dacrydium*, *Dammara* (a conifer producing much pitch or resin); *Arthotaxis* (in growth like a cypress); *Actinostrobus*; *Diselma*; *Microcachys*; and *Pherosphæra*.

[2] The palms of Australia, according to a list kindly drawn up by Dr. Stapf, belong to the following genera: *Calamus* (the climbing rattan or "cane" palms of northern Australia); *Kentia*, a genus of six species of fan-shaped fronds, one of which was Cook's "cabbage palm" with "nuts that were good for pigs"; *Clinostigma*; *Ptychosperma* (a genus extending to Tahiti and Fiji); *Areca* (probably Cook's "second cabbage palm"); *Arenga*; *Caryota*; and *Licuala*. This last genus of low-growing palms was probably the third kind described by Cook, with fronds like a fern and nuts like chestnuts.

good food for pigs. The second palm, also producing an edible cabbage, had larged pinnated fronds like those of the coconut; and the third kind, which, like the second, was found only in northern Queensland, was seldom more than 10 feet high, with fronds resembling those of a large fern. It bore no cabbage, but a plentiful crop of nuts the size of a large chestnut only rounder, nuts that were probably roasted and eaten by the aborigines. Nevertheless, when eaten by Europeans, they proved almost poisonous, causing them to vomit and to be purged with great violence.

The conclusions at which Cook arrived in regard to the aborigines of Australia were singularly accurate, considering that he had only landed about five times on the coast of New South Wales and Queensland, and had in addition only the scanty records of Dampier and the Dutch seamen regarding the western coast of Australia. He argues from the utter savagery of these coast natives, and from the Dutch accounts of the desolate, parched nature of the south and west coasts of Australia, that the interior is probably mainly desert and uninhabitable. Their houses, which were seen at their best at Botany Bay, were just high enough for a man to sit upright in, and not large enough for him to lie down at full length. They were built with pliable rods as thick as a man's finger, in the form of an oven, the two ends being stuck into the ground. These withes were then covered with palm leaves and broad pieces of bark, and the door was nothing but a large hole at one end. In other words, they were precisely like the houses built by the pygmies in some parts of the Congo Forest. Inside tnese huts they slept three or four in number, coiled up. Their only implements seemed to be made of bark or netted fibre. Pieces of bark were tied at the two ends with some lithe twig which served as a handle, and these bark basins or buckets would then hold water. In addition the natives roughly knitted together long fibres into bags, which they slung by a string over the head. But their fish hooks were very neatly made of shell, and some exceedingly small. For striking turtle they had a barbed wooden harpoon, the detachable end of which was fastened into a staff of light wood, to which was tied a line of fibrous string, while the other end of the bush rope was fastened to the harpoon. After striking the turtle the barbed end of this weapon would become detached in the animal's body, while the staff, being of light wood, rose to the surface and served as a float by which the victim could be traced, and also as a drag on his speed. They were able to make string from some fibre which ranged from the thickness of a half-inch rope to the fineness of a hair, and argued some skill on their part. Their cooking was done by broiling on coals or baking in a hole with the help of hot stones. They had no nets for catching fish, though they used a hook and line and also the harpoon. The boomerang was almost their only weapon for bringing down birds. They produced fire by whirling a drilling-stick into a piece of soft wood, getting a spark in less than two minutes. "We have often seen one of them running along the shore, to all appearance with nothing in his hand, who, stooping down for a moment at the distance of every 50 or 100 yards, left fire behind him, as we could see first by the smoke and then by the flame amongst the driftwood and other litter. We had the curiosity to examine one of these planters of fire when he set off, and we saw him wrap up a small spark in dry grass, which when he had run a little way, having been fanned by the air that his motion produced, began to blaze. He then laid it down in a place convenient for his purpose, enclosing a spark of it in another quantity of grass, and so continued his course."

By setting fire to the bush the natives managed to surround and kill a number of animals — kangarus, emus, lizards, &c.

The lances of the Australians were of wood, sometimes with a shaft made of cane or the stem of a bulrush. The actual weapon itself was of hard wood, the point of which would be smeared with a resin which gave it a polish and made it enter deeper into what it struck. In the southern regions these lances usually had four prongs, each pointed with bone or sharp shells, and barbed. All such insertions of substances into the wood were held in their places by resin (Eucalyptus or *Dammara* gum). They could become terrible weapons, for they were thrown with great force, and, owing to the smooth resin, entered far into the flesh of the person aimed at, and could never be drawn out without tearing the flesh or leaving sharp ragged splinters of bone or shell behind. When fighting at close quarters the lances were aimed with the hand, but at a greater distance were thrown by an instrument which Cook calls a throwing-stick. This was a plain, smooth piece of hard wood, highly polished, about 2 inches broad, ½ inch thick, and 3 feet long, with a small knob or hook at one end and a crosspiece about 3 or 4 inches long at the other. The knob at one end caught into a small dent or hollow, which was made for that purpose in the shaft of the lance near its point, but was not made sufficiently deep or rough to detain the lance when violently projected.

When it was intended to hurl a lance by this means it was laid along the machine, being held in position by the knob entering the small hollow in the shaft, and the person throwing it held both lance and throwing-stick over his shoulder. He then, after a preliminary shake, hurled both the throwing-stick and the lance with all his force, but the stick being stopped by the cross-piece, which came against the shoulder with a sudden jerk, the lance went forward with incredible swiftness and with so good an aim that at a distance of 50 yards these black Australians were more certain of their mark than the white men often were with their guns. The only tools the people possessed seemed to be adzes with stone blades, wooden mallets, sharp shells, and fragments of coral; but for polishing their throwing-sticks and the points of their lances they rubbed down the wood with a leaf of a kind of wild fig tree, the underside of which had a very rough surface, which bit upon the wood almost as keenly (remarks Cook) as the shaving grass of Europe which was formerly used by English joiners.

As the *Endeavour* sailed along the south coast of New Guinea the breezes from the shore would be strongly impregnated with the trees, shrubs, and herbage, which was pleasantly aromatic. At some point on the south coast of New Guinea about 130 miles to the east of Valsche Cape (False Cape) the *Endeavour* anchored for a short time whilst Cook, Banks, and a small party of men went on shore, in all twelve persons well armed. The coast was very low, and covered with a luxuriance of wood and herbage that can scarcely be conceived. They were obliged to wade 200 yards till they reached the strand, where they saw the prints of human feet. Walking along the outskirts of the forest they came to a grove of coconut trees on the banks of a little brackish stream. They looked at the fruit very wistfully, but, not thinking it safe to climb, were obliged to leave without tasting a single nut. Suddenly three Papuans rushed out of the forest with a hideous shout, and as they ran towards them the foremost threw something out of his hand which burnt exactly like gunpowder but made no report. The other two instantly threw their lances, and as there was now no time to be lost the Eurupeans fired their guns, which were loaded with small shot. Several still came on. Bullets were used, and then they ran away, whilst the white men retreated to the water and a boat. As they waded away from the shore a number of Papuans came out to attack them, which they did by discharging some flaming substance through a short piece of stick, probably a hollow cane. "This wonderful phenomenon was observed from the ship, and the deception was so great that the people on board thought they had firearms." Having made this attack they retired, and the people of Cook's party picked up the fire-producing weapons. They were found to be light darts about 4 feet long, of reed or bamboo, pointed with hard wood in which were many barbs. They were apparently hurled with a throwing-stick like the lances of the Australians.

Passing by the south end of Timor they saw unexpectedly an island, which they thought at first was a new discovery. It was Savu, midway between Timor and Sumba, or Sandalwood Island. To their great surprise they saw not only people dressed more or less after the fashion of Europeans, but numerous flocks of sheep. The second lieutenant landed and was received with great civility. Moving round to a better anchorage they saw the Dutch colours. The raja or chief of the island, who had with him a Portuguese interpreter, explained that he would be delighted to afford them stores and other assistance, if they could first obtain the permission of the Dutch East India Company, without which he was not able to trade with any other people. This Company was represented in Savu at that time by a German named Lange. He came on board and behaved with great civility, bringing with him the raja of the island. But in spite of fine words it was with the utmost difficulty, and after many delays, that Cook's party obtained any supply of fresh provisions, the Dutch Company's agent pretending that he had received instructions from his superior officers on the Island of Timor to render no assistance. In fact, Cook would have fared very badly had it not been for the inherent good nature of the Malay people of the island. He pleaded with the raja for liberty to purchase one pig and some rice, as they were so urgently in need of fresh provisions. The king replied graciously that he would give them a dinner himself.

"About five o'clock dinner was ready; it was served in six-and-thirty dishes, or rather baskets, containing alternately rice and pork, and three bowls of earthenware, filled with the liquor in which the pork had been boiled; these were ranged upon the floor, and mats laid round them for us to sit upon. We were then conducted by turns to a hole in the floor, near which stood a man with water in a vessel made of the leaves of the fan-palm, who assisted us in washing our hands. When this was done, we placed ourselves round the victuals, and waited for the king. As he did not come, we enquired for him, and were told that the custom of the country did not permit the person who gave the entertainment to sit down with his guests; but that, if we suspected the victuals to be poisoned, he would come and taste it. We immediately declared that we had no such suspicion, and desired that none of the rituals of hospitality might be violated on our account. The Prime Minister and Mr. Lange were of our party, and we made a most luxurious meal; we thought the pork and rice excellent, and the broth not to be despised; but the spoons, which were made of leaves, were so small that few of us had patience to use them. After dinner, our wine passed briskly about, and we again enquired for our royal host, thinking that though the custom of his country would not allow him to eat with us, he might at least share in the jollity of our bottle; but he again excused himself, saying, that the master of a feast should never be drunk, which there was no certain way to avoid but by not tasting the liquor. We did not however drink our wine where we had eaten our victuals; but as soon as we had dined made room for the seamen and servants, who immediately took our places: they could not despatch all that we had left, but the women who came to clear away the bowls and baskets, obliged them to carry away with them what they had not eaten."

At length the old man who was the king's Prime Minister, and who was won over by the present of a spyglass and a broadsword, intervened with a show of force, and the Dutch-German factor and his Portuguese colleague had to give way. Cook purchased 9 buffaloes, 6 sheep, 3 pigs, 360 fowls, a few limes, some coconuts, dozens of eggs, a little garlic, and several gallons of palm syrup—a most welcome addition to the food supply of the ship, which by this time had been reduced in the matter of fresh provisions to a single sheep, and probably the saving of life for many invalids on board. The sheep which he bought on the island were like those of Southern India, with hair instead of wool, very long, pendent ears, and arched noses.

This small island of Savu was densely inhabited, and could raise from out of the five principalities into which it was divided an army of at least 7700 men armed with muskets, spears, lances, and pole-axes. The people were somewhat elaborately dressed, and had a great variety of food owing to the abundance of domestic animals and of vegetables. They were made hideous by the abuse of the betelnut, the chewing of which with lime darkened their teeth and wore them down to the gums. But they were very proud of their pedigrees, which they traced back for generations. Each raja set up in the principal town of his province a large stone which served as a memorial of his reign. Many of these stones were so large that it is difficult to conceive by what means they were raised to their present position on summits of hills. Muhammadanism had not yet reached them, nor had Christianity. Their religion was described as "absurd", inasmuch as each man chose his own god and determined for himself how he should be worshipped. Nevertheless, their morals were irreproachable. They were honest, and although warlike in disposition kept the peace amongst one another. Their style of living was remarkable for delicacy and cleanliness. They appeared to be healthy and long-lived.

From Savu the *Endeavour* reached without difficulty Batavia, the capital of Java and of the Dutch Indies. But her arrival at Batavia, together with the facilities which were given to Cook by the Dutch Government for repairing his ship—to say nothing of the pleasure of finding oneself amongst Europeans and even Englishmen for the first time after having sailed half round the globe—were of small consolation in the presence of a terrible sickness which seized on all of them owing to the unhealthy nature of the place. Tupia and his boy Taito, who had come with them all the way from Tahiti, and who had been through such wonderful adventures in New Zealand and elsewhere, and who showed themselves so intensely delighted with the varied aspect of civilization at Batavia, both succumbed to illness, and died. Banks and Solander were so bad that they also nearly died; Monkhouse, the surgeon, and several seamen perished. Cook himself was very ill. Every individual, in fact, of the *Endeavour's* crew was ill except the sailmaker, an old man between seventy and eighty years of age. Five Englishmen out of the crew were buried at Batavia, besides the two Tahitians.

From Java they sailed to the Cape of Good Hope, where they stayed for rest and refreshment, and after calling at St. Helena the *Endeavour* anchored in the Downs off Deal, and at that place Cook landed on 12 June, 1771, after his circumnavigation of the world, which opened a new epoch in colonial history.

Cook was commended highly by the Admiralty for his services, and he was made a Fellow by the Royal Society, very small rewards for such a wonderful achievement. [To excuse their niggardliness in this respect the Government of the day said, *after Cook was dead*, that had he lived to return from his third voyage he might have been made a baronet!] But perhaps the most striking evidence of the insolent indifference to Cook's interests was displayed by the Board of Admiralty in regard to Cook's Journals and Banks's elaborate records of the ethnology, botany, and zoology observed in the course of the wonderful voyage. All this material was placed in the hands of a Dr. Hawkesworth by Lord Sandwich, the dissolute and vicious Minister[1] at the head of the Admiralty, simply because Hawkesworth had been introduced to him by the actor Garrick as a writer of plays for the stage. Wishing to help Hawkesworth with funds, without putting his hand in his pocket, Lord Sandwich handed over to him Cook's Journals, and induced Banks to do the like with his own work. Hawkesworth then sold the joint work of Cook and Banks to publishers and booksellers for £6000, which he invested on his own behalf, and which—for he died soon afterwards—passed to his widow without benefiting Cook (Banks being rich did not need it) in the least. Banks, it must be remembered, had spent something like £8000 on the expedition.

[1] As is well shown in Admiral Wharton's editions of Cook's *Journals.*

CHAPTER VIII

Cook's Second and Third Voyages

NOT long after Cook's return to England in July, 1771, he was appointed to command a ship of 462 tons, built at Whitby by the same person who had constructed the *Endeavour*[1]. She was named the *Resolution*, and with her was associated a smaller vessel of 336 tons, called the *Adventure*. Almost immediately after Cook's return it had been decided by the Admiralty to equip a still better furnished expedition to complete the discovery of the Southern Hemisphere. A lieutenant who had sailed with Captain Wallis in 1766, TOBIAS FURNEAUX (no doubt a descendant of French Huguenots), had been promoted to command the *Adventure*. At first it was thought that the expedition should be accompanied by Mr. (afterwards Sir Joseph) Banks and a number of assistants, who should make a careful examination of the botany and zoology of the countries to be visited by the ship under Cook's command. And Banks spent several thousand pounds in getting his share of the expedition ready, the British Government being then, as now, very loath to spend much money on these branches of scientific research, in the value of which it is only beginning to believe. But at the last moment difficulties were put in Banks's way. He was offered so little accommodation on the *Resolution*

[1] The *Endeavour*, it might be mentioned, was sent out soon afterwards as a store-ship to the Falkland Islands, where she ended her days.

that he decided not to accompany Captain Cook, and went later on to Iceland instead.

Still more determined to combat scurvy, Cook included amongst his stores such things as malt and a concentrated extract of wort and beer, which, diluted with water, might in fact make for the men throughout the voyage a drink of a wholesome and a palatable nature. They also took sour crout (cabbage cut up and pickled with salt, juniper berries, and aniseed) and salted cabbage, orange and lemon peel, mustard, and "marmalade of carrots". This was the juice of yellow carrots evaporated until it was as thick as honey or treacle, and it had been strongly recommended by a learned person of Berlin as being a great remedy for scurvy, but when put to the test was not found to be of much use.

A landscape painter, William Hodges, was appointed to this expedition in order to make drawings and paintings of the scenery and people of the countries which might be visited, and in place of Joseph Banks and his party a naturalist of German extraction—John Rheinhold Forster—and his son,[1] were both engaged to make botanical and zoological researches. (At the Cape of Good Hope, Cook also allowed Forster to engage in this department a Swedish naturalist, Sparrman.) The expedition, which was to search, amongst other things, for the South Pole, left England at the end of June, 1772, called at the Cape of Good Hope, and then directed its course to the south-east, getting amongst icebergs, over which the terrific waves of the Southern Ocean broke even when they were 60 feet high, soon after it had passed the fortieth degree of south latitude. Cook had been preceded in these waters nearly

[1] They were poor creatures compared to Banks and Solander, and the elder Forster made himself so ridiculous that he became the butt of the seamen.

forty years before by the French navigator Bouvet, who had reported the existence of land in the far south. But Cook, on this voyage, though he penetrated as far south as 64°, did not even encounter one or other of the island groups which dot the surface of the ocean at rare intervals between South Africa and Antarctica. Yet he must have been near these islands, some of which he discovered on his next voyage, on account of the abundance of sea birds which they saw, including penguins, which never travel out into the ocean far from land.

The expedition sighted the coast of the South Island of New Zealand on 20 March, 1773, and anchored in Dusky Bay on the following day, having been 117 days at sea, and sailed 10,980 miles without once seeing land. Yet only one man had been seriously ill with scurvy on this long voyage, and the excellent health of the ship's crew is justly attributed to the antiscorbutics they had carried with them, especially to the weak beer and to the portable broth. Immediately after they came to an anchor in Dusky Bay one of the ship's officers killed a seal (of which there were many lying about on the rocks), the meat of which was most welcome to the messes. Cook had brought with him numbers of domestic animals and birds from England to introduce into these new lands, but a good many of them had been killed by the stormy and cold weather through which the expedition had passed, and had even suffered from a form of scurvy, so that when the sheep, for example, were landed in New Zealand their teeth were so loose and their gums so tender that they could not masticate the grass of the country, and could only feed feebly on leaves. The geese were landed on the South Island of New Zealand in the hope that they might increase and multiply and so furnish this part of the world with a valuable domestic bird. But apparently they died out without leaving any issue, and about the only creature that Cook's expedition succeeded in introducing permanently into New Zealand was the pig. But this part of New Zealand was found to abound in native ducks of five different kinds.

"The largest are as big as a Muscovy duck, with a very beautiful variegated plumage, on which account we called it the painted duck: both male and female have a large white spot on each wing; the head and neck of the latter is white, but all the other feathers, as well as those on the head and neck of the drake, are of a dark variegated colour.[1] The second sort have a brown plumage, with bright-green feathers in their wings, and are about the size of an English tame duck. The third sort is the blue-grey duck or 'whistling duck', as some called them from the whistling noise they made. What is most remarkable in these is that the end of their beaks is soft, and of a skinny, or more properly, cartilaginous substance. The fourth sort is something bigger than teal, and all black except the drake, which has some white feathers in his wing."[1]

Cook also noticed the characteristic wingless rails of New Zealand, which he called wood hens. "As they cannot fly they inhabit the skirts of the woods, and feed

[1] There are at least nine species of duck-like birds in New Zealand. The four specially cited by Cook are probably classified as follows, in the order mentioned by him: *Fuligula novæzelandiæ*, the New Zealand scaup; *Anas superciliosa*, the New Zealand mallard; *Hymenolæma malacorhynchus*, the celebrated "Blue duck" of New Zealand (though it is not strictly speaking a duck but more related to the slender-billed merganser and smew); *Nyroca australis*, the Australian pochard. The remaining five species are the New Zealand ruddy sheldrake (*Casarca*), a tree duck (*Dendrocygna*), a shoveller (*Spatula*), and two teal (*Elasmonetta* and *Nettion*). But New Zealand once possessed black swans like those of Australia, and a huge flightless goose (*Cnemiornis*) like the existing Cereornis goose of Australia, and a musk duck (*Biziura*). But all these became extinct long before the white man came on the scene.

on the seabeach; and are so very tame or foolish as to stand and stare at us till we knocked them down with a stick."[1] The natives were even then fast destroying them. Amongst the small birds Cook particularizes the wattle-bird, poë-bird, and fan-tail, on account of their singularities of form and plumage.[2]

In Pickersgill Harbour, close by, the seamen thought that they descried a small mammal about the size of a cat, mouse-coloured, and with short legs and a bushy tail, "more like a jackal than any animal they knew". This may have been a runaway dog, of degenerate type, belonging to the natives; or just possibly some mammal indigenous to New Zealand which soon afterwards became extinct. Yet with the exception of bats (and the dogs and rats introduced by the natives, and the seals which frequented the seacoasts), no indigenous beast has ever been discovered in New Zealand, either existing there in the past or at the time of its discovery.

During the stay of the expedition at Dusky Bay and

[1] The Weka-rails, *Ocydromus*. There was also a monster Porphyrio, the *Notornis mantelli*, unable to fly, and consequently soon killed out by the colonists.

[2] The Wattle-bird or Huia was so-called because it had two wattles under its beak as large as those of a bantam cock. It was larger and longer in body than an English blackbird. Its bill was short and thick, and its feathers of a dark lead colour; the colour of its wattles being a dull yellow, almost orange. This description of Cook's refers to the chough-like *Heterolocha*, in which the male has a short, sharp, straight beak, and the female one which is long and curved like a sickle. The Poë-bird or Tui was about the size of a starling, and belonged to the family of honey eaters. The feathers were (wrote Cook) "of a fine mazarin blue", except those of its neck, which are of a most beautiful silver grey, and two or three short white ones, which are on the pinion joint of the wing. Under its throat hang two little tufts of curled, snow-white feathers, called its "poes", which, being the Tahitian word for ear-rings, was the origin of the name given by Cook's people to the bird, which is not more remarkable for the beauty of its plumage than for the sweetness of its note. "The flesh is also most delicious, and was the greatest luxury the woods afforded us." Of the "fan-tail" warblers mentioned by Cook there were different sorts, but the body of the most remarkable one was scarcely larger than that of a wren, yet it spread a tail of beautiful plumes, "fully three-quarters of a semicircle, of at least of 4 or 5 in. radius". These fan-tails were probably flycatchers of the *Muscicapidæ* family.

elsewhere in the South Island the small black sandflies were a serious pest. Wherever they bit they caused a swelling and such intolerable itching that many of the people who had landed were at last covered with ulcers like smallpox. Nevertheless the whole crew soon became strong and vigorous. A local conifer, styled a "spruce" by Cook, but in reality a *Phyllocladus*, furnished an astringent beer in a decoction of its leaves, the bitterness of which was tempered by using an equal quantity of the tea plant.[1]

On the way north from Dusky Bay towards Queen Charlotte Sound, six or seven waterspouts were seen. According to Cook, they were caused by whirlwinds which created a kind of funnel or tube of water, which ascended in a spiral stream up to the clouds. In one of them a bird had been enclosed, which the seamen saw being whirled round and round as it was carried upwards. It appeared to Cook that, although these spouts reached the clouds, it was not from the rainwater of the clouds being drawn down to them, but by the column of whirling water ascending from the sea to the clouds above.

When in the southern Indian Ocean Cook had arranged with Captain Furneaux that if they should be separated by weather (as they were) they should rendezvous at Queen Charlotte Sound. The *Adventure* was separated from the *Resolution*, and after searching for her in vain set out on a lonely voyage of 4200 miles through an utterly unknown sea and reduced to an allowance of 1 quart of fresh water a day. They steered for

[1] Cook describes this as a small tree or shrub with five white petals shaped like those of a rose. The leaves were like a myrtle, and made an agreeably bitter beverage. If this was strongly brewed it acted like an emetic.

Tasmania, reached the south coast of that island, and landed there on 10 March, 1773, finding the soil very rich and the country well clothed with woods, and plenty of water falling from the rocks in brilliant cascades 200 or 300 feet perpendicularly into the sea. They were the second white men to land in Tasmania. The *Adventure* anchored for five days in the bay since called after her. The trees of the forest they found mostly burnt or scorched near the ground, owing to the natives setting fire to the underwood, so as to make passage easy through the forest. There seemed to be little variety of trees, which were mostly of the eucalyptus kind; but there was an abundance of birds, Australian "crows" with their sharp white beaks, several kinds of duck, parakeets, and a large white bird about the size of a small eagle and very like one.[1] As for beasts, they only saw one, which was a kind of opossum (phalanger), but from the traces they saw of others (kangarus) they believed the land to contain deer. There were many signs of the natives—rough wigwams or huts,[2] in which there were bags and nets made of grass, stones and tinder for striking fire, spears sharpened at the end with a shell or stone—but the people themselves kept out of the way of the Europeans and were not once seen.

The *Adventure* after this repose skirted the coast and islands of Tasmania, as far as the opening of Bass's Strait and the string of islands named after Captain Furneaux. The last-named did not ascertain definitely that Tasmania

1 Probably *Haliætus leucogaster*, a white and grey fish-eating eagle.

2 "The boughs of which their huts are made are either broken or split and tied together with grass in a circular form, the largest end stuck in the ground and the smaller parts meeting in a point at the top, after which they are covered with fern and bark, but so poorly done that they would hardly keep out a shower of rain. In the middle is the fireplace surrounded with heaps of mussel, scallop, and cray-fish shells, which I believe to be their chief food."—*Captain Furneaux.*

was an island and not any longer a peninsula of Australia. From a point very near the Australian coast the *Adventure* sailed straight across to New Zealand and duly rejoined the *Resolution* in Queen Charlotte Sound. The crews of both ships felt "uncommon joy at their meeting" after a separation of fourteen weeks.

From New Zealand the two ships made their way to Tahiti. On arriving there the Tahitians enquired about Tupia, the invaluable interpreter on the first voyage; but his friends and relations were quite satisfied when an account of his death at Batavia was given to them. Civil wars had brought about certain changes in the government of the island, and one of the most prominent chiefs known to the *Endeavour* expedition was dead. This was Tutaha, and his mother came to meet Cook, bursting into tears as she seized him by both hands, and said: "Tutaha Tutayo no Tuti, matti!" (Tutaha, the friend of Cook, is dead).

Goats were landed on this island to introduce a breed of valuable domestic animals. The expedition then passed on to the adjoining island of Huahine, and here they obtained another invaluable interpreter for their further voyages—Omai, a native of the island of Ulieta, and of rather negroid or Melanesian type, but a most useful member of Cook's second and third expeditions.

In the interval between Cook's first and second visits to Tahiti a Spanish ship had called at that island and had introduced several noxious European diseases. The degeneration and depopulation of the Society Islands was about to begin, and even their food supplies were beginning to get short, owing to the demands made on them for pigs and fowls by European ships, and by the civil wars which caused much loss of live stock.

From the Society Islands the *Resolution* and *Adventure* sailed westward, discovered Hervey's Island, and rediscovered the Tonga archipelago already visited by Tasman. Here they met with such a kindly reception, the natives coming out to meet them in canoes,[1] and running along the shore displaying small white flags, that the group was afterwards christened the "Friendly Isles". [The Tonga archipelago under a native king is now a British protectorate.] The people supplied them with abundance of fowls, pigs, bananas, and coconuts.

Cook gives the following description of a house of worship on Tongatabu Island built on an artificial mound about 18 feet above the level of the ground:—

It was of an oblong shape and enclosed by a wall or parapet of stone about 3 feet in height. From this wall the mound rose with a gentle slope and was covered with green turf, and on the top of it stood the house. . . . Three elderly men came and seated themselves between the Europeans and the temple and began a kind of prayer, which lasted about ten minutes, then led the way so that the house of worship might be examined. In front there were two stone steps leading to the top of the wall. From this the ascent to the house was easy. It was surrounded by a fine gravel walk and was built in all respects like a dwelling-house of the country, with poles and rafters, and covered with palm thatch, with eaves coming down to within 3 feet of the ground, and sides or walls made of strong matting. The floor of the house was laid with fine

[1] Cook describes the sails used by the Polynesians of the Tonga archipelago as being lateen, extended to a lateen yard above and a boom at the foot. When they change tacks they throw the vessel up in the wind, ease off the sheet, and bring the tack end of the yard to the other end of the boat. There are notches or sockets at both ends of the vessel into which each end of the yard is put. He describes the sails as being exactly similar to those in use at the Ladrone Islands.

gravel, except in the middle, where there was an oblong square of blue pebbles raised about 6 inches higher than the floor. In two corners of the house stood images rudely carved in wood, which did not seem to be treated by the natives with much respect. The space of blue pebbles was a sort of altar, and on this the Europeans laid their offerings of things that the natives would be likely to prize.

Cook describes Tongatabu Island as a little paradise. There was not an inch of wasted land. The beautifully made roads occupied no more space than was absolutely necessary, the fences were only about 4 inches wide and mostly consisted of useful trees or planfs, and the ground round the houses and temples was planted with large and shady fruit trees, which besides the customary bread-fruits, coconuts, and the Tahiti *ahiya*, included shaddocks (a large kind of orange). The people also grew sugar cane and made pottery. They were of the same good-looking Polynesian type as those of Tahiti. The men applied dyes to their abundant crops of head hair, which either bleached it white or stained it red, or even blue. They had here the custom so widespread in North America, and amongst the Bushmen of South Africa and the people of Australia, of mutilating the fingers, especially the little finger, by cutting off the two first joints to mark their mourning for children, husbands, or wives.

Cook also noticed the lepers of the Tonga archipelago, some of whom had the whole face and nose reduced to dreadful smooth scabs, surrounding nearly embedded eyes, and emitting an intolerable stench.

From Tongatabu the two ships sailed to New Zealand, and on the journey the *Adventure* was lost sight of. Cook, unable to wait (after searching for this ship along the coasts of New Zealand), left messages behind in bottles, buried in the camps to which they had most resorted, and then, on 26 November, 1773, sailed once more into the Southern Pacific to search for Antarctica. He reached ultimately to latitudes as high as 72°, where he found vast mountains of ice or land covered with ice. He had, in fact, probably reached the coast of Wilkes's Land. Some of the innumerable ice islands they passed on this southern voyage could not have been less than 200 feet in height, and terminated in peaks like cupolas or domes.

Being now well satisfied that no land was to be found in this direction, except unapproachable through icefields and quite uninhabitable, Cook turned his vessel to the north to reach the Tropics once again, and on 13 March, 1774, anchored off Easter Island,[1] where the ship was at once met by a canoe paddled by two men, who brought out a bunch of plantains. This gave the crew of the *Resolution* a good opinion of the Easter Islanders, who, as we know, were not unfamiliar with Europeans, having been visited already by Spaniards and Dutchmen. In fact, when they landed they found one man with a good broad-brimmed European hat on, whilst another wore a Spanish jacket, and a third a red silk handkerchief. The people, though very friendly, were rather thievish, not only towards the European, but each other. For instance, finding that Cook's party was very willing to buy sweet potatoes, they unhesitatingly raided a man's plantation near the landing place, and sold them for what they could get.

[1] For the convenience of the reader I might repeat the statement that Easter Island, in 27° S. latitude, is, as regards human inhabitants, the farthest prolongation eastwards of Polynesia, and is situated 2374 miles from the west coast of South America, and 1326 miles from Pitcairn Island, the nearest land.

Cook, being ill himself at the time, sent a party of officers to explore Easter Island thoroughly. They had not proceeded far on their journey before a middle-aged man, tatued from head to foot, and his face painted with a white pigment, appeared with a spear in his hand, on which he hoisted a piece of white cloth as an emblem of peace. He then drove away a crowd of natives that followed, and constituted himself a guide. The surface of the island appeared to be a barren, dried, hard clay covered with stones, except where the natives had cleared the ground and made plantations of sweet potatoes or had planted banana groves. On the highest part of the south end of the island the soil was a fine red earth and more fruitful, bearing a longer grass, and was not strewn with stones. But the most remarkable feature in this somewhat desolate island, which has an area of about 45 square miles, were the statues of stone and ruins of masonry. These were mainly on the east side of the island and near the sea. Here the officers of the *Resolution* met with three platforms of stonework, and on each had stood four large stone statues, mostly, however, now lying prone on the ground and some broken. Each statue[1] had on its head a large cylindrical stone of red colour, wrought into a perfectly circular form. One of these stone statues was 27 feet long and 8 feet across the breadth of the shoulders, yet there were others larger than this still standing, one of them so big that its shade at two in the afternoon was sufficient to shelter the whole party of twenty persons from the rays of the sun.

Throughout the whole island there was scarcely any supply of really fresh, sweet water. In fact this landing party only met with one such pool or well, and this was

[1] Some of these figures are outside the British Museum.

very dirty, owing to the habit of the natives going there to drink and at the same time washing themselves all over. If a numerous party came up for this purpose the first arrival leapt right into the middle of the hole, drank, washed himself without the least ceremony, and then gave up his place to another, so that the lastcomer had a very filthy liquid to quench his thirst. But for the most part the wells or watering places were brackish or even salt. The natives seemed to drink the salt water without any reluctance.

In the course of this journey taken by the party from the *Resolution* the natives frequently came up with roasted potatoes, sugar cane, and supplies of water. They distributed these supplies of food and drink with great punctiliousness, being careful that those in the rear should be as well served as those in front of the expedition. Yet all the time they were taking trouble to minister to the wants of the white men they endeavoured to steal from them by snatching at their bags or any loose gear which they could easily detach from their persons; so much so that at last it was necessary to fire a musket loaded with small shot, which did not in the least interrupt the otherwise friendly relations.

On the whole the natives of Easter Island (Rapanui, Hwaihu, and Teapai, as it was sometimes called) were living in a somewhat miserable condition when revisited by Cook, as though they had very much degenerated. Their food supply was poor, not even fish being abundant on the coasts. They had a few fowls and rats, and lived chiefly on sweet potatoes, yams, pumpkins or gourds, bananas, and sugar cane. The speciality of the island was the sweet potato, which Cook thought the best he had ever tasted. It seemed to Cook as though there were not more than 700 natives left on this island (probably there were then from 2000 to 3000). Their houses were low, miserable huts, or a kind of vault built of stone partly underground. Their fuel (as there were scarcely any trees left in the island) consisted of grass, and, above all, the stalks of the sugar cane. They had a few canoes made of boards, and it was a mystery where they could have got the wood from which to build them, unless it was driftwood.

But of course the greatest mystery of the island, then as now, were the stone terraces and platforms and the gigantic stone statues. The workmanship of the mortarless masonry appeared to the officers of the *Resolution* to be not inferior to the best stonebuilding work then known in England. The stones were morticed and fitted into one another in a very artful manner. The side walls were not perpendicular, but inclined inwards. The statues were, as a rule, erected on these stone platforms. It is noteworthy that the ears of these stone figures had their lobes prolonged downwards out of all proportion, but resembling closely the artificially elongated ears of the living Easter Islanders. Another puzzle was how the red stone cylinders could have been placed on the tops of the heads of these statues when they stood sometimes 25 feet or more above the ground. It must have required also considerable art to raise these immense carved stones to a perpendicular position. The statues did not seem to be regarded as idols by the people, but as the memorials of dead chiefs, and to have been in some way connected with the burial places of notabilities. The stonework on this island, nearly 1400 miles from the nearest land—Pitcairn—which has also remains of a similar nature, remains one of the world's great unsolved mysteries in the history of the human species, and it is remarkable that such small effort has been made by excavation to find some clue as to the origin and affinities of this vanished race of stonebuilders, whose works stretch across the Pacific from the Ladrone Islands to Easter Island.

From Easter Island, Cook proceeded to the Marquezas archipelago, already known through the explorations of the Spaniards. Here the natives were of the usual type of friendly, boisterous thieves, not provoked to much dismay or anger if any of their companions were killed or wounded by the muskets which Cook was obliged to order to be fired at them, to stop their carrying off things of great importance to the ship. All the islands and most of the ports bore Spanish names. The people were Polynesians, but far better supplied with food products than the miserable Easter Islanders. They had pigs, fowls, bananas, yams, numerous edible roots, bread-fruit, and coconuts.

From the Marquezas the *Resolution* sailed back to Tahiti, and, after another visit round most of the Society Islands [where Cook's relations with the natives were so peculiarly cordial and intimate that he left them with some shedding of tears on both sides and many appeals and promises to return], once more sailed for New Zealand. On the way thither, Howe Island and Savage Island (so called because of the ferocious attack made on a landing party by the natives) were discovered and named. The *Resolution* visited the northern islands of the Tonga group, but curiously missed seeing the large islands of Fiji, though Cook discovered and named Turtle Island, the southernmost of the group, on his voyage from the Friendly Islands to the New Hebrides. In like manner Cook never visited the Samoan archipelago, though, with

A CHIEF AT ST. CHRISTINA IN THE MARQUEZAS ARCHIPELAGO

A MAN OF EASTER ISLAND

(Natives of the remotest Pacific Archipelagoes. From drawings by W. Hodges, who accompanied Captain Cook's Second Expedition)

these two exceptions, he was the discoverer or rediscoverer of almost all the Pacific islands.

The *Resolution* reached the New Hebrides archipelago in July, 1774. The first island at which any stay was made was the second largest of the group, Mallikolo. The people of this island and of the rest of the group Cook at once saw were markedly different from the tall, handsome, European-like Polynesians. They seemed to their discoverers the most ugly and ill-proportioned people they had ever seen; very dark-coloured and rather diminutive, with long heads, flat faces, and monkey countenances. Their hair, black or brown, was short and curly, though not so tightly curled as that of a negro. They had strong, crisp, and bushy beards. What added to their deformity was a belt or cord which they wore round the waist, tied so tightly that they were wasp-waisted. The men practically went quite naked, but the women, who were not less ugly than the men, and had their heads, faces, and shoulders painted red, wore a kind of petticoat and a bag over their shoulders in which they carried their infants. They had ear-rings and bracelets of tortoiseshell, and armlets made of thread and studded with shells; the bridge of the nose was pierced, and through it was thrust a circular piece of white stone. They were armed with wooden clubs and spears, bows and arrows, and the bow, which was about 4 feet long, was remarkable for not being circular, but had a great bend in its lower half, so that the bow and bowstring together in outline were like the half of a pear cut lengthwise. The arrows were reeds pointed with hard wood or bone, and the tips were covered with a poisonous substance. Their language was utterly different from that of the Polynesians, and it was noticed that they expressed their admiration by hissing like a goose. They had no dogs or domestic animals of any kind apparently (probably, however, they had fowls, like the New Caledonians).

At another of the islands, Efate, an attempt was made to lure them on shore, no doubt believing that their weapons were ineffective, and that they might be easily robbed, killed, and eaten. But at Tanna Island, the southernmost of the group, pleasant relations were entered into with the people, who were of a somewhat different race and spoke a different language to those of Mallikolo. They were taller, better shaped, and with more agreeable features, and were no doubt mixed with Polynesian blood. Their skin colour was very dark, their hair curly and crisp. They had pigs, but no knowledge of dogs, goats, or cats, calling them all pigs. They were frankly cannibals, and asked Cook and his people if they did not also eat human flesh.

There was an active volcano on this island which during the stay of the *Resolution* vomited up vast quantities of fire and smoke, making at every eruption a long rumbling noise, like that of thunder or the explosion of mines. The air was sometimes loaded with ashes or a kind of fine sand, and it was exceedingly troublesome to the eyes. The volcano also hurled huge masses of rock into the air, and when it rained it rained mud, on account of the degree to which the atmosphere was charged with sand and dust. Whichever way the wind was the ship's crew were plagued with the fall of ashes. Nevertheless the natives seemed quite indifferent to these volcanic manifestations. Unfortunately, at the close of their stay at Tanna, their relations with the natives ceased to be friendly, owing to the inexcusable shooting of one of them by a sentry. Cook throughout his books has to complain on several occasions of the frequency with which the marines, or even the midshipmen, fired at the natives without sufficient cause.

From Tanna the *Resolution* sailed north to the large island of Espiritu Santo, and stayed in St. Philip's Bay, the harbour discovered by de Quiros. The natives of this island were very dark-skinned, and their hair short and woolly, yet there were others of more Polynesian appearance, with long hair tied up on the crown of the head and ornamented with feathers like the headdresses of the New Zealanders. These taller people spoke a language apparently of a Polynesian type. Their canoes had outriggers.

Sailing away from the New Hebrides in the direction of New Zealand, land was discovered to the south on 4 September (1774). This was the large island named by Cook New Caledonia. The people were found to be obliging and civil, and with little reluctance came off to the ship to receive presents and to bring supplies of fresh food for sale. They had not the least knowledge of pigs, goats, dogs, or cats, and not even a name for one of them, but had apparently (so it is stated in Cook's journal) domestic fowls of a large breed. The men went naked, but were nevertheless much attracted by presents of cloth, especially if it was red in colour. When Cook landed he was received by a vast concourse of people almost entirely unarmed and very attentive to the orders of their chief. But the country was not so attractive in appearance as the beautiful Pacific archipelagos farther north and east. Cook at once noted in his journal that "it bore in general a great resemblance to parts of New Holland (Australia) under the same latitude", the forest being without any underwood and the trees being of much the same species [there are, however, no Eucalypti in New Caledonia]. The mountains and other high places seemed for the most part incapable of cultivation, consisting chiefly of rocks, the little on them being scorched and burnt up by the sun, though it bore tufts of coarse grass and a few trees and shrubs.

Whilst anchored off New Caledonia Cook very nearly lost his life from eating a fish of a poisonous nature. "It was of a new species something like a sunfish, with a large, long, ugly head. Having no suspicion of its being of a poisonous nature, we ordered it to be dressed for supper; but very luckily the operation of drawing and describing it (undertaken by Mr. Forster) took up so much time that only the liver and the row were dressed", of which the two Forsters and Cook merely tasted a little. But about three in the morning they were seized with an extraordinary weakness and numbness, and almost lost the sense of feeling. They could not distinguish between light and heavy bodies, so far as they had the strength to move, a quart pot and a feather seeming to be the same in weight. They immediately took emetics, and afterwards recovered the full use of their senses; but one of the pigs on board, who had eaten a portion of the inside of the fish, died soon afterwards, and they learnt from the natives that it was a deadly food.

Besides giving the chiefs dogs for breeding purposes, Cook landed couples of pigs in order to supply this island with domestic animals.

These people of New Caledonia were very like negroes in appearance, but their head hair grew much longer and the men had abundant beards. The men went nearly naked, the women wore a short petticoat. Their language seemed to be a mixture between that of the Melanesians of the New Hebrides and the Polynesians of New Zealand. As regards weapons, they had something like a boomerang, and a wooden club shaped like a pickaxe. They used slings and stones, harpoons for striking fish, spears and darts. Their houses were circular, but kept full of smoke from the ever-burning fire in order to drive away the mosquitoes. They had clumsy dug-out canoes, generally used double, secured to each other by cross spars which projected a foot over each side. On these spars would be laid a deck or platform made of planks, on which they could even have a hearth of clay with a fire burning on it. These canoes were navigated by one or two lateen sails. Bananas and sugar cane were here, and also bread-fruit and coconuts, but all such things very scarce, and the natives lived chiefly on roots, the bark of a tree, which they roasted and chewed, and on fish. They had no other drink but water.

The coasts of New Caledonia, however, were beset with reefs and shoals, so that it was practically impossible for a sailing ship like the *Resolution* to make any close survey without running risks of being lost altogether. Cook therefore sailed away from New Caledonia, and discovered the Isle of Pines at its southern extremity: a series of islets, really, on which grew very tall conifers.[1] One little island, scarcely more than three-quarters of a mile round, was covered with a forest of these tall pines 60 to-70 feet in height. The wood was white, close-grained, tough and light, and exuded turpentine. On this southward cruise Cook, curiously enough, missed seeing the Loyalty Islands, which lie at no great distance to the east of New Caledonia,

[1] There is an extraordinary development of southern conifers in New Caledonia and the adjacent islands and islets. They belong to the genera *Araucaria* (eight species), *Podocarpus* (seven species), *Agathis, Dacrydium, Libocedrus* (five species), *Callitris*, and *Acmopyle*, a remarkable assemblance for a land area of about 6450 square miles.

almost midway between New Caledonia and New Zealand. But he discovered Norfolk Island, which was uninhabited. Here his people noticed the aloe-like "flax" plant of New Zealand and a great abundance of splendid pine trees—the now celebrated Norfolk Island pine (*Araucaria excelsa*). The woods were full of pigeons, parrots, rails, and small birds. There were also "cabbage" palms, not thicker than a man's leg, and from 10 to 20 feet high, probably of the *Areca* genus, "with large pinnated fronds".

New Zealand was once more reached on 11 October, 1774. There were evident traces in Queen Charlotte Sound that the *Adventure* had been there. The natives received them with a certain reserve, though at first very joyfully. They told a story, however, of a white man's ship which some months ago had been beaten to pieces on the rocks. The white men had landed, but after their muskets had ceased to be of any use they had been attacked, killed, and eaten by the natives, though not by the people of Queen Charlotte Sound.[1] There being nothing now to detain Cook at New Zealand, he left Queen Charlotte Sound in November, 1774, and, sailing across the Southern Pacific, reached Tierra del Fuego, at the extremity of South America, and, after visiting the Falkland

[1] The actual truth of this story was that the *Adventure*, returning to New Zealand to keep her tryst with the *Resolution*, had sent a boat with a landing party to get wood and water. These had landed, and, for some reason not explained, had been attacked by the natives, who had killed them all but one, and eaten a good deal of their remains. Apparently a midshipman, Woodhouse, escaped slaughter, and afterwards managed in some way to get in a native canoe to other islands and return to England in a foreign ship. The *Adventure* was obliged through shortage of supplies to give up the idea of meeting her consort and make the best of her way to England. Accordingly, she steered through the southern latitudes for South America and the Cape of Good Hope. With a continual wind blowing eastwards she was almost blown across the Pacific, and reached Cape Horn in only a month from New Zealand, and from here sailed onwards till she reached the Cape of Good Hope, and, eventually, England. Her gallant captain, Furneaux, afterwards died in the American war, at the early age of forty-six.

Islands and discovering the large island of South Georgia, he continued his journey round the southern waters of the globe till he reached the Cape of Good Hope, from which he made his way to England, having been absent three years and eighteen days, during which voyage he had lost but four men, and only one of them from sickness. "The nature of our voyage carried us into very high latitudes, but the hardships and dangers inseparable from that situation were in some degree compensated with the singular felicity we enjoyed in extracting inexhaustible supplies of fresh water from an ocean strewed with ice."

On Cook's return from his second voyage he received, from the hands of King George III, his commission as a post captain in the navy, and soon afterwards was appointed to be a fourth captain at the Royal Hospital for Seamen at Greenwich, with a salary of £200 a year, a residence, and certain allowances, subject, however, to the right of the Admiralty to call on him for further sea service should they require him. And the call—provoked by the eagerness of Cook—was not long delayed, for in the following year (1776) he was appointed to command once more the *Resolution*. To this ship was added a smaller consort, the *Discovery*, which had a capacity of only 300 tons, to be commanded by Lieutenant Clerke, formerly of the *Resolution*.

In the Third Voyage, which began in the summer of 1776, the exploration of the Pacific was to be continued, but more with the intention that Cook should explore the western coast of North America and find out conclusively if there was or was not any sea way which would give a passage for ships across the North American continent.[1]

[1] This matter has been dealt with in my work on the *Pioneers in Canada*.

The new voyage to be undertaken by the ships *Resolution* and *Discovery* was designed to proceed to the Pacific by the Cape of Good Hope across the Indian Ocean in southern latitudes, and past New Zealand and Tahiti to the west coast of North America. Rumours had begun to reach England about French discoveries in the South Indian Ocean, notably those by du Fresne and Crozet and by de Kerguélen-Trémarec in 1772, which it was desirable to investigate. An interesting member of Cook's crew was a Tahitian—Omai—who had been brought to England by the *Adventure*, and had not been spoilt by the kindliness of his reception. Omai was to return with Cook to his native land, and proved himself as useful, plucky, good-natured, and well-mannered an interpreter as had done the unfortunate Tupia, whose bones lay buried at Batavia. After the usual stay at the Cape of Good Hope, the *Resolution* and *Discovery* made their way into the Southern Indian Ocean through mountainous seas and bitter cold weather, and discovered or rediscovered Prince Edward's Island,[1] the Marion du Fresne and the Crozet Islands, and came to an anchor off the large island in 48° S. latitude, which had been already noted by the French sea captain, de Kerguélen-Trémarec. This last-mentioned island now bears Kerguélen's name. Captain Cook and the great French explorers who had preceded him had found no vast southern continent in the Southern Indian Ocean, but all unknowing they had found the last remaining vestiges of such; for Kerguélen, St. Paul, and Amsterdam Islands, the Crozets and Prince Edward's Islands, are the only portions remaining above the sea of a great Antarctic land which probably once united South America with Australia and New Zealand. All these scattered oceanic islands rise

[1] After the father of Queen Victoria—the Duke of Kent.

from what is called the Kerguélen Plateau, a region of the bed of the Indian Ocean in which the depth does not much exceed 8000 feet.

Kerguélen is the largest of these islands—about 1400 square miles in extent. Its mountains attain altitudes of 2400 to 6120 feet. One of them is an active volcano, and the whole of Kerguélen has been subjected in recent times to much volcanic activity, lava having covered much of its surface. This eruption of plutonic forces seems to have followed a severe glacial period, during which the island was covered with ice. It is therefore not to be wondered at that between them fire and ice destroyed a once abundant plant growth; for Kerguélen, in Tertiary times, maintained great forests of trees of South American affinities.

On this desolate wind-swept island of snow mountains and crumbling lava the crews of the *Resolution* and *Discovery* spent Christmas, partly to obtain fresh water ("every gully afforded a large stream") and fresh meat —the flesh of penguins and other sea birds and seals. The seals (chiefly sea elephants and sea leopards) also provided quantities of fat or blubber, from which oil was obtained for the ship's lamps. The principal feature in the vegetation (there were no trees, except fossil ones) was a plant called the Kerguélen cabbage, actually a kind of cabbage (*Pringlea antiscorbutica*). This was a great boon to the ship's company, who ate it boiled and also raw in their eagerness for vegetable food. Amongst the birds of the island was a land bird, the sheathbill (*Chionis*), the size of a large pigeon, with white plumage, black beak, and white feet, a bird which is related both to the gulls and the plovers. There were also giant petrels, king penguins, albatrosses, gulls, cormorants, and a peculiar species of teal.

On 24 January, 1777, the coast of Tasmania was sighted, and on the 27th the second party of Englishmen (the men of the *Adventure* being the first) landed in that southernmost portion of Australia. The following day a party of natives appeared, who approached them unarmed without betraying fear. They were quite naked and wore no ornaments, but their bodies were decorated by large weals or ridges of skin in straight or curved lines. They were of average size, rather slender, with black skins and black woolly hair. Their features were not ugly. The language was wholly unintelligible, and seemed even to be different from that of the natives of New South Wales.

After a further visit to New Zealand, and a long stay in the Friendly Islands (the Tonga archipelago) and the Society Islands, Cook turned the course of his expedition northwards, discovered Christmas Island, and sailed across a stretch of open ocean till at last, in January, 1778, he sighted a wonderful new land in the archipelago of Hawaii. To this he gave the name by which they were long afterwards known—the Sandwich Islands. After a stay in this region of eight principal islands and many islets, with its wonderful volcanoes (the highest of which is snow-crowned and 13,823 feet in altitude), its peculiar vegetation, and its Polynesian people, he passed on to the exploring of the western and north-western coasts of North America, with the results which have been described in my book on the *Pioneers in Canada*. Returning again southwards to continue the explorations of the Pacific archipelagos, he met his fate in a miserable skirmish on the west coast of the large island of Hawaii, the easternmost of the Hawaii group.[1]

[1] The Hawaiians, though very friendly, were very thievish, and their robberies on the *Resolution* and *Discovery* and attempts to take away boats became so serious that

A DANCING GROUND AND DRUMS AT PORT SANDWICH, MALEKALA (MALLICOLO) ISLAND, NEW HEBRIDES. TAMBU HOUSE (TEMPLE) IN BACKGROUND

Cook's adventures and those of his officers, after reaching northern latitudes such as the Hawaii archipelago, can scarcely be brought within the limits of Australasia, so that Cook now passes from our narrative. But he remains the most remarkable figure in the past history of Australasia. He was perhaps the greatest of British navigators, for he made not only all the most remarkable discoveries of the Pacific Ocean between the ice fringe of the Southern Continent and the Bering Straits; but he did so with singularly little hardship to his men, whose health he studied with the utmost care, while in his contact with the natives he has left behind him an admirable reputation for kindliness and sympathy. From the point of view of science he fully deserved the Fellowship of the Royal Society. The books composed from his journals read like those of modern travellers of the best type, so shrewd are his observations and so accurate his descriptions. He stands in the first rank of the world's heroes, and it is interesting to remember that, though there are not many greater Englishmen in our national records, he rose from being the son of a Yorkshire farm labourer, a boy serving out groceries in a little shop, an apprentice on board a collier, to command, as an officer in the king's navy, vessels which performed voyages far more wonderful than that of Columbus, and which revealed to the knowledge of science the coasts of the Arctic and Antarctic Oceans, the Continent of Australia, the Dominion of New Zealand, and most of the islands and archipelagos of the Pacific Ocean.

Cook landed with a party of marines and attempted to secure the person of a king or chief as a hostage. In the struggle that followed he and four marines were killed. The flesh from Cook's body was afterwards sent back to the ship, but his bones were preserved by the priests as relics.

CHAPTER IX

Bligh and the "Bounty"

COOK'S first and second expeditions had drawn special attention to the bread-fruit as an article of food. The English planters in the West Indies thought that the bread-fruit tree would be a valuable addition to their food supply; for, owing to the foolish economics of slave labour, periodical famines occurred in Jamaica and other West India islands from one cause and another. Accordingly, in 1787 the British Admiralty dispatched WILLIAM BLIGH, in command of a king's ship named the *Bounty*, to the Pacific Ocean to obtain young bread-fruit trees, and then convey them to the West Indies. Bligh had commenced his experiences in Australia by accompanying Captain Cook on his second expedition in 1772 as sailing-master or navigating officer of the *Resolution*. In 1772, and after Cook had started on his third expedition, Bligh was promoted to be a commander and sent out in H.M.S. *Providence* to Tahiti in connection with Cook's last voyage. On 23 December, 1787, he left England in the *Bounty*, but owing to the frightful storms off the extremity of South America his ship was unable to proceed direct to the Pacific and obliged to cross the Southern Atlantic to the Cape of Good Hope and remain there thirty-eight days to refit, to replenish the provisions and refresh the crew. Starting again from the Cape on 1 July, 1788, they reached Adventure

Bay in Tasmania on 20 August, after a remarkably swift passage across the southern Indian Ocean. Another uneventful voyage of short duration took them to Tahiti.

With him there sailed a Mr. Nelson, a horticulturist, who had been with Cook in his third expedition and had planted shaddock trees in Tahiti (now found to be, eleven years afterwards, well grown and full of fruit). Nelson at once set to work with the assistance of the natives to dig up quantities of young bread-fruit plants. He obtained 1015, besides many specimens of other Tahitian plants. The *Bounty*, on 4 April, 1789, sailed away from Tahiti, "where for twenty-three weeks we had been treated with the utmost affection and regard, which seemed to increase in proportion to our stay". After calling at Anamuka in the Tonga archipelago the celebrated mutiny occurred. In the early morning of 28 April, when Bligh had just turned in for a sleep, he was suddenly awakened by Fletcher Christian, the master's mate (one of the officers on board, and probably a Manxman), who, accompanied by several gunners and seamen, tied his hands behind his back and threatened him with instant death if he spoke a word. In spite of his shoutings, however, he was not hurt, but dragged up on deck, where he found that twenty-five officers and men had mutinied against his command and had resolved to put him and seventeen others into an open boat and cast them adrift.

The cause of this mutiny undoubtedly was Bligh's own behaviour to officers and men, but above all to his officers, since leaving England. He was obviously a man of the most violent temper and of very coarse habits and mean disposition. Being purser as well as commander, he evidently tried to make money out of the rations issued to officers and men. He was perpetually charging his officers with stealing coconuts or yams. He would subject the midshipmen to the most cruel punishments, almost enough, one would think, to have killed them; and it is obvious that mutiny was in the hearts of many on board long before it actually broke out. Bligh gave as his explanation that during the long stay at Tahiti most of the men on board had contracted attachments towards the native women and wished to return and settle down there permanently. But it has been remarked that if this was the case they might have all deserted in a body whilst on the island, or have mutinied before the ship left these waters instead of doing so after leaving the Tonga archipelago at a distance of three weeks' sailing from Tahiti. The mutiny was undoubtedly precipitated by Bligh's complete loss of temper whilst the ship was in the Tonga archipelago, and his threats to make the life of all on board "a perfect hell" for the rest of the voyage, which, by way of the Dutch Indies and the Cape of Good Hope to Jamaica, would have been a tremendously long one.

Bligh, together with the sailing-master, the acting surgeon, the botanist, and several other officers and petty officers, in all nineteen persons, were thrust into a launch which, when loaded with passengers and goods, was brought so near to the surface of the water as to endanger her sinking with only a moderate swell of the sea. Yet in this crazy boat Bligh and his companions sailed for a distance of 4000 miles till they landed at Timor—one of the most noteworthy sea adventures on record. Before they left the *Bounty* they were given 150 pounds of bread, 32 pounds of pork, 6 quarts of rum, 6 bottles of wine, 28 gallons of water, and four empty barrels. Thus provisioned they sailed for the island of Tofoa, intending to obtain bread-fruit and coconuts. When the natives met them, Bligh, wisely or unwisely, accounted for his plight by telling them that the *Bounty* had capsized and that they alone were saved. They were therefore regarded rather contemptuously as shipwrecked sailors, and only received small quantities of bread-fruit, bananas, and coconuts. Moreover, an attempt was made to seize the boat, in which one of the seamen was killed. In terrible distress they implored Bligh, who with all his faults had great force of character, to get them back to England *somehow*. He told them that their nearest hope of salvation was the Island of Timor, 4000 miles distant, more or less, and that if they were to reach that they must obey his orders implicitly and maintain the most absolute discipline. They agreed.

Soon after leaving the last islet of the Tonga archipelago a terrible storm burst on them, and the sea curling over the stern of the boat the fatigue of baling became very great, and some of the provisions were spoilt. They would probably have succumbed to their miseries but for the rum, which was served out to them in teaspoonfuls. When the weather improved they suffered from want of room, their limbs being fearfully cramped, for scarcely any man could stretch out to his full length, and the nights were cold, especially to men soaked with seawater. They passed near the Fiji Islands, from which they were chased by cannibals in canoes. They were soused with heavy rain, and, though it increased their stock of fresh water, this added to their miseries.

In order to serve out allowances methodically Bligh made a pair of scales with two coconut shells, using pistol balls as weights. He also interested the crew by his description of what was known of both New Guinea and Australia, giving all the information stored in his mind, so that in the case of his death the survivors might still reach Timor. Their rations sometimes consisted of a quarter of a pint of coconut milk, a little decayed bread, and the kernels of four coconuts. Occasionally half an ounce of salt pork was given to each man. The storms and the rain continued, and Bligh proposed to the men that when wet through with rainwater they should wring their clothes out in salt water before putting them on again, a proceeding from which, he says, they derived much warmth and refreshment, though every man complained of violent pains in his bones. Incessant baling had to be carried on, both because of the deluge of rain and the waves breaking into the boat. They were sometimes so covered with rain and saltwater that they could scarcely see, and suffered extreme cold. Sleep fled from them in their misery.

One day about noon some noddies (terns, a kind of gull) came so near the boat that one was caught by the hand. It was about the size of a small pigeon. Bligh divided it with its entrails into eighteen portions, which were impartially distributed amongst the crew, Bligh himself, in drawing lots, having nothing but the beak and claws. Later they caught a gannet, which was also divided into eighteen portions, though its blood was given to the three people who were most distressed for want of food. After that they caught more and more gannets, and found their crops containing flying-fish and small cuttlefish, all of which were welcome additions to their diet.

On 28 May they heard the sound of breakers on the Barrier Reef which surrounds north-eastern Australia.

c 487

CAPTAIN BLIGH AND HIS MEN SEARCHING FOR OYSTERS OFF THE GREAT BARRIER REEF

With intense thankfulness they found a break in the reef a quarter of a mile in width. Through this the boat sailed to the westward and came immediately into smooth water, so that all the past hardships seemed at once to be forgotten, and on this account a short religious service was held on board. Soon afterwards they landed on the sandy point of an island off the Australian coast, and to their intense delight discovered oysters on the rocks. By the help of a small magnifying glass a fire was made. One of the men had managed to bring away with him a copper pot, and into this put a mixture of oysters, bread, and pork, from which a stew was made sufficient to give each person a full pint of nourishing food. Moreover, they obtained berries or fruits on this island, which out of gratitude Bligh named Restoration Island. Calling soon afterwards at another island they discovered one of the species of "cabbage" palms already referred to in this book, and from the palm cabbages and oysters they made excellent meals, which restored almost everyone to health.

On one of these islands they saw, just as they were embarking after filling the boat with oysters, twenty naked savages running and hallooing and beckoning the strangers to come to them; but as each one was armed with either a spear or a lance it was thought better to hold no communication with them. At one of these islands off the north coast of Australia, to which was given the name of "Sunday", a mutinous feeling began again, which Bligh allayed by inviting the mutineer to fight a duel with him. In spite of this unpleasant occurrence on Sunday Island they obtained oysters, clams, dogfish, and wild beans. A party was sent out by night to catch birds, and returned with only twelve of the noddy terns. The reason they did not get more was that one of the men rushed amongst the birds precipitately and disturbed them in order to secure for himself as large a number as possible. In his frightful hunger he acknowledged that he had eaten *nine* of these little gulls! Nevertheless, after again putting out into the open sea on their course to Timor, hunger again attacked them, and there was a terrible decline in health. On 10 June Bligh noticed a visible alteration for the worse, his people showing extreme weakness, with swelled legs, hollow and ghastly countenances, a constant inclination to slumber, and a weakness of understanding. He administered wine, and cheered them up by saying that from his calculations he believed they were now close to Timor.

He proved to be correct, for on 12 June the coast of Timor was discovered at a distance of only 6 miles, and two days afterwards they came to an anchor at the Dutch settlement in Kupang Bay, where they were received with every mark of kindness, hospitality, and humanity. They stayed at Kupang for two months to recruit their strength, and then obtaining a small schooner they sailed to Batavia, from which island they were sent home in the ships of the Dutch East India Company. Bligh himself was landed at the Isle of Wight on 11 March, 1790. Nelson the botanist, however, died at Kupang, and five of the other officers and men succumbed to disease at Java or on the way home, so that besides the man who was killed on the Island of Tofoa, six only out of the nineteen men set adrift by the mutineers failed to reach a home which was some 14,000 miles distant from the place at which they had been cast adrift.

After setting Bligh and his companions adrift, Christian took command of the *Bounty*, and her course was directed, not to Tahiti, but to the Tubuai archipelago farther south. The mutineers threw overboard the greater part of the bread-fruit plants, but, quarrelling with the natives of Tubuai, they sailed to Tahiti. Here Otu, the principal chief, became very inquisitive about the fate of Captain Bligh and the bread-fruit plants. They told him a garbled story about meeting Captain Cook and handing the plants over to him, and that Mr. Christian had now returned to Tahiti to obtain an additional supply of pigs, goats, fowls, and more bread-fruit. So overjoyed were the Tahitians to hear that their dear friend Captain Cook was not dead, but alive (which of course was a lie) and about to settle on an island so near to them, that in the course of a very few days the *Bounty* received on board 312 pigs, 38 goats (derived of course from the animals landed by Cook originally), 96 fowls, a bull and a cow, and a large quantity of bread-fruit and bananas. The *Bounty* also received on board eight men, nine women, and seven boys. They then returned to Tubuai, where they ran the ship on shore, landed the live stock, and set about building a fort. But they soon quarrelled with the natives, of whom they shot many with their firearms. Their position became untenable; so once more they returned to Tahiti, in September, 1789. Here sixteen of the mutineers were landed at their own request, while the remaining nine decided to continue their voyage in the *Bounty*, which once more sailed away with seven Tahiti men and twelve women, intending to discover some unknown or uninhabited island in which there was no harbour for shipping.

British ships of war sent out after the return of Bligh to search for the mutineers brought away fourteen out of the sixteen who had been landed at Tahiti. All these were put on their trial: three were executed and the remainder either pardoned or only received short terms of imprisonment. But they were conveyed to England under circumstances of great brutality, and, curiously enough, on their way back, the *Pandora* (the ship of war which conveyed them under the command of Captain Edwardes) struck on the Barrier Reef off north-east Australia, and the mutineers, like everyone else, had in one of the ship's boats to perform a voyage to Timor almost equally remarkable with that of Captain Bligh. Once more the Dutch officials at Kupang (who must have got rather tired by this time of shipwrecked mutinous British seafarers) received them with the greatest kindness and sent them towards England in a vessel of the Dutch East India Company.[1]

Meantime the people in England were still in ignorance of what fate had attended the last of the mutineers. This was not revealed until 1809. An American ship, the *Topaz*, of Boston, by a mere chance approached the shores of desolate little Pitcairn Island, and on landing there to obtain water they discovered, to their astonishment, an old Englishman calling himself Alexander Smith, and the only survivor of the nine mutineers who left Tahiti in 1789 in search of a distant and desert island, accom-

[1] A midshipman on board the *Bounty*, Peter Heywood, who really took no part in the mutiny other than not offering to accompany Captain Bligh, and who surrendered himself to the *Pandora* by swimming off to that ship when she arrived at Tahiti, was afterwards tried for his life in London under very affecting circumstances. He might quite easily have been sentenced to death but for the unflagging efforts of his sister Nessy, a young girl with some gifts as a poetess, who resided in the Isle of Man. The journey of Nessy Heywood to London, the way in which she petitioned and interviewed ministers and secretaries of state, and ultimately so worked on the feelings of the great people in the capital, that although her brother was convicted he was afterwards pardoned and restored to the naval service, is as much worthy to be made the subject of an historical novel as the conduct of Jeanie Deans in the *Heart of Midlothian*. Unhappily Nessy wore herself out in this struggle, and a few months after her brother's restoration to liberty died of consumption. Peter Heywood afterwards distinguished himself in the naval wars with France, became a post-captain, and died in 1831.

panied by twelve Tahitian women, six men, and a number of boys. Smith stated to the captain of the *Topaz* that the *Bounty* was run on shore at Pitcairn and broken up in 1790, but about four years afterwards a good deal of jealousy and ill humour arising between the Tahitians and the English seamen, the former suddenly revolted and killed every Englishman, except Alexander Smith, who was severely wounded. [Alexander Smith had for some reason, then or earlier, changed his name to that of John Adams, by which he is better known in history.] The same night the Tahitian widows of the slain Englishmen rose up and put to death the whole of the Tahitian men, leaving Smith the only adult man alive on the island, together with eight or nine women, and several children who were the offspring of the English mutineers and the Tahitian women. These survivors now applied themselves sedulously to tilling the ground, so that in course of time it produced plenty of yams, coconuts and bananas, while they bred hogs and poultry in abundance. The population at the time of the *Topaz's* visit amounted to thirty-five, who all acknowledged Smith as their chief and "father". They all spoke English, and Smith had done his best to educate them in a religious and a moral way. He died in March, 1829.

The little colony had been joined before that time by a seaman from a whaling ship, named John Buffet, who deliberately settled there and constituted himself chaplain and schoolmaster. He certainly contributed a good deal in course of time to the education and good morals of this colony of handsome half-breeds, a colony which was from time to time visited by British war vessels.

As to Christian, it was at first said that he had committed suicide soon after arriving at Pitcairn Island, but the true story was that he was killed by one of the Tahitians. But he left behind him a son who grew up to be a handsome young fellow, and greatly astonished the naval officers whose ship visited Pitcairn in 1814 by coming off in Tahitian undress and saying in excellent English: "Won't you heave us a rope, now?" He then sprang with alacrity up the side of the ship and said, in reply to the question "Who are you?": "My name is Thursday October Christian." He was fully 6 feet high, with almost black hair, a handsome face, and wearing no clothes except a straw hat and a piece of cloth round his waist. His manner of speaking English was exceedingly correct both in grammar and pronunciation, and he was accompanied by a fine handsome youth of seventeen or eighteen, who called himself George Young, who was the son of one of the midshipmen of the *Bounty*.

Pitcairn was named after a midshipman in the ship of Captain Philip Carteret, who first sighted the island in 1767. It rises to 2000 feet in height, and its area is only 2 square miles. It is 100 miles from the nearest island of the Paumotu group. It possesses the remains of carved stone pillars similar to those of Easter Island, together with stone axes, showing that at a remote period it was inhabited. When first discovered its surface was clothed with rich forest, the soil was very fertile, but the coast was rock-bound and dangerous of approach.

There were no springs or streams in Pitcairn Island, and when the forest began to be cut down by the settlers the rainfall decreased and there was a scarcity of water. An attempt was made by the mutineers' descendants to return to Tahiti in 1830, but it was given up, and the Pitcairn Islanders continued to inhabit the little island until 1856, when the whole of them—by this time 194 in number—were landed on Norfolk Island, between New Zealand and New Caledonia. There most of their descendants live to this day. But in 1858 two families of these handsome hybrid people returned to Pitcairn, which now has a population of 170, who no longer speak English but an extraordinary mixture of Polynesian and English. They have also a good deal degenerated from the high standard of morality which was maintained in earlier days.

As to Bligh, he was sent back to Tahiti in command of the *Providence* in 1791, and promptly obtained another supply of bread-fruit plants which he conveyed safely to Jamaica, thus introducing the bread-fruit tree into the West Indies. After distinguishing himself markedly in the British naval service he was appointed Governor of New South Wales in 1805, but became so intensely disliked there by the violence of his temper and his arbitrary acts that another mutiny arose against him headed by the principal military officer. Bligh was kept in prison by the mutineers for two years, but returned to England in 1811, where he was promoted to be an admiral. He died in London in 1817.

CHAPTER X

The Results of the Pioneers' Work

ABOUT the time that Bligh was dispatched in the *Bounty* to obtain bread-fruit plants great developments were instituted in regard to Australia as the result of Cook's earlier voyages. The revolt of the American colonies and other circumstances had deprived the British Government of a region across the seas, to which convicted criminals might be sent as a cheap and easy way of getting rid of them. It was accordingly suggested to the British Government by various persons, including Sir Joseph Banks, that New South Wales (as Cook had called the eastern part of Australia) would be an excellent region in which to found a penal settlement, as well as to take steps for the ultimate founding of a free colony, a region to which British emigrants might go.

Australia and Tasmania need no longer take it to heart that their foundation as nations dates from such a cause as the transportation of convicts, since from a remote period in the history of civilized peoples this is how many and many a new colony has been founded. More especially was it so in the case of British America and the oldest of the British West India Islands. These settlements were chiefly valued for nearly 200 years by the British Government because they were places to which persons convicted of felony or of political crimes could be transported. Moreover, the free emigrants of good character who colonized Australia and Tasmania from the first considerably outnumbered the convicts who were sent to Tasmania, New South Wales, Victoria, and West Australia. Amongst these again the criminal convicts for the most part died out without leaving issue. It was the political prisoners among the transported persons who chiefly prospered and founded families. In short, the colonization of Australia resembled in its processes the colonization of the United States. The person appointed to superintend the first settlement of Australia was Captain ARTHUR PHILLIP, the son of a German teacher of languages in London, who had entered the British Navy and served with great distinction. He commanded the first expedition to New South Wales, and left England in 1787 with a fleet of two men-of-war and six transports, conveying 550 men and 200 women convicts, and three store ships. There were also some free emigrants; in all about 1100 persons. The ships sailed round the Cape of Good Hope and reached Botany Bay on 18 January, 1788. Less than a month afterwards Phillip had already chosen and named the wonderful harbour of Sydney as the capital of the future colony, and almost on that very day there arrived at Botany Bay two French ships under the command of the Comte de la Pérouse, who had been sent out from France on a scientific expedition similar to those of Captain Cook. It is possible that but for the punctual arrival of Governor Phillip the French flag would have been hoisted over Australia. Though, as it would certainly have been pulled down again a few years later by the British conquest of the seas, the possibility is not one to give rise to sensational writing. But Governor Phillip was a man of energy. He not only asserted the

British claim to all the coasts of eastern and southern Australia, but sent a party to take possession of Norfolk Island and its splendid sources of timber supply, and here a number of convicts were set on shore.[1]

The interest of the French Government in the lands of the Pacific Ocean did not cease with the remarkable voyage of Bougainville. In 1785 JEAN-FRANÇOIS GALAUP, COUNT OF THE PEROUSE (a native of Albi in the south-west of France, who had done gallant service for his country in Canada), took command of an expedition of two vessels, *La Boussole* and *L'Astrolabe*, which was to explore more especially the northern parts of the Pacific. Although France had recently been expelled from Canada by the success of the British arms, and had transferred Louisiana to Spain, she still hoped in some way to regain her position in North America; and in spite of Cook's inability to find a navigable strait of water across the vast breadth of the North American continent from the Atlantic to the Pacific, the opinion still persisted in France that such a sea route across the continent did exist.[2] De la Pérouse was also directed to explore the coasts of north-eastern Asia, China, Japan, New Guinea, and Australia. His explorations of north-east Asia were very remarkable, but do not come within the scope of this narrative. He reached the Samoa archipelago in the winter of 1787. Here the officers and crew of the *Astrolabe* quarrelled with the natives, and as a result eleven of the Frenchmen were killed. From Samoa the French expedition passed by way of Tonga and Norfolk Island to the coast of New

[1] They were afterwards transferred to Tasmania.

[2] We know that it does, but that it is very far north and perpetually obstructed by ice.

South Wales, and, as already related, arrived at Botany Bay only a few days after the British expedition under Governor Phillip. After a brief stay in Botany Bay the Comte de la Pérouse sailed away northwards, and his expedition was heard of no more, nor was his actual fate ever completely made known. Apparently the two ships were wrecked on the coral reefs of Vanikoro, a small island in the Santa Cruz group to the north of the New Hebrides. The natives of the Santa Cruz Islands showed themselves very hostile to strangers and white men in earlier times. It was here that Bishop Patterson was murdered in 1871, and it is possible that after the two French ships were driven on to the coral rocks by some storm their crews perished at the hands of the savages.

In 1791 another expedition, under the command of BRUNI D'ENTRECASTEAUX, Governor of Mauritius, was dispatched from Mauritius with two ships, *La Recherche* and *L'Espérance*, to search for de la Pérouse. D'Entrecasteaux obtained no information about the fate of his predecessor's ships, but his voyage added considerably to our knowledge of Australasia. He did much to complete Cook's very imperfect outline of the coast of New Caledonia, he surveyed a good deal of the Tasmanian coast (though he failed to find out that this was after all an island), and he explored the south coast of Australia, which, except for the preceding voyage of Vancouver, had remained almost entirely unknown since the hasty exploration of Pieter Nuyts in 1628.

GEORGE VANCOUVER (whose great work as a British pioneer is associated more with the north-west coast of America) had in 1791 mapped a good deal of the south-west Australian coast and had pointed out the value as a harbour of King George's Sound. He also added to our knowledge of New Zealand, and then continued his route across the Pacific towards what is now the coast of British Columbia.

The troubles which ensued in France, owing to the Revolution and the uprise of Napoleon, diverted the attention of the French from oversea discovery for something like eight years. The British took advantage of this lull to increase their knowledge of the Australian coast and their claims to this region, which even in 1788 were defined as extending from Cape York on Torres Straits, round the east coast of Australia to the southernmost point of Tasmania, and to comprise all the adjacent islands of the Pacific Ocean. A remarkable discovery of an outcrop of coal on the Australian coast near Tasmania by shipwrecked sailors attracted the attention of GEORGE BASS, the surgeon of a small Government vessel. This bold man, embarking in a mere whaleboat, passed along the Australian coast until he found the outcrop of coal. In the following year, 1798, his explorations of these regions convinced him that Tasmania was an island. Bass was accompanied on his circumnavigation of Tasmania by Lieutenant MATTHEW FLINDERS. This first circumnavigation of Tasmania, which lasted for five months, was undertaken in a little vessel which had been constructed in Australia from the timber of the Norfolk Island pine, and was only of 25 tons burden. In this same vessel the gallant Flinders[1]—one of the most remarkable amongst Australian pioneers—in 1799 explored the coast of what we now know as Queensland, which was then called the Moreton Bay district. In 1802 Flinders had become the commander of H.M.S. *Investigator*, a ship of 334 tons. He christened the continent for the first time definitely

[1] Born at Dorrington, near Boston, in Lincolnshire, in 1774.

with the name of AUSTRALIA; and having already added to Cook's exploration of the Queensland coast, he now turned his attention to that of South Australia, which at the commencement of the nineteenth century was most imperfectly known, being only vaguely delineated from the surmised outline put down in the early part of the seventeenth century by the Dutch explorers, together with a little work achieved by Captain Vancouver and the Frenchman D'Entrecasteaux. Amongst other points Flinders discovered Kangaru Island off the coast of South Australia.[1] The French seem to have had some conception of the indentation of the South Australian coast known as Spencer's Gulf, and from this hint arose the theory put forward at the end of the eighteenth century that New South Wales was one vast island and New Holland another, separated by a strait of water uniting Spencer Gulf on the south with the Gulf of Carpentaria on the north. Flinders's exploration of Spencer's Gulf definitely proved the continuity of the whole Australian area.

With Flinders on board the *Investigator* was a young midshipman (his cousin) of the name of JOHN FRANKLIN, long afterwards to become a governor of Tasmania and to achieve deathless fame as one of the great Arctic pioneers.

In 1800 there was dispatched from France another scientific expedition for the exploration of Australia. This was under the command of Captain NICOLAS BAUDIN, and consisted of two ships, *Le Géographie* and *Le Naturaliste*, and contained twenty-three geographers, zoologists, and draughtsmen; but owing to bad arrangements in regard to her supplies of food the crews of the two ships suffered to a

[1] An island with an interesting fauna. It possessed a peculiar species of Emu, which has since become extinct.

horrible extent from scurvy before they reached Australia, and indeed might have perished but for the assistance they received from the British settlement at Port Jackson (Sydney). This French expedition also explored the southern coast of Australia, but, with the exception of about 160 miles of coast which it was the first to examine, added little to geographical knowledge as regards priority of discovery, though for a long time Captain Louis de Freycinet, the mapmaker who accompanied Baudin, posed as having been the first to map much of the Tasmanian and South Australian coasts. It is evident that his commander, Baudin, or Freycinet himself, had borrowed and copied the charts made by Flinders, and had amused themselves by giving the names of French personages to many a bay, promontory, and island already discovered and named by the British.

In the autumn of 1802 Flinders, having completed his survey of the whole south coast of Australia from Cape Leuwin to Sydney, started once more in the *Investigator* to complete his circumnavigation of the island continent. He made a careful exploration of the Great Barrier Reef, and then proceeded to explore the coast of the Gulf of Carpentaria. After a brief rest at the Island of Timor the *Investigator* sailed round the west and south coasts of Australia and once more reached Port Jackson in 1803. Flinders had thus been the first commander to circumnavigate Australia and to prove that it was an undivided area, and that there were no more surprises or mysteries in its outline.

Flinders left Port Jackson again in August, 1803, to proceed to England in H.M.S. *Porpoise*, which was accompanied by a merchant vessel, the *Cato*. But both these vessels struck a coral reef about 800 miles north from Port Jackson and were completely wrecked. The crews managed to land in safety on a small sand-bank only 4 feet at most above high-water mark, and here they were obliged to camp under a blazing sun with all that they could save in the way of provisions and important papers. Flinders, getting into a six-oared boat with a few seamen, actually rowed and sailed 800 miles across the sea back to Port Jackson, obtained a small vessel there, returned to the reef, and brought off safely all the officers and men who had been left there. In this same vessel, the *Cumberland*, a schooner of only 29 tons, he started for England with ten seamen and a collection of papers, charts, and geological specimens. In this little unseaworthy vessel he actually sailed across the stormy Indian Ocean and reached Mauritius, where he put in for rest and refreshment.

Mauritius at that time—December, 1803—was still in the possession of the French. Although Flinders had been granted a French passport when he left England in the *Investigator*, the Governor of Mauritius refused to recognize this as he was no longer in that ship. This Governor—General Decaen—on the contrary, put Flinders in prison, charging him with being a spy, and seized all his papers and charts. But although these last were kept from him until the close of 1807, and one of his logbooks was never returned to him, it is now shown that they were not made use of in compiling the atlas for the report of Baudin's expedition. What the French had borrowed from him was due to his friendly communications when the two expeditions met on the south-east coast of Australia.

Nevertheless, Flinders was detained more or less as a prisoner in Mauritius, eating his heart out, for nearly seven years. He reached England in October, 1810, after Mauritius had been surrendered to a British fleet. His treatment by the Government of his country on his return to England staggers one with its heartless ingratitude. The first circumnavigator of Australia—who had encountered perils which only a heroic spirit could have overcome, who had nevertheless taken the utmost care of the health of those serving under him, and had consequently had little loss of life to report, who had really by his presence on the Australian coasts at many points on different occasions assured to his mother country undisputed possession of that continent by forestalling the expeditions of France, who had traversed the Indian Ocean from Torres Straits to Mauritius in a little boat of 29 tons—was given no reward or honour, and was told that his long imprisonment in that island had barred him from all promotion. He settled down to work for the Admiralty at Portsmouth, and he devoted himself with unceasing industry to the compilation of a book describing his explorations and reproducing his original charts of the Australian coastline. On the very day on which this book was published—in July, 1814—Flinders died, only forty years old. His constitution had been greatly impaired, not so much by the incidents of his circumnavigation of the Australian coast as by the long and unhealthy imprisonment in Mauritius; and his health was undoubtedly further affected by the utter lack of recognition which his great journey met with on the part of the British Government.

Soon after the fall of Napoleon, in 1815, the French Government again sent out exploring expeditions to the Pacific, and each one caused fresh British settlements on the Australian coasts and on those of New Zealand. This last region had been visited at the close of the eighteenth

c 487

WHALING IN THE SOUTH SEAS

century not only by Captain Vancouver but by Spanish and even Russian ships, while the infant marine of the United States, chiefly interested in whaling enterprise, were attracted to New Zealand on account of the abundance of seals and whales on its coasts or in the adjacent waters of the Pacific. They found in New Zealand (which in spite of occasional episodes of savage anger against the white man, and cannibalism, was becoming more and more used to trade and the settlement of the white man) a useful base for their operations, and their attention was directed not merely to the obtaining of oil from whales and seals, but to the value of the New Zealand flax and timber.

It was, however, the foundation of the British colony of New South Wales which most powerfully influenced the fate of New Zealand. Communication rapidly sprang up from the beginning of the nineteenth century onwards between Sydney and New Zealand. In 1814 there arrived a party of English missionaries, under the leadership of the Rev. SAMUEL MARSDEN, which settled in the North Island. In spite of frequent disappointments and rebuffs these missionaries actually succeeded in about twenty-five years in bringing the two islands into something like a condition of peace by composing the quarrels between native tribes, many of whom became converted to Christianity. EDWARD GIBBON WAKEFIELD, who had already carried out several successful colonizing experiments in South Australia, desired to do the same in New Zealand, but was opposed by the missionaries and by the British Government. He eventually succeeded in his purpose, and may almost be called the creator of the New Zealand Dominion, though he would have failed had it not been for the co-operation of that great Governor, Sir George Grey. The British Government hesitated to annex New Zealand, until forced to do so by learning that a French colonial expedition was on its way to take possession of these islands for France. New Zealand was therefore added to the British empire on 11 August, 1840. The French settlers arrived at Akaroa, in the South Island; but, in spite of the British flag having been hoisted only two days before, fifty-seven of them decided to remain, and their descendants at Akaroa now number six hundred.

Between 1835 and 1853 the French obtained some small satisfaction for their eighteenth-century explorations by establishing a protectorate over the Tahiti archipelago and annexing the large island of New Caledonia, to which possessions they subsequently added the Marquezas, the Paumotu, and Tubuai archipelagos, and the Loyalty Islands near New Caledonia. It was really French scientific expeditions which definitely discovered the Fiji archipelago, so curiously overlooked by the great British explorers. But when a French expedition, under DUMONT D'URVILLE, examined these islands in 1827 it found them already under British influence; for from time to time convicts had escaped from the Australian penal settlement and had sought refuge in Fiji, where they had become in some cases the advisers of the native chiefs. A better influence, however, came among them in 1835, in the shape of the Wesleyan missionaries, who migrated to the Fiji archipelago from the Tonga or Friendly Islands, where they had met with complete success.

In 1813, three explorers—BLAXLAND, WENTWORTH, and LAWSON—had succeeded in pushing their way through the difficult country of the Blue Mountains in New South Wales, which although not excessively lofty had nevertheless daunted even Bass, the companion of

AUSTRALIA
and
NEW ZEALAND
Scale, 1:46,000,000
English Miles
0 100 200 300 400 500 1000
Long. East 140° of Greenwich
INDIAN OCEAN
PACIFIC OCEAN
Coral Sea
Timor Sea
Arafura Sea
Java
New Guinea
Solomon Is.
New Hebrides
New Caledonia
Loyalty Is.
Tropic of Capricorn
Gulf of Carpentaria
Great Australian Bight
AUSTRALIA
WESTERN AUSTRALIA
NORTH AUSTRALIA
SOUTH AUSTRALIA
QUEENSLAND
NEW SOUTH WALES
VICTORIA
Tasmania
Bass Strait
Perth
Brisbane
Sydney & Port Jackson
Lord Howe I.
Norfolk I.
NEW ZEALAND
North I.
South I.
Cook Str.
Stewart I.

Flinders, and discoverer of Bass's Straits. As the result of the crossing of the Blue Mountains a road was made through this mountainous region, and the pastoral interior of the eastern half of Australia was forthwith opened up. A maritime surveyor, Lieutenant JOHN OXLEY, R.N., in 1823, once more continued the exploration of Queensland. A colony—Victoria—had grown up round the great harbour of Port Phillip from 1803 onwards. Tasmania had been explored from 1803 onwards, Lieutenant BOWER being the pioneer, and had been selected as a penal settlement in 1805. Hither had been removed the convicts first stationed on Norfolk Island. In 1829 the first settlement in West Australia was founded on the Swan River, where Perth, the capital of that State, now stands.

In 1828–30 Captain CHARLES STURT made a remarkable overland journey from New South Wales to what is now known as South Australia, during which he discovered the Murrumbidgee, Darling, and Murray Rivers, the most important streams in Australia (Sturt also, in 1845, travelled from the banks of the Darling to the very centre of the stony, desert heart of Australia). One of the results of Sturt's first journeys was the foundation of the colony of South Australia, which began in 1836. In 1840 EDWARD JOHN EYRE (long afterwards to be Governor of Jamaica under unhappy circumstances, yet to survive triumphs and troubles alike, and to die in England in 1901) travelled overland the whole way from Spencer Gulf in South Australia to King George's Sound in West Australia, and discovered the salt Lake Torrens, and caught a glimpse of the larger Lake Eyre—believing, indeed, that he had had a vision of a mighty inland sea, instead of four separate, shallow, brackish lakes. In 1844–5 Dr. F. W. L. LEICHARDT, a German explorer, made a wonderful journey, 3000 miles in length, from near Brisbane, in Queensland, to the Gulf of Carpentaria, and then across Arnhem land to Port Essington, in the extreme north of the continent. In 1847 Leichardt attempted to cross Australia from east to west, but got lost in the bush in the interior of Queensland, and died, probably of thirst.

After these journeys, and the further explorations of the great JOHN M'DOUALL STUART (Central Australia, and the crossing from south to north) in 1858–62; R. O'HARA BURKE and W. J. WILLS (also Central Australia) in 1860-1—they were the first explorers to traverse Australia from south to north; A. H. HOWITT, 1861; J. M'KINLAY (South and Central Australia), 1862; W. C. GOSSE (West Australia), 1873; Major P. EGERTON WARBURTON (Central to West Australia), 1873; Sir JOHN FORREST (Central to West Australia) in 1873–4; and ERNEST GILES (West and South Australia) in 1875; the main features and characteristics of the Australian continent became known to the civilized world.

The first value attached to Australia was for its wheat-growing and cattle-rearing possibilities. Next followed, early in the nineteenth century, the introduction of merino sheep, and for forty years or so the main interests of Australia were pastoral, while the breeding of horses for the use of India ("Walers" they were called, as an abbreviation of New South Wales) became an important object of the settlers. The timber of Eucalyptus, Araucaria, and Casuarina was good enough to export; and the capacity of southern and south-eastern Australia as a vine-growing country soon became apparent. But in the middle of the nineteenth century the discovery on a large scale of gold threw all the other assets of this southern continent into the shade. Australia proved, moreover, to be rich in silver, copper, tin, precious stones, and coal, besides gold; and happily the desert and stony regions, which were quite worthless for agricultural or pastoral purposes, turned out to be better endowed with minerals than the fertile land. In 1812 the total white population in all Australia scarcely exceeded 12,000; in 1912 it is not far off 4,500,000. A hundred years ago this continent of 2,947,000 square miles was a barely known and derelict land, the coasts of which were roughly indicated on the map, the interior being completely unknown. To-day it is the home of a young, white nation, which may some day rival in power and resources the United States of North America.

As regards New Guinea, no close attention was given to the geography of that great island until the surveying expedition of H.M.S. *Fly*, in 1842–6, commanded by Captain F. P. Blackwood, R.N., and that of H.M.S. *Rattlesnake* under Captain Owen Stanley, R.N., in 1846–50. This last-named expedition included in its staff as surgeon the great professor, Thomas Henry Huxley. Huxley named the high mountains of south-east New Guinea after his commander, who died before the expedition returned to England. South-east New Guinea (Papua), the portion nearest to Australia, was annexed by Great Britain in 1884.

In the settlement which followed the conclusion of the Napoleonic wars Great Britain decided to restore to Holland the Island of Java, which she had occupied since 1811. She also gave up all other Dutch possessions in the Malay Archipelago, and compensated herself by the establishment of Singapore and the elimination of Dutch rule from the Malay Peninsula. Thenceforth—from

1818—the kingdom of Holland extended its sway through the nineteenth century over all parts of Malaysia, except the Philippine Islands (which belonged to Spain down to 1898), the Portuguese portion of the Island of Timor, and the northern parts of the great island of Borneo. It is difficult to understand why the Dutch left North Borneo alone. That region had been, however, for centuries, more or less under the dominion of a once powerful Muhammadan prince, the Sultan of Brunei, and it may be that he was too strong (possessing, as he did, in the early part of the nineteenth century, a great fleet of pirate ships) for the Dutch to tackle. This potentate occasionally entered into relations with the East India Company, but was not infrequently called to account for the piracies committed by his subjects or his allies the "sea-gipsies" (see p. 55) in the narrow seas between Borneo and Indo-China.

The possibilities of North Borneo attracted the attention in 1830–2 of a notable pioneer of the British Empire, James Brooke, who had been an officer in the service of the East India Company, but was taking a journey to China on account of his health. Learning that the Sultan of Brunei wished for assistance to enable him to put down piracy and overcome rebellious chiefs, Brooke, having inherited his father's fortune, fitted out an expedition at his own expense in England and left the mouth of the Thames in 1838 for North Borneo in a ship of his own, a sailing yacht of only 140 tons. It would somewhat daunt the modern adventurer to embark on a little sailing vessel of that size and voyage round the Cape of Good Hope and across the stormy southern half of the Indian Ocean to the Sea of China. Brooke found on his arrival at Brunei that the uncle of the sultan was engaged in a difficult war with the Dayaks in the western part of northern Borneo (Sarawak). On condition that he subdued the rebels and pirates in the western part of his dominions the Sultan of Brunei agreed to confer on Brooke the chieftainship of this region; and this delegation of authority developed (not altogether, however, to the liking of the Sultan of Brunei) into the creation of the very remarkable State of Sarawak, which ever since 1841 has been a sovereign state in Malaysia, under the rule of an English raja. Indeed, although Sarawak was founded in 1841, it has only known, so far, two rulers, firstly, Sir James Brooke, and secondly, his nephew Sir Charles Johnson Brooke. Ever since 1888 Sarawak has been under British protection. The British Government had annexed the Island of Labuan, near Brunei, in 1846, as a basis from which they might attack the pirates who infested the Malaysian seas. In 1881 a charter was granted to a company of British merchants for the foundation of the State of North Borneo, originating in concessions made by the sultans of Brunei and Sulu. The historic Sultanate of Brunei itself was brought under British protection in 1888, and finally under British administration in 1906, so that the whole of the northern third of Borneo is now within the limits of the British Empire.

Germany first began to take an interest in Australasia about 1850, when German steamers or sailing vessels from Hamburg and Bremen found their way to the South Seas. Especially noteworthy was the house of Godeffroy, founded originally by French Huguenots. Although this firm eventually failed, it did much to lay the foundations of German commerce in the Pacific, and took an especial interest in the Samoa archipelago. As a result of its work the German Government decided to acquire possessions in this direction where other European nations were not already established. The Marshall Islands were annexed in 1885; and the Caroline Islands, with the exception of the island of Guam (which was ceded by Spain to the United States), came under the German flag by purchase in 1899. The Dutch had laid claim to the western half of New Guinea during the middle of the nineteenth century, when all that region was being explored with great advantage to science by ALFRED RUSSELL WALLACE; but at the same period it was almost taken for granted that the eastern half, and especially the parts of New Guinea nearest to Australia, would eventually become British.

The Government of Queensland, indeed, annexed all the eastern half of New Guinea in 1883; but their action was disavowed by the British Government. Shortly afterwards, however (in 1884), seeing that other European powers were considering the possibilities of New Guinea as a suitable region for annexation, the British flag was raised there, and eventually, by agreement with Germany, Great Britain added to her empire the south-eastern parts of New Guinea, together with nearly all the Solomon Islands and the Santa Cruz archipelago. Germany, in the same year (1884), had annexed north-eastern New Guinea (Kaiser Wilhelmsland) and the Bismarck Archipelago (New Britain, New Ireland, the Admiralty Islands, &c.). She also acquired Bougainville and Buka Islands in the Solomon archipelago. France attempted about the same time to claim the New Hebrides, but Australia objected, with the result that the New Hebrides are at present administered jointly by Britain and France. In 1899 Germany annexed the two principal islands of Samoa, the smallest of the three falling to the United States, which, by its successful war with Spain, had acquired the Philippine archipelago and the island of Guam. Fiji had been ceded to the British Government in 1874 by its chiefs and people. In 1899–1904 the Tonga or Friendly Islands became a British protectorate; and at earlier and later dates many small Pacific islands and groups not important enough to need special mention were brought within the British Empire.

The people of Hawaii archipelago, where Cook lost his life, had been converted early in the nineteenth century to Christianity by missionaries, British and American. The islands were ruled in a more or less civilized fashion by a native dynasty of kings, but at the same time were increasingly settled by white men as planters and merchants. The white population became too difficult of government by these half-civilized Polynesians, a revolution was brought about, for a few years Hawaii was an independent republic administered by Americans, and finally was annexed by the United States in 1898. Consequently there remains at the present day no territory whatever in Australasia which is not under the flag of some European or American power. In Australia—which became a homogeneous state by the institution of federal government in 1900—we have the beginnings of a mighty nation; likewise in the Dominion of New Zealand, which now has a white population of over 1,000,000. New Guinea is still a land mainly inhabited by savages, and it is probable that owing to its unhealthiness it will remain more or less a domain of the black man, and the same may be the case with the Solomon Islands. But elsewhere, though the Polynesian and Melanesian peoples are far from being exterminated, they are diminishing in numbers from one cause and another, and those that survive will probably fuse in blood with the white colonists. Many of these Pacific islands are earthly paradises, so far as climate and fertility of soil are concerned. They will doubtless some day become densely inhabited, and their prosperity will justify the efforts, the sufferings, and even the crimes and mistakes of the Pioneers.